System

of

Horsemanship

Louis Seeger

Translated by

Cynthia F. Hodges, J.D., LL.M., M.A.

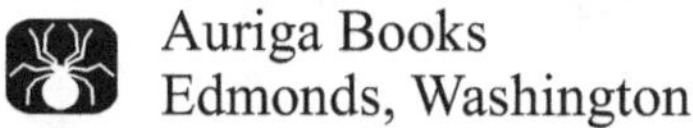

Auriga Books
Edmonds, Washington

Seeger, Louis. *System of Horsemanship.*

Original: Seeger, Louis. *System der Reitkunst.* (Berlin 1844).

Translated from the German by Cynthia F. Hodges, JD, LLM, MA

Translation copyright © 2019 by Cynthia F. Hodges, JD, LLM, MA

ISBN-10: 0-9763920-7-0
ISBN-13: 978-0-9763920-7-1

Published in the United States by
Auriga Books
Edmonds, WA 98020
www.cynthiahodges.com/auriga

Cover Art:
"Trakehner Stallion"
Oil painting by Bonnie Hodges © 2019
bonniehodges.com

Description

Louis Seeger was an important 19th century dressage figure in Berlin. He was the son of a court horseman in the service of Prince Heinrich of Prussia, the brother of King Friedrich II. After training at the Spanish Riding School in Vienna with Max Ritter von Weyrother, Seeger founded his private riding school, *Seegershof*, where he preserved Old School training principles. His most famous student was Gustav Steinbrecht, the author of *Gymnasium of the Horse*.

Seeger authored a number of books about horses. In addition to *System of Horsemanship* (1844), he wrote *Rathgeber fuer die Stalldienerschaft* (1848), *Zuechtung, Erziehung, Ausbildung des Pferdes im systematischen Zusammenhang* (1850), and *Monsieur Baucher and His Arts: A Serious Word with Germany's Riders* (1852) (translated by Cynthia F. Hodges). Seeger was also a board member of the Berlin Racing Club and was awarded the Gold Medal of Honor.

This book lays out a training system that begins with breaking the colts and continues all the way to the Airs Above the Ground of High School dressage. Seeger reveals Old School methods in this systematic theory on horsemanship. Proven strategies to put the horse in perfect balance are outlined in this book. Seeger also explains how horses that are not suited to dressage can be made serviceable.

Seeger's classic horse-training treatise, *System of Horsemanship*, was once only available to an elite group of European experts. Now that Cynthia F. Hodges, JD, LLM, MA has translated this pillar of equestrian literature, the classical principles of Old School dressage training contained herein are available in English for the first time.

Most respectfully dedicated to His Royal Highness,

The Prince of Prussia

Most Serene Prince and Gentleman!

Because Your Royal Highness had the grace to accept the dedication of my work most magnanimously, I have the joyous view that one will honor it by heeding the principles contained within it, testing them, and I hope, recognizing them as being true.

If I succeed in bringing about a new recognition of riding as an art form with my new system, then this success will be almost entirely attributed to the approval that His Royal Highness, the illustrious connoisseur and patron of the arts and sciences, has most graciously bestowed upon my work, and will be less likely to fail.

With the same feelings of the deepest gratitude and dedication, I respectfully remain

Your Royal Highness'

most humble and loyal servant.

Louis Seeger
Seegershof,
February 20, 1844

Foreword

Amongst the arts, there is no keener nor more general interest than in horsemanship. Due to the need to ride under differing conditions and to achieve various purposes in life, certain principles have been set that are mostly abstracted from mathematics and mechanics. Adhering to these exactly results in speed, flexibility, and stamina in the horse, as well as energy and skill in the rider. This gradually elevates it to an art form. Horsemanship gains supporters due to the general widespread fondness for horses, the many conveniences that riding affords, the great value of good and noble horses, and above all, the indispensability of horsemanship for the training and maintenance of the cavalry, among other things.

Riding as an art form includes not only the School, but also riding in balance and riding in the natural position of the horse.

Failing to recognize this principle even with eager and general participation in horsemanship is what causes most riders to pursue a one-sided course. Rather than acknowledging that all three styles of riding belong to the art form, they usually pursue only one of them and neglect the others. However, these three styles of riding, namely riding in the natural position of the horse, riding in balance, and the School, are to be regarded as a harmonious whole whose individual parts are worthy of the same respect. The artistic position of the horse can never be successfully attained without the natural position of the horse under the rider, because the latter is the initial preparation. It also provides the correct standard by which to judge the former.

Those who are entirely dedicated to horsemanship should heed this in particular. They seek to attain the principles of the School through continuous practical exercises, such as riding in balance, but should not neglect to practice riding the horse in the natural position as well.

Even if the rider has practiced the differing styles of riding many times and has developed the most skilled technique possible, he will still never achieve a clear picture of his art without certain knowledge of the aids. This is indispensable for the riders who wish to rise to the higher levels of the art. This knowledge of the aids is partly obtained by experience. However, it often requires half of a lifetime to recognize the true and to reject the false. In addition to a most thorough School education and continuous practical exercises in School and campaign riding, this deals primarily with:

> The rules of attending to and caring for horses;
> Knowledge of veterinary medicine and breeding;
> Military riding service;
> Selecting horses for various riding purposes, etc., etc.

In designing this study plan, I thank, in addition to the examples worth emulating, my father and brother (both distinguished career riders), who taught me the mechanics of the horse's gaits from my earliest youth on, and the training of the deceased Max. von Weyrother of Vienna, who died much too early for the art of riding.[1]

However, it is only after twenty years of experience, which was gained by testing and comparing all of the other known riding methods, that I have succeeded in systematically ordering my views regarding the principles of horsemanship.

---

[1] Even the Baron v. Biel rightfully paid tribute to Weyrother's teachings in his 1827 work, which appeared in Vienna, *Ueber edle Pferdezucht*.

If this makes it easier to learn riding and to successfully complete the horse's dressage training more quickly, but does not fail to recognize the old principles of horsemanship, then perhaps it will succeed in unifying the adherents of horsemanship, who often become enemies due to their differing opinions on the various styles of riding. If this is done, then the purpose of my book will be achieved.

The authors of older riding theories applied the principles recommended in their works only to the dressage training of well-built and strong horses. The explanations of their special methods are, however, mostly insufficient, and the illustrations are a poor substitute even for the experienced rider.

They either only partially address how to divide the movements into levels and use them with strong horses that one does not intend to train to the greatest perfection or to weak horses that cannot be trained by means of the School, or not at all.

The need for great numbers of cavalry horses does not allow for the selection of individual horses. It is true that the majority of them will be well-built and strong, but only a minority will be suitable for being trained in the School to its greatest perfection. One will fail to the same degree with a weak horse or if the rider does not understand the often unintelligible articulations of the old riding texts and the teachings of the new instructors.

It is, therefore, time to make the dressage training principles of the School available in a comprehensible manner with a thorough explanation. These principles, when based on the methods of the old masters and the proven rules of the older works on horsemanship, must be modified, even if the basic idea has been preserved. This is because, in our time, the rider's demands on the horse are usually very different from those that were made in former times, and also because today's noble horse differs in its conformation and temperament from those used for riding service in the past.

It was necessary to divide the training into half-school or campaign-training, if one intended to apply the School to more than one discipline. However, because the School was neglected and almost forgotten, every offshoot lost its theories (and at the same time, its foundation). The result was that people just fished around for methods.

By following the rules that were contained in the works on horsemanship up to now — whereby the frequent misunderstanding of these rules, however, is not to be overlooked — the majority of riders did not succeed in acquiring the results for which they had hoped and that are demanded in modern times. On the contrary, there is clear evidence that the old principle, "Without flexion in the haunches, the horse cannot go in balance under the rider," has been neglected.

If balance is lacking, even a good rider loses out on such advantages as the multi-faceted use and longevity of the horse.

It seems fitting for the riders, who are interested in the dressage training of the horse in particular, as well as those, who use differing riding methods depending on the purpose that they are pursuing, that a systematic, orderly work should serve as a guide. Certain true and irrefutable principles form the foundation of all parts of this work, published with the title, *System of Horsemanship*. The book is divided into a General Section and a Special Section.

The General Section is to be seen as the basis upon which the contents of the three following sections are systematically built.

The Special Section contains three parts. The first part deals with the campaign-training or how to bring the horse into balance. The second part makes up the School, through which the greatest perfection of dressage is attained and the balance that has been developed in the horse is permanent. The contents of the third part show how differing purposes of riding can be achieved. However, they do not entail correct dressage training of the horse, which is contained in the previous sections. Using these methods leads to quick wear and tear on the horse that is largely unavoidable.

An illustration and a short description of the horse's skeleton is included at the end of this work to help facilitate a better understanding. It is included in the General Section so that the mechanics of the horse's gaits are explained simply and clearly using the theory of the lever. Accordingly, the bones should be regarded as the lever and the muscles as the power source. The horse should be divided into two parts, i. e. two double-armed levers that are joined together.

The conditions under which the lever-action for the horse's dressage training can take place follow, as well as an explanation of this effect as it relates to the horse's movement and forward motion.

The first two sections belong to the Special Section, which primarily involves the horse's actual dressage training. The normal order and naming of the lessons are retained. However, there is a superscript corresponding to the purpose of dressage when necessary for clarity. This is related to how the carrying capacity of the hind legs works.

Because dressage should regulate the horse's forward motion, which only comes from the hind legs, the principles of dressage can only be drawn from the correct movement of the hind legs.

In general, it is impossible to put the horse in balance under the rider without partial flexion in the haunches. This is sufficiently explained in the first and second parts of the Special Section. If a horse has a well-built back and hindquarters, then this bending in the haunches can be achieved in a relatively short period of time via School exercises.

If a horse has a weak back or if the horse's hind legs are not strong due to an abnormal position of the bones, then the School can still be used, but only to a certain degree.

In addition to the first handling and breaking of the young horses, the third part contains instructions for how horses are to be ridden in their natural position in shortened or lengthened gaits.

The completely different riding styles that are dealt with in these three sections, alternatively depending on conditions, lead the rider to be able to correctly judge when a horse is in balance, when it is on the haunches, and when it is on the forehand, and how it must be positioned in these three situations in order to move well. If the rider can recognize by feel where his and the horse's center of gravity is in every one of these situations, then he has achieved the correct rider feel. This is discussed more thoroughly in the chapter, "On the Resistance of the Horses."

Green horses' hind legs, which have by nature both carrying and pushing power, do not step correctly when burdened by the rider, i. e. they use too much pushing power.

All of the School lessons are aimed more at developing the horse's carrying capacity rather than the pushing power of the hindquarters. In other words, they are geared more towards flexing in the haunches rather than extending, and especially towards the momentary bending of one hind leg and then the other or both at the same time. In this work, the purpose of the exercises is usually indicated by the title that precedes a more detailed explanation.

The alternating loading and bending of the hind legs brought about by the weight of the forehand can only take place if the horse steps into the foot prints of its forefeet with its hind feet. In this case, the horse cannot oppose the rider by using the strength of its neck muscles. The rider is able to use the natural flexibility of the neck to determine the degree to which to load and bend the haunches, as well as the forward motion.

The correctly increased use of the rein on one side increases the flexion in the hind leg on that side. This is indicated by the horse turning its head to that side, thus making it easier for the rider by bending that hind leg.

This is essentially the only way to flex in order to put the horse in balance. By contrast, if one gives the horse's neck a bent position, but it either does not step forward enough or steps too far forward and under, or if it does not go forward at all, then this is not only of no use, but it actually robs the horse of its desire to go forward if done to an exaggerated degree.

The differing head and neck positions, namely the lowering and raising of the head, the high and deep head carriage, and bending the neck sideways, are suited to all horses by nature. They will only refuse to obey the rider's rein aids in the beginning if the hind legs do not step far enough forward and under. As a consequence, they can use their neck muscles to resist.

Every horse should be trained in dressage until its hind feet step into the footprints of the forefeet, i. e. it goes in balance. The dressage training should continue until this almost becomes a habit for it and is enduring. It is impossible, however, if the horse is lacking sufficient natural ability and hind leg defects prohibit them from flexing.

In the lesson, "On Bridling with the Curb," at the end of the first part, a curb bit is described that is appropriate for any well-built horse or one that has been prepared for going in balance via work on the snaffle in the previous lessons. The other type of curb is mentioned in the third part.

The end of the first part, "Training in Campaign Riding," seems especially worthy of being followed by prospective riders. This part has an eye toward the further instruction and perfection of horse-training pedagogy.

In order to finally instruct the rider in the more exact assessment of the horse's value, and to serve as a guide in the selection of horses for various riding purposes at the same time, it seemed necessary to include a summary that was as brief as possible on the horse's exterior in the Appendix.

I hope that the following work, which has now been handed over to the publisher, achieves its purpose and will be useful to riding.

The Author

Contents

General Section

All of the riding books that deal with the riding horse's training establish putting the horse in balance as the main purpose of training. In general, it is recognized that the horse can only move the lightest, surest, and with the greatest strength and stamina when it moves in balance. Few riding books differ in the methods they recommend to achieve this main goal. However, the rules for this usually lack the necessary systematic order.

Because the ease with which the horse can be balanced depends on its conformation, the teachings have to deal with the horse's exterior. However, this is not included here because it is beyond the scope of this book. It is also not as necessary as the relevant content that is contained in this book.

A good conformation generally entails both the quality of the individual parts of the horse's body, as well as how they are put together. The horse uses these parts to move forward, and in this, its ability is most clearly expressed.

The person uses this for various actions, but mainly for carrying and pulling. This depends on whether he intends to use the horse as a riding horse or as a carriage horse. Every use involves moving forward. It will always be the case that, among horses that are suited to the same work, the horse with the best gaits will be preferred.

Along with all of the various qualities of the conformation that the knowledgeable horse-person recognizes as being good, the ability to go forward must be considered. This is because the horse's quality is dependent on its fitness for service, assuming that there are no afflictions and one is only judging by the horse's exterior.

One gains an understanding of good movement when one has a clear idea of how the horse moves in its gaits. From experience, one can imagine generally good movement by which all of the other gaits that are required for various uses are to be judged. This good movement is partly due to physical reasons and partly due to mechanical ones. The rider must be able to recognize perfect movement, which is that of a horse in balance. This is because it serves as a yardstick by which all of the incorrect gaits can be judged in order to improve them. For this reason, this movement must be defined in general. Such a general determination must not be based upon arbitrary individual opinions, but rather must be grounded in the general fundamentals of the animal's mechanical structure.

Because everything depends on the horse's balance, it is necessary to first determine exactly what balance actually is, both at rest and in motion.

Balance requires a resting point, and can, therefore, only be understood insofar as it is applied to a horse that is standing at rest under the rider with its weight distributed equally on all four feet. Balance in motion depends upon the weight being distributed alternately on the carrying legs in such a way that the conditions for balance are not negatively impacted.

Horsemanship, as well as the art of riding and training horses in dressage, cannot establish the necessary principles alone, but rather must borrow them.

The first principle of horsemanship can be taken from structural analysis, and indeed from the general phrase: "The closer the center of gravity is to the center of the body's mass, the more stable it is." This principle applies to both horse and rider, and particularly to their structure to determine their position.

The explanation is as follows: The term, "center of gravity," means the point on the body that is in such a position that, when it is supported, all parts around it are in balance. If the center of gravity is supported, then the entire body is supported. It rests on its point of support in such a way that it seems as though the entire weight of the body were united with it. A perpendicular line drawn from the center of gravity to the base of the body is called the line of the center of gravity.

Structural analysis proves this principle regarding balance, namely that a body can maintain its most secure position or condition when the line of the center of gravity is in the middle of the base, and that a body that is standing will fall, if the line of the center of gravity falls outside of this area.

If one applies the above principle to the horse, one must first ask oneself, "Where is the horse's center of gravity?"

If the horse has a normal conformation, one can assume that the center of gravity lies between the eleventh and twelfth ribs, i. e. under the fourteenth vertebra of the spine. This point is clearly indicated by the position of the dorsal process of the vertebra, in that the first thirteen processes have a slanted position from front to back, as opposed to the processes of the last four vertebrae and the lumbar vertebra, which are slanted from back to front. Only the fourteenth dorsal process sticks straight up. The horse rests upon that point, if one thinks of a scale. It is supported on this point and in balance. If a perpendicular line were drawn from this point down, it would be the line of the horse's center of gravity. The horse's center of gravity lies closer to the forelegs than to the hind legs due to the weight of the head and neck. The base is bound by the legs, which are either standing or carrying.

The line of the horse's center of gravity must fall between the legs that are carrying, if the horse is to go forward safely. The closer the line gets to the center of the base, the lighter and more surely the horse will maintain its position.

The green horse at rest usually carries itself with its head and neck sticking out and with most of its weight on the forelegs. Because it sometimes places them farther out in front in order to better support its weight, they will fall outside of the base. The heavier the head and neck are, the more the balance is disturbed. The weight of the head and neck pulls forward, so if they are less overweighted, then the center of gravity will fall more on the center of the base. One cannot make the head and neck of the individual horse lighter in an absolute sense, but one can make them lighter in a relative sense by putting them in a different position. Determining this is the first principle for how to position the horse's body.

In which position does this weight become relatively lighter?

Imagine the horse's head and neck acting like a lever, the point of support for which lies where the head and neck vertebrae are connected (as will be shown farther down in the movement of the joints). According to the principles of how levers work, the relative weight of the lever arm has less effect the more acute the angle is that both arms of the lever create. This is because the weight is reduced to the same degree that the weight's horizontal axis is shortened. In order to bring this about, the head and neck must be carried higher, which the horse will do on its own as soon as it wants to go forward with energy.

For the sake of greater clarity, imagine that the following illustration represents the horse: d f is the neck that is fully extended. Some of the weight falls in f, and the whole length of d f falls outside of the base (o p). However, if this part of the weight goes from f to i, in other words, if the head and neck are raised to the i d position, then the weight of i falls vertically on n. Thus, the distance that the weight lies outside of the base o p is now only n d. Finally, if the same part of the weight goes from f to c, where the weight falls on c m, then the weight's distance from the point of support is only m d. Thus, it is shorter than m f, which is what it was at the beginning.

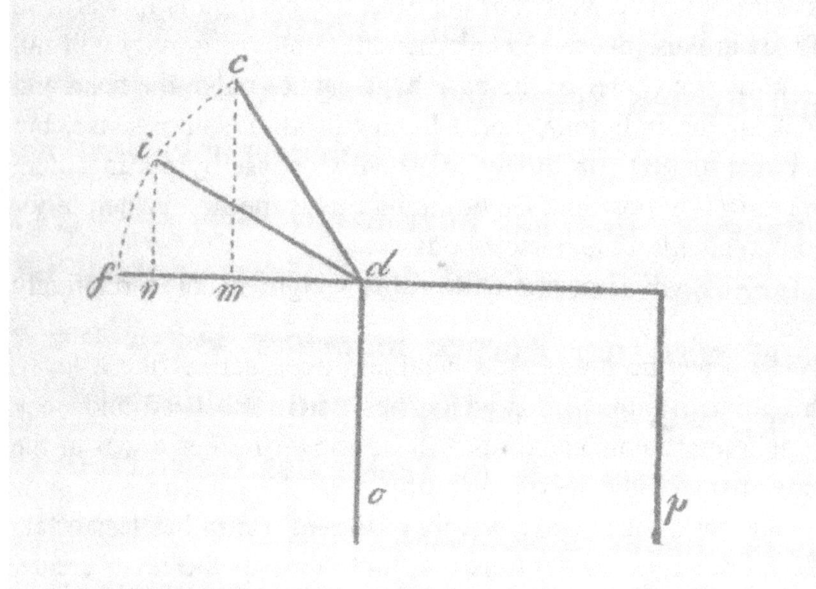

The weight behaves in the opposite manner from how it did as it moved away from the point of support. That is, the weight of the head and neck becomes proportionally lighter as they return to n.

Therefore, in order to prepare the horse to have good movement, the first principle in positioning the horse's body is to lift the head and neck. The relationship, how far one can and should go in this, depends on the movement of the joints. In this position, the center of gravity must, out of necessity, fall more in the back, i. e. behind the center of the body's base.

This is because the weight, which brought the balance point forward, is minimized.

If the horse is not to fall while in motion, then the point of balance must always be on the leg that is on the ground. The more this occurs, the more equally the horse's weight is distributed on its legs. For this, the leg that is on the ground must carry the most weight by virtue of its position. The more the center of gravity falls inside the region bounded by the legs, or the more evenly the weight is distributed on the legs, the more securely the body will remain in its upright position and the stronger the gait becomes with increased endurance. For example, in the trot, the weight of the horse's body must always be equally distributed on the diagonal legs that are on the ground, and the evenness of this should not be disturbed by the alternating movement of the legs.

The second principle for the proper movement and position of the legs is as follows: "The distance between every step may indeed be different, but the power of the movement should be the same under all circumstances, insofar as the physical strength of the horse is the same."

Because the hind legs push more than they carry in the natural gaits, and because the burden of the rider now has to be evenly distributed, the hind leg must assume an equal part of the weight from the foreleg diagonal from it at the same moment that its non-diagonal leg is set down. The hind leg that is being lifted up should not overload the front leg that is on the ground. Therefore, it has always been accepted that the third principle of good movement in balance under the rider is: "The hind foot should always step straight into the hoof print of the forefoot."

The first condition for good movement is that the horse's legs move as freely and nimbly under the rider as they would in the case of healthy and strong animals that are in a state of freedom, and move forward in accordance with the energy of the individual animal. One must wonder, "How and when can the movement of the limbs be the least obstructed and, therefore, the strongest? What effect does the lever arm that is formed by the head and neck have on this, and what effect does the rest of the bone structure have on it?"

The answer to these questions will show us with which means we will succeed in giving the horse good gaits, commensurate with its individual abilities.

First, it is necessary to determine which of the systems of the horse's body the positioning of the head and neck most clearly affects, or in other words, which parts of the horse's body the rider can most successfully affect.

The basis of the animal's innate strength, upon which the muscular strength acts secondarily, are the fixed parts — the skeletal system. The muscular strength acts upon this according to the laws of mechanics, which determine how the limbs move.

The rider must know the laws that determine how the horse moves so that he can thoroughly assess his horse and handle it accordingly.

Although a precise knowledge of the soft tissue parts of the horse's body cannot be demanded of every rider, he should nevertheless acquire such knowledge as it pertains to the skeletal system. For this reason and for clarification purposes, a figure of a skeleton has been included.

The laws of mechanics that apply to how the horse's power acts upon the skeleton arise chiefly from the theory of the lever. It is necessary to mention this theory in part, especially as it pertains to the horse's skeleton.

One differentiates between

1) Levers of the first kind. To these belong, for ex., the balance beam, where the point of support lies between the two forces that move in opposite directions.

2) Levers of the second kind. With these, the pivot point is on one end and the force acts upon the other end. The force and the weight move in the same direction, as is the case, for example, when a pole is used to push a weight forward along the ground. The ground at one end comprises the support for the lever; the moving force works on the other end, which lifts the weight in the same direction.

These different types of levers have other names. The most common are as follows: the lever of the first kind is a double-armed lever, while the second type is an oscillating lever.

The power of the double-armed lever to move depends upon the various relationships its arms have to each other. If both arms are the same length, then the lever is called an equal-armed lever. If force and weight are equal to each other, then the entire lever is at rest. If the arms of the first type of lever do not run in a straight line, but rather form an angle to each other from the base, then it is called a broken or angular lever.

The row of skeletal bones that runs mostly horizontally from the first cervical vertebra, where the head is located, to the sacrum, is the spinal column.[2] It is supported on two points by columns made of bone, namely the bones of the front and hind legs.

Thus, the whole skeletal system can be regarded as two double-armed levers that are connected to each other and, through their articulation, act upon each other. The support of these levers is formed by the bones of the forefeet and hind feet. The first double-armed lever is comprised of the cervical spine going to the last spinal vertebra. The forelegs constitute the base. The point of support lies in the middle between the two shoulders, where the neck and back vertebrae meet.

The front arm of this foremost lever consists of the cervical vertebrae, while the posterior arm consists of the eighteen spinal vertebrae.

The six lumbar vertebrae form the foremost-arm of the rear double-arm lever. The pelvis is the rear arm, and the resting place is where the legs join with the loins, i. e. on the sacrum. The bones of the back legs form the base of this lever. Thus, the rear arm of the front lever is connected to the front arm of the rear lever. If the force and the load on the double-armed lever are equal to each other, then there will be a state of rest in the entire lever, and then the support will be able to move freely in any direction.

---

[2] The term "column" can really only be applied to the human skeleton. With horses, on the other hand, it would be more accurate to call it a beam — a beam that connects the forehand and the hindquarters. There is no sufficient explanation of the parts of the skeleton as is normally taught in anatomy as it pertains to the training of the horse. There would be no interaction or interplay between the parts of the horse if it were divided into fore-, middle- and hindquarters, even if this would simplify the description of individual parts. The division into two parts, the forehand and the hindquarters, is more appropriate for our purposes.

With regard to the horse, the legs would be able to move the most unhindered and with the most freedom and endurance, if the opposing forces of both double-armed levers counteract each other at the same time, or in other words, if there is balance between forehand and hindquarters.

This view makes it clear what the main purpose of the dressage training is and safely guides us in choosing the following methods.

In the front lever, the length of both arms is about the same. However, their weight is different, in that the head causes the front lever arm to be overweighted.

This gives rise to the first obstacle to the proper action of the lever, and therefore, the first limitation of the free movement of its support, that is, of the front legs. This is all the more true the greater the front lever arm outweighs the rear one.

With respect to the front lever, this proves that the position of the front arm can reduce its weight.

Looking now at the rear lever, which is positioned in the opposite direction, and particularly the connection between the two, they are so closely connected that a change in the direction of the arm of one of the levers must necessarily affect the one connected to it.

The eighteen dorsal vertebrae of the rear arm of the front lever run in a line with the lumbar vertebrae, which form the anterior arm of the posterior lever. Therefore, any change in the position of the dorsal vertebrae must also extend to the position of the lumbar vertebrae.

For example, if the head and neck were too high, too much weight would be transferred from the front lever arm onto the rear arm. This would cause the latter to lose its straight line and be pushed down more than the correct amount.

Therefore, the front arm of the rear lever must follow this position, and the rear arm, the pelvis, must be lifted. The consequence of this is that the hind legs are too far back and do not take on their fair share of the burden. Balanced gaits are then no longer possible. The forward movement is also hindered.

The pelvis can only approach the perpendicular position to a certain degree. At this point, the carrying capacity of the hind legs reaches its maximum, and the forward movement ceases. If this degree is exceeded, then movement will occur, but in the opposite direction. It will cause the horse to fall down.

Horses that naturally have a low, hollow back do not usually track up (i. e. step into the hoof print of the fore hoof with the hind hoof). Lifting the head and neck higher will only result in an even greater gap between the two footprints. With such horses, the head and neck must be lowered so that the back forms more of a straight line.

By contrast, the hind legs of horses with high backs, the so-called donkey backs, will over-track so much that they track over the print of the forefoot. Such horses must be given more of a raised position so that the back becomes more level.

In both cases, the hind legs are in a faulty position. They are not positioned such that a perpendicular line drawn straight down from the sacrum falls exactly between the two square hind hooves. This line designates the correct connection of the hind legs to the body, and is understood to be the normal line of the correctly positioned haunches.

On the other hand, one often finds horses with donkey backs whose hind feet do not track up, just as there are swaybacked horses that over-track. Both cases are caused by the abnormal position of the pelvis. In the first case, its position is almost horizontal. In the second, it is almost vertical. In both cases, the line of the haunches does not fall exactly between the two hind hooves.

One cannot claim that horses with abnormal back conformation have surpassed those with correctly positioned hindquarters in speed and endurance. For although the animal's body moves according to the laws of mechanics, it is subordinate to life. The energy, the animal's innate strength, which is imparted through the muscles and the bones, is so predominant in some animals with poor proportions that it makes up for a lack of good conformation. So, too, can the horse's will, its spirit, which determines how the innate strength is used (we may infer that animals are analogous to us in this regard), causes a horse with a poor conformation to actually surpass a horse with a far superior conformation.

From the division of the individual parts of the skeleton into two double-armed levers, one sees that, first, if the head and neck are lifted to the correct extent, the horse comes more into balance and allows the shoulder to move more freely. Secondly, if this lifting is overdone, however, then it will hinder the movement of the hind legs.

The horse's training is subject to some conditions of this first set of rules that cannot be precisely determined. Instead, they must be carefully considered depending on each individual horse's conformation. In general, however, it can be stated that, in order to put the horse in balance and to bring about the best possible gaits, it is usually necessary to first lift its head and neck. Even though this lifting alone is not enough to balance the horse in motion, it will nevertheless most certainly be necessary to prepare the horse in this way, especially horses with heavy forehands.

As for the vertebral column, which determines the position of the horse's entire body by its connection and position, we see that it is lower in the front between the shoulders than it is behind at the small of the back. As long as this condition is not remedied, the horse can never be in balance. This is especially true if it is to carry a rider, whose weight is pushed forward by this position of the spine. Consequently, it cannot be equallly distributed on all four legs. In this case, one should not consider the line that is formed by the vertebral processes, but rather the one that is formed by the corpuses of the vertebrae. In every horse without exception, this is lower in front than in the rear.

It is, therefore, of the utmost importance to remedy this obstacle to put the horse completely in balance, especially under the rider. We have seen that by lifting the head and neck, the position of the back becomes more level. However, this only occurs to a small degree, and thus, requires the use of another method to achieve the horizontal position of the spine. This method is as follows:

The horse's hind leg has three angles, two of which are directed outwards or backwards and one inwards or forwards. The first angle is created by the femur joining with the pelvis, and is directed towards the rear. The second angle is formed by the femur connecting to the fibula, and is pointed towards the front. The third angle is created by the fibula and the cannon bone, and is directed towards the back.

The individual skeletal connections of the hindquarters are, therefore, capable of greater mobility. This is due to how the angles can be decreased and increased. In the first case, the bones come closer together. In the second case, they move farther apart. If the angles are made more acute, then the hindquarters are lowered and the spinal column forms a level line. Only by means of this flexibility of the hindquarters can the forehand be lifted and the horse be put in balance.

The fourth principle of the training is thus:

"One must affect the flexibility in the horse's haunches."

Yet another characteristic of the horse's conformation is not an insignificant obstacle to its training. This is the fact that it is narrower in the front than in the rear. Therefore, two lines running along the length of its sides would converge and intersect. Because of this characteristic, the horse is fast and agile, but it is also easy for it to evade the effect of the haunches. Therefore, it is necessary for a rider who wants to balance his horse to first straighten it.

The horse is straight when the distance between two parallel lines drawn from the shoulders to the hips is equal. For example, if one imagines the horse standing between two parallel walls that touch the hips on each side, then the distance from the shoulders to the wall on each side is equal. The spine forms the middle line that lies exactly between the two parallel lines.

In this way, the horse will walk with its body straight; only then is the position in balance and, thus, the bending in the joints of the haunches possible. In contrast, this is impossible or detrimental, if this is demanded when the horse's body is in a crooked position, whereby the distances between the two shoulders to the two parallel lines are unequal. The lateral flexions of the horse, which are incorrectly done in this case, are of little use. The horse is only correctly bent, or bent-straight, if the distances from the shoulders to the curved parallel lines remain the same.

With correct bending, the requirement of how the horse's feet are to step is not done away with, but only partially modified. Only the inside hind leg steps into the footprint of the forefoot on the same side, or at least follows the forefoot in the same direction, if this perfection in the gait has not yet been achieved.

If the joints in the haunches are flexed, then both hind legs resemble a spring. The spring force is awakened by the flexing of the hip and stifle joints along with the hock joint. As a result, the entire body moves forward in balance only by loading and unloading one hock joint or the other, or both together. It is, therefore, possible to apply the following theory of spring-action to the movement of the horse's hind legs:

The springiness of a body, no matter what it is made of, is manifested when it changes its position and shape due to the influence of an external burden. It always seeks to remove this influence and, after its removal, return to its former state. For example, a spring, when compressed, tends to resist pressure and resumes its previous shape when the pressure is removed. Thus:

1) When the body, which compresses a spring, presses it again after its first counteraction, the spring will express its first force anew.

2) If the compressing pressure and the releasing tension of the spring are equal, then the body that causes the compressing pressure and the spring that strives to release it will result in an equal motion.

There is only one spring in the horse's hind legs, namely, the hock. The other joints are extended only by the extensor muscles. The hock differs in structure from the other joints in that it is not comprised of only two joint bones like the others, but out of seven joint bones that lie in two layers that overlap each other. These bones are kept in place by tendons and ligaments, which surround them like a capsule, whereby the whole joint gains in elasticity.

The hock is where the weight of the body and the counteraction of the ground meet.

Applying the above laws of motion to the hock, and especially with regard to the forward motion, the most important principle is: The direction of compression determines the direction toward which the spring releases.

Every hock can be loaded to a certain degree. If the weight is gradually increased, then it will be in a position to carry the heaviest load. However, if the hock is burdened suddenly, then it will lose either all of its elasticity or most of it.

The correctly loaded hock manifests its power in that it compresses under the load and pushes back to the same degree when it releases. The load is pushed back in the same direction from which it was placed on the hock.

The characteristics of the spring can, therefore, be applied to the horse's hind legs when they are in a spring-like position. The main rules of dressage, to achieve the desired gaits, are based on this hock action. The horse cannot go with an even tempo until it has gained the necessary flexibility in its hindquarters. Neither can it track up without the necessary position of the hindquarters, which can only be attained by way of flexibility in the haunches.

When considering the gaits of the still green horse, especially under the rider, we see that the stretched-out head and neck is not the only obstacle to balance, but so is the stiffness, or rather inflexibility, in the hind legs. In this case, the hind legs push too much and overload the forehand.

Dressage training gives us the means with which to remedy all of these unfortunate circumstances to achieve the main goal of dressage, which is good movement. Before we occupy ourselves with this, however, we should mention the mechanism of the horse's movement in its natural gaits, and especially those we use at the beginning of its training, namely the walk and trot. This is based on the following natural laws.

If we watch the horse in its natural state, we find that it has three main gaits that differ according to how the legs move. They are the walk, trot, and canter.

Variations in these gaits only arise due to the sequence of the leg movement (the momentum of the gait) being faster or more lengthened. Deviations from the normal leg sequence do not belong to the natural gaits, because they usually do not arise from a manifestation of the animal's will. They do not deserve further mention because they lie outside of the purpose of the training and can be sufficiently explained by the description of the correct gaits.

The first forward moving gait that green horses choose when left to their own devices is the gait that is divided into four visible beats — the walk.

The horse prepares to walk out of a stand still by redistributing its body weight onto its four legs in such a way that the body leans forward and assumes a crooked position. It throws its head and neck up, back and to the side toward the front leg that it wants to burden. The horse moves the leg that is now unburdened forward by pushing its head, which is now held high, forward. It then steps under its body with the diagonal hind leg and lifts it forward. This describes the second beat. The other two diagonal legs move in the same way, which comprise the third and fourth beats.

As the horse unloads its forelegs by lifting them up and stepping forward, one clearly sees how the hindquarters push toward the forehand with each step, depending on the horse's energy.

From these transitions from rest to motion, the truth of the following laws arises:

1) The body itself does not move with the leg movements.

2) In the moment the body moves, i. e. when the rump moves forward before the first front leg is raised, the legs do not step forward, but rather remain on the ground.

3) Accordingly, the body and the limbs are sometimes fixed and sometimes mobile, and alternate in relieving each other of the burden.

The above three laws of motion can be seen even more clearly in the trot. The trot is the second forward gait. It differs from the walk in that it only has two beats. The two diagonal legs lift at the same time and are set down at the same time in order to unburden the other two. The mechanism in this gait is the same as in the walk, except that the position of the loaded legs comes closer to the perpendicular line. The body actually moves forward on the second beat, so that in the lofty trot of quick and powerful horses, there is a moment when all four feet are in the air. This is caused by one hind leg moving before the other is set down. The horse's body moves in a similar way in the canter stride, which is maintained by the outside hind leg. The sequence in which the four legs move in the walk and trot, which defines these two gaits, cannot and must not be changed. They can only be improved, both in general and in particular, by how the horse's entire body moves, and not just its individual limbs.

The horse can go in the first two natural gaits more safely and with more endurance than in the canter, which should never be practiced until the horse can walk and trot to the degree of perfection of which it is capable. The explanation of this third gait is, therefore, saved for a special chapter on the canter.

First Part

On the horse's training for the campaign riding service

On the handling of the green horse and preparing
it to flex its inner hind leg without the rider

The rider must demand unconditional trust and obedience from the trained horse. The first impressions made on the green horse by how it is treated in the beginning will either lead to trust, and therefore, true obedience, or the opposite. Every time the horse offers resistance, it is due to fear of man, ignorance of what is asked of it, or being unable to do what is demanded of it. These three causes of resistance in the green horse must, therefore, be carefully avoided. Bad habits must also be nipped in the bud, or, if this is no longer possible as in the case of an already frightened horse, be eliminated by better treatment.

The primary purpose of the first handling of the green horse must be to make it trusting and obedient. To achieve this first goal, one should lunge the horse on a circle. This is because no other method brings about the horse's submission as well.

By going on the lunge line, not only is the foundation of the horse's obedience laid, in that it constantly moves forward as it turns, but it also learns to follow the lunge line's lead, which is the beginnings of being guided.

This type of training is actually only aimed at the horse's obedience. The horse's trust must be fostered, for the most part, by being treated well in the stable. The stablehands must also treat the horses well.

The work on the lunge line on a circle, the green horse's first training, has to take into account the three causes of resistance that were listed above. Therefore, it must be carried out carefully. This is especially true because first impressions are the strongest and often the most lasting. It goes without saying that the horse must already allow the cavesson and girth to be put on, which, incidentally, must be done while it is being constantly praised. The cavesson should be fastened high enough so that it rests on the firm part of the nasal bone, such that the use of the lunge line does not cause too much sensitivity. It should also not be fastened so tightly that the horse cannot eat the oats that are offered as treats. Neither should it be so loose that it slips down the nose.

The girth must be loose at first, then gradually tightened so that the horse slowly becomes accustomed to it and finds it less uncomfortable. If the girth were to be fastened tightly right from the start, then this could give rise to resistance, or at least, cause the horse to blow up while being girthed up. If the horse tolerates the snaffle, then attach the two reins loosely to the girth. Then have a quiet man lead it to the middle of the circle in the arena without any force, where it should then stand quietly. At the beginning of the work on the lunge, there should be three people: The trainer who holds the lunge line, the trainer with the whip, and the one who led the horse in. The one with the whip should now walk behind the horse at some distance without frightening it at all. The trainer holding the lunge line should then approach the horse while softly talking to it and feeding it, attach the line to the middle ring of the cavesson, and then stand in front of the horse, trying to gain the horse's trust. The handler fastens the rein with which he led the horse just as loosely as the snaffle rein to the girth ring. This should be done on the left for the first time, because the horse is easier to handle on the left. It should be noted here that he should not immediately grab for the girth. Instead, he should first slowly and softly caress the horse's forehead while praising it, then run his hand along its cheek to the neck and so on until he reaches the girth. If the animal has tolerated this patiently, then it should be rewarded with oats. Now have this man lead the horse out onto a wide circle at the walk going to the left. Make the circle as wide as possible, because a wide circle is more comfortable for the horse. This is because the horse does not need to bend as much on a wide circle as on a smaller one. In addition, its natural inclination to go forward straight ahead is not hindered as much.

The trainer with the lunge line stays at some distance and goes in the same direction as the horse is being led. The trainer with the whip follows the horse's hindquarters and tries to make it move forward more quickly with encouraging calls and by tapping the whip on the ground, but without actually touching the horse. He doubles his efforts to drive it forward until it goes forward on its own. Now the one leading the horse begins to gradually leave its side and join the trainer with the lunge line. The trainer holding the whip then points the whip at the horse's girth in order to drive it not just forward, but also out. In the event that the trainer does not have any assistants to lead the horse out, then it is better to lead it around himself with a shortened lunge line. Once the horse has gone around the circle a few times, the trainer with the lunge line (during which the one with the whip no longer drives the horse forward, but only prevents it from stopping or coming into the circle) seeks to bring the horse to a quiet walk by softly talking to it, lets it walk around a few more times, and then brings the horse to him using a certain word, e.g. "stop" or "halt," while the trainer with the whip steps to the side.

He must choose a specific word right from the start, so that the horse does not come in when he hears other words that are spoken to it, which are just meant to calm it down. At this point, he praises the horse and rewards it with food. Then he lets it walk around to the right, just as he did before to the left. He then calls it back to him in the same way and lets it be led back to the stable.

The trainers with the lunge and the whip have to observe the following rules in the beginning of the training:

The former must hold the lunge line in one hand while the horse is walking around, while the other hand holds the loop. The leading hand must never be in front of the horse's body, and never let the lunge line touch the ground. The lunge can either be gently shaken to moderate the horse's gait, or one can raise the hand to lift the head and neck.

The hand that holds the lunge line must usually be directed toward the horse's girth. However, in the case of greater resistance, it should be directed toward the hindquarters.

If the horse goes against the lunge and leaves the circle, which often happens in the beginning, then the trainer must try to bring it in with intermittent tugs. He should not hold on steadily, as the horse will learn to look for support on the line. The trainer with the lunge line pivots around the foot that is on the same side that the horse is moving. In so doing, he should always face toward the horse as it goes around the circle

The trainer with the whip must hold the whip in the hand opposite of the direction in which the horse is going. He must always stay behind the horse's shoulder so that he can drive it forward at the slightest hesitation on the part of the horse.

It is of the utmost importance that the horse moves forward off of the whip, because this can prevent bad habits. One must always gradually increase the use of the whip to drive it forward, first by quickly moving it towards the horse's head, then by lifting the whip, then by hitting the whip on the ground, and finally, by actually touching the horse. The whip, which can be used more strongly depending on the circumstances, should only touch the horse from behind the shoulder to the flank. Using the whip anywhere else does not drive the horse forward and out, but rather frightens it more. This can easily give rise to resistance. For example, hitting it on the croup can cause it to kick out.

Another reason for this is that, by touching the horse's flanks and sides with the whip, the horse is trained to move forward off of the rider's legs.

If, after several lessons, the horse has been handled as described above, has learned to go on the circle, and has become more familiar with the lunge line, then the trainer holding the lunge line will begin to do it on his own. He should gradually lengthen the line and return to his spot. If the horse tries to come in, then he should hold his hand up towards the horse's head, while at the same time, the assistant with the whip drives the horse back out. While softly speaking to the horse and gently shaking the lunge line, the trainer lets the horse walk out, but only allows the horse to transition to trot at his command. He does not let the horse come in until it has calmly walked around on a wide circle a few times, which it may not leave of its own accord. The horse is no longer allowed to arbitrarily choose its own gait, but rather only transition from one gait to another on command.

If the horse acts contrary to the trainer's will, then one should not correct it immediately. Instead, assess whether it was forced to make the transition.

For example, if the horse suddenly breaks out of a lengthened trot into a canter, then one must not try to bring it back to the trot immediately. Instead, let it first take a few canter strides. This is not only because it had to choose this gait due to the over-rushed trot, and therefore, had to transition without incurring any blame, but also because it will be too difficult for it to suddenly return to the trot.

When the horse has progressed in its lessons to the point of going out onto the circle as directed by the trainer, remaining in the lengthened gaits, and is trusting enough to permit people to approach it from both sides, then one begins to make the snaffle reins shorter, so that they gradually begin to affect the horse's mouth more and more, but without setting the head in any particular position. The horse must learn to go forward despite the pressure on the reins, which must be slight. The inside rein must be shorter when the horse is standing straight. This is because it bends with its body curved outward on the circle by contracting the inner side and allowing the outer feet to reach farther forward. The horse must not be robbed of these characteristics by a shorter outside rein.

Once the horse that has been chosen to be a riding horse is trusting enough, it is time to saddle it. It goes without saying that the first saddling must be done with all possible care, as it is something with which the horse is unfamiliar. One should first show it the saddle from a distance, then bring the saddle closer and slowly place it on the horse while softly talking to it and offering it food. The saddle should not have anything on it, neither girth nor stirrups that could scare the horse by touching it too soon. One should not make the girth too tight. The horse should be praised as it is led at a walk on a short lunge line, then gradually let it transition to trot when it is no longer afraid of the saddle.

If the horse resists in spite of all precautions, then the horse may be gently punished, but should be immediately calmed down again.

If the horse is used to the saddle, then one can start working on its carriage, and thereby, on its gaits.

Up until now, it is still in its natural carriage, which has not changed during the previous work. The trainer has now become acquainted with the horse's carriage and its natural gaits. His job now is to improve faults and imperfections as much as is possible while working without a rider. However, he should not forget to differentiate between the deficiencies that are due to the horse's conformation and those that are due to its carriage and movement. To determine this exactly, one can consult the laws of the mechanics of motion regarding the sequence of the footsteps in the walk and trot. (See the General Section).

The first goal of working the green horse in-hand is to lift the neck, as this is necessary to achieve balance.

The trainer's opinion about how much this or that horse can be lifted is important. As a general rule, every green horse learns to gradually lift itself to the degree that its conformation and way of moving allow.

A horse that is going more on the forehand must necessarily be lifted more than one that has freer forward movement. Because the hindquarters are loaded to the same degree that the forehand is lightened, the hindquarters determine how much or how little the forehand is lifted. Thus, a horse with strong hindquarters that only goes on the forehand because the hindquarters are inflexible can be lifted more than one that has weak hindquarters.

A well-positioned neck with a light head also permits the forehand to be lightened more than a short, stiff neck with a heavy head. The head and neck should only be lifted to the extent that the movement is not hindered.

The trainer can use the lunge line to lighten the forehand. He can use the whip to drive the hindquarters under the horse while checking the forward movement with the lunge line to the same extent. This will lift the forehand. Only by driving the hind legs under the horse will the forehand be lightened. However, in the beginning, this may only occur to the degree that the hind legs have become flexible. The whip can be used on the hindquarters to drive the hind legs under the horse. Usually, the trainer taps the rump with the whip, touches the horse's side behind the girth, or lastly, the flanks. The trainer with the whip drives the horse's hindquarters forward, but does not just try to get the hind legs to step under actively, but also to develop a rhythmic gait with an even tempo. At the same time, the trainer with the lunge line must work together with the trainer with the whip in such a way that the horse does not become too rushed as a result of being driven forward with the whip. The forehand should become lighter due to the hind legs stepping forward. In contrast, if the horse falls into a hurried gait, the forehand will become heavier. Using the specified bridling, the horse's head and neck must be gradually raised a little higher in each new lesson until the position is achieved in which it has the freest movement of the forehand. With respect to this free movement, it is understood that this includes not only lifting the front leg from the shoulder freely, but also stepping forward and down freely with the whole foreleg.

Now the horse begins to straighten its back and to step under more with its hind legs. This occurs with the leg being as stiff as it normally is at the beginning of the training: The angles formed by the hind legs become wider due to the fact that they reach under the horse farther. Now the hindquarters must become more flexible to achieve the desired tempo for the gait. In putting the horse in the raised position, the inside rein brings the head more to the inside, while the outside rein holds against it. This is for the following reasons:

A half-halt on one rein, if not countered by holding against it with the other rein, works less on the entire body and more on the head and neck, and especially on the diagonal hind leg. This causes the horse to become crooked. However, if this counter-action takes place, then the rein works on the horse's entire side, and the effect is that the ribs and the vertebrae are drawn together on that side.

If the inside rein is attached so that the horse is positioned to the inside while the outside rein holds against it, yet the inside front leg is not too restricted in its freedom of movement, then the horse will be prepared to carry its weight more and for a longer time on the inside hind leg, which must bend out of necessity, especially as the horse goes on the circle. It is the whip's job to prevent the inside hind leg from dragging behind. This is because, if it is not properly placed under the horse, it will not bend correctly. Since this exercise becomes difficult for the horse, one must not go in the same direction for too long, but rather one must change direction regularly and often. Through this work, not only is the initial flexibility in the haunches achieved, but also the whole forehand is lightened, whereas the first exercises in lifting only affected the horse's head and neck.

There may be several exceptions to the work that was just described. For example, a horse that naturally has free shoulder movement and a free and straight head and neck position does not need this lifting. However, it will not naturally have the flexibility in its haunches that it can attain through purposeful training. Therefore, this training will always be necessary. There can be no better preparation than the work on the circle described above. In this way, the horse becomes more balanced, more obedient, and is prepared to be ridden. Its gaits become lighter and nicer, and the young horse becomes stronger through this work, which is suited to its nature.

Chapter II

On mounting the horse and the preparation for bending the inside hind leg under the rider (on one track)

After this preparatory work, it is time to accustom the horse to being mounted. This important undertaking must not scare the horse, because its trust in humans would suffer and would give it a reason to resist. Do not choose a young boy as the rider, but rather a light-weight man who is strong and agile. Too much weight in the beginning just makes horses more suspicious and more inclined to resist. Carefully examine the saddle and bridle before use, and make sure that they are in the best possible condition. In the first lunging session prior to being mounted, the saddle girth will usually become loose. It must be gradually tightened, as horses with sensitive backs tend to buck when the weight of the mounting rider causes the saddle to shift. The saddle must be constructed and fit the horse in such a way that it does not pinch the withers or the backbone, and does not restrict the shoulder movement. Therefore, it should be positioned four fingers' width behind the mane, on the fossa supraspinata, which can be clearly felt behind the shoulder blade. Regarding the bridle, one uses the normal loose-ring snaffle on green horses. It should be as mild as possible and should not have any sharp places on its joints.

While the trainer with the lunge line is holding the horse's head and neck with both hands on the cavesson, and while an assistant is helping him by holding the snaffle with the right hand and holding the stirrup leathers with his left hand at the same time, the rider attempts to mount the horse without whip or spurs, all the while praising the horse. After he has secured himself by holding onto the reins and mane, he puts his left foot into the left stirrup, whereupon the knee should press upon the saddle flaps with the heel pushed down. In this way, the hand that is holding the mane and the knee form two axes around which the body must turn as it swings up. If the horse remains calm, then the rider begins to slowly and gradually pull himself up until he is standing in the stirrup. Make sure the trainer holding the lunge line is standing directly in front of the horse and is holding the lunge line in such a way that he can keep control of the horse and can soothe and pet it at the same time. Meanwhile, the trainer with the whip stands to the right of the horse's hindquarters, so that he can prevent the horse from escaping to the right or stepping back. The rider should make sure that he does not put his foot too far into the stirrup, but rather sets the ball of the foot on the tread so that he does not jab the tip of his boot into the horse's side and run the risk of getting caught in the stirrup if the horse bolts. The rider should not stand in the stirrup for too long, because it becomes difficult for the horse to carry all of the weight on one side for a long time. He can judge by the horse's behavior whether he should try to sit on the horse or not. If the horse remains quiet, then he should grab the cantle with this right hand and use his right foot to energetically swing up. If the horse, which has guessed the person's intention, does not appear to become angry, then the rider should swing up onto the horse and lower himself softly into the saddle. The rider's weight is supported in the beginning by the right hand, the four right fingers, the left thumb, which is placed on the pommel, and then on the sides of the saddle between the trapezoid formed by the legs, and finally on the seat. Carefully and without scaring the horse, the rider should take the snaffle reins with his right hand as quickly as possible, and let go of the mane with his left hand so that the free use of the left rein is not hindered. At the same time and with as much caution as speed, the assistant must give the rider the right stirrup and then make himself immediately available to help the trainer with the lunge by holding the horse's head, feeding it oats, praising it, etc. If the horse remains quiet, then the greatest reward is to dismount, which must occur with the same care as the mounting did. The rider takes both reins in the left hand, secures it in the mane at the withers, places his right hand as before on the pommel to support his weight, takes his right foot out of the stirrup first, once the assistant has taken ahold of the stirrup leathers, and swings his body up out of the saddle without touching the croup with his right leg. While the right leg is over the horse, it is very difficult for the rider to balance himself if the horse moves unfavorably in this moment. Therefore, the right hand must quickly reach for the pommel when mounting in order to help support the rider. When dismounting, the cantle can be used for support. However, the dismount should not be hurried, especially if the horse shows impatience through restless movements. In this case, it is better to sit in the saddle again rather than to leave it, and wait until the horse has calmed down before trying again.

If the horse can be mounted and dismounted several times without resistance, then one should use the lunge line to get the horse to step backwards a few steps. This is not done to make the haunches flexible in this case, but rather to achieve more obedience to the lunge line. The trainer should be satisfied with just a few steps. He should avoid letting the horse rush backwards, which the trainer with the whip can help prevent. However, the trainer with the lunge line is in a better position to prevent it if he does not suddenly and abruptly force the horse backwards, but rather slowly and gradually increases the pressure on the nose until the horse obeys his will.

As soon as the horse allows itself to be quietly mounted and no longer tends to be distrustful and resistant, the trainer should try to lead the horse forward with the rider. He should seek the help of an assistant for this, who will hold a rein that is attached to the lunging cavesson on the opposite side. The trainer with the whip mainly takes care that the forward motion is not hindered. If the rider wants to make use of the lunging cavesson, then he can take both reins in his hands. They will serve him well in staying in the saddle, especially if the horse offers resistance. It will also help if he sets himself against the horse strongly from the beginning, with the hips firm and set slightly back, and keeps the reins short. This is so that he can lift the horse's head and neck without bringing his upper body out of the position mentioned above, but can also yield to the horse. He should not hold the reins so short that his arms stick straight out, because every jolt on the reins the horse makes would be jarring to the rider's upper body and would make him less secure in the saddle. If the rider's arms are bent at the elbows, then the jolts on the reins would be lessened, the upper body would not be pulled out of position, and there would be no lack of strength with which to lift the horse up again. The reins must also not be kept too long, nor the hands held too high. In the first case, the rider has too little control over the horse. In the second case, the pressure on the reins affects the rider's upper body too much.

The rider should hold his legs out in front slightly, but softly, in order to better set his upper body against the usual resistance that horses offer in the beginning. However, he should avoid lifting his knees, because this would make him lose his position and security in the saddle. Unnecessary gripping with the legs will lead to fractiousness. The rider should not give any leg aids as the horse is being led. The horse should only be driven forward with the whip. For the same reason why it is good to first start training the horse on the lunge on a circle, so too, is it a good idea to do it with the rider. In the beginning, one should just have the horse walk, but later, when the trainer can see that the horse is no longer afraid of the rider, then he can let it start to trot. If one begins to trot too soon, then it will scare the horse when the rider touches the saddle and will try to get rid of the rider. It goes without saying that the horse may not be worked in such a way until it is used to being ridden astride. From time to time, it will appear to be calm, but then it will refuse the food that is offered while mounted, regardless of whether it otherwise likes to eat out of the hand or not. If this is the case, then it is enough to repeat mounting and dismounting.

If the horse is accustomed to the rider, then the rider must begin to work the horse himself — with help from the trainers with the lunge line and the whip. He still rides on the lunge on a circle. His first task is to lighten the horse in front using alternating checks on each rein that follow each other in quick succession. This is done in accordance with his position and direction. The half-halts cannot be made right from the start with firmly set upper arms from the elbow to the wrist. This is because, in order to affect the head and neck with these quick half-halts, one must have free use of the arm. The trainer with the lunge line must support the rider in this work. The trainer with the whip must make sure that the horse moves forward well and steps under with its hind legs. The half-halts may not be made on both reins at the same time, because, if the horse pulls on the reins, it will pull the rider out of the correct position. However, in the other case, the horse will only pull on one rein, which will give the rider enough time to meet the resistance with the other hand. When the horse moves forward obediently off of the whip under saddle, the rider should begin to gradually support this with the legs. He does this by taking his legs, which had just hung down previously, and beginning to slowly press them against the horse at the same time that the whip drives the horse forward. If necessary, the whip should actually touch the horse's flanks to teach it to move forward off of the legs. With these aids, the horse is ridden on a circle in walk and trot and lightened in front, but the horse is not given any other position. The only thing the rider has to watch out for is that he works more on the outside rein than the inside rein. This is done so as to make the lunge line more effective, because it can only be used successfully if the outside rein acts with the necessary counter-action.

The trainer allows the transitions to occur as in the beginning and lets the rider halt often. He supports the rider in this by saying "halt" and by using the lunge line. At the same time, the trainer with the whip prompts the horse to go forward. In this way, the horse learns to pay attention to the rider's legs, especially when the reins are yielded. It also learns to move forward off of the leg without being driven forward by the whip.

Up to now, the trainer has not allowed the horse to halt immediately out of the trot. Instead, he has brought it back to the walk first before being halted. Trotting directly from the halt has also not been permitted. It is now time to practice this, but it is still more prudent to first collect the horse from a lengthened trot before coming to a halt. In so doing, many horses have the bad habit of stiffening, sticking their necks out, and leaning on the reins. The trainer can only counter this by lightening the horse's forehand with the lunge line before the halt. Should he not achieve this intention, then he can correct it with the lunge line prior to the halt. Before he resorts to this harsh method, however, he must be convinced that neither the rider's hard hands nor a sudden strong pulling on the reins is to blame. Furthermore, he must know whether he has properly prepared the horse to be obedient in this lesson.

In order to gradually accustom the horse to the leg and rein and to make the assistants less indispensable, the trainer with the lunge line can allow the rider to go on a small square rather than on a circle. The rider must keep the horse on a straight line from one corner to another, which is only possible when it is properly between the leg and rein. Any deviation from the straight line is to be strictly avoided. One should be careful to maintain the rounded position of the horse's head and neck. In order to be able to keep this position in the future in each gait, this arching of the head and neck is necessary from here on out. It can only be considered to be a main method of training when it is practiced more in motion than when the horse is at rest, and that is for the following reasons:

The principle that the rider follows in the training, which one tries to bring into a systematic order, is to constantly work toward the goal of putting the horse in balance. This can only be achieved by lightening the forehand and loading or flexing the haunches at the moment when the hind legs are stepping forward and down, as was explained in the General Section. The closer they stay together, the less they can evade the flexion. The weight that is used to burden the hindquarters (besides the hindquarters themselves) is the head and neck, later, the entire forehand of the horse, and then the rider's weight, too. Their position determines their effect. If the head and neck are to be arched in a useful manner, then it must be done in combination with the forward motion. If one tries to do so without the hind legs stepping forward and under, then the weight will not be transferred to the hindquarters, but rather will rest on the shoulders. Rather than furthering the horse's balance, it will work against it. The horse is taught the desire to move forward on the lunge line. Loading and flexing the inside hind leg more is prepared by the shorter inside rein. It can be useful to do in-hand flexions of the head and neck. If the horse bends its neck at the halt, then the horse must move without forward motion. It transfers its weight to the inside feet, namely to the inside hind hoof as it bends. If forward motion is allowed, then this foot will remain more heavily loaded, as the rump at rest does not change the weight distribution. (When the legs are moving, the rump is the resting point and vice versa. See the General Section). This achieves the purpose of loading the inside hind leg.

If the flexions are undertaken without the prior lunging, then they can only be of use in the case of a horse that has a forward-moving disposition and goes against the bit to do what it wants, even if this causes pain. It is understood that the horse must also be good-natured. The lunge line and whip are unnecessary with such horses, but more adversarial characters cannot be made submissive without them. The flexions can be done at the end of every lesson in the following manner:

The horse should be halted and positioned straight so that the weight of horse and rider is evenly distributed on all four legs. The rider then playfully gives and takes on one rein to bring the horse's head around so far that he can pet it.

At the beginning, just as with every exercise that is new to the horse, this flexion cannot be expected to be perfect. This can only be achieved by proper training. One should make sure that, when bending the horse's head toward the rider at the beginning, the entire neck is evenly bent from withers to poll. If it is not, then the horse will put more weight on its outside hooves and will become crooked in an effort to evade the flexion. This type of flexion may be done both right and left. It is considered to be an ideal method, which affects only the head and neck, to bend the horse with the inside rein and, at the same time, to lift the horse with the outside rein. The head is brought around only as far as is allowed by yielding on the outside rein. It is again positioned straight ahead after the flexing exercise.

As indicated above, flexing on the spot can only be of use if the horse is inclined to bend, but not if it tries to evade by moving the shoulders and hindquarters. This mistake is easy to correct in the beginning, but it is made by many riders who do not know how to recognize it when flexing their horses. This leads to serious consequences. If the horse turns around as a result, loses its balance, and even falls down, the riders often do not recognize the cause and do not know how to correct the horse. The goal here is to determine what causes this mistake as it arises, i. e. crawling back with the hindquarters or going behind the bit.

The first thing the horse does that is against the rules is to pull against the reins with its lower jaw. The second thing is to move its body to evade the flexion and free up the inside feet, but without actually moving the feet. The third is to move its legs incorrectly to follow the weight of the rider. The horse will stagger sideways or backwards, or pivot on its outside legs on the spot, which often puts the rider in danger of falling with the horse. These movements are quite contrary to the ones practiced before. In those, the horse followed the position of its head, loaded the inside feet more, and had to go forward on the hand. This was beneficial for turning. The correct movements and the desire to go forward must be the yardstick for every flexion; the same goes for the individual parts of the horse's body and, later, for the entire horse.

Such flexion exercises can be done at the end of every session. They can help the horse and rider become more familiar with each other. Touching upon the essential flexion in the forward motion, the pressure that the individual reins exert on the inside lower jaw forces the horse to bring its head around and bend its neck properly only if the inside hind leg is more heavily loaded. Since this can only occur if the inside hind leg steps into the hoof print of the forefoot, the horse must be driven forward by pressure from the rider's inside leg and by the whip. It is important that the croup does not fall out when applying pressure on the inside rein, which is supported by the lunge line. The outside leg must prevent this and contact must be kept on the outside rein. Supporting the inside rein with the lunge line can only be effective when the inside hind leg is set down and the outside hind leg is lifted up.

The flexion lesson should not last too long on one side. The flexing may be done for a longer period only if the horse is less flexible on one side. For this reason, one should alternate often if the horse is equally flexible in both haunches so that an evenness in position and direction on both sides is achieved. As the horse is exercised in this lesson, it is necessary to make it feel the outside rein more and more. This is done so that it learns to become more put-together and goes with more certainty.

If the horse obeys the individual rein according to the degree of its use and willingly obeys it and the leg, then it is time for the rider to begin to turn the horse without outside help. In so doing, one must make sure to only give checks on the inside rein and not work against it with the outside rein until the horse is to be ridden off of the straight line or circle line, depending on whether it is on a square or circle. The rider should be advised to first look at the line onto which he wants to ride. This is necessary if he wants to be exact in the direction the horse goes. If he is successful in making the first and easiest turns on his own without help from the assistants, then the trainer will let him make the more difficult turns. The most advantageous change of rein right or left is on the diagonal across the whole arena. This is because the rider must make sure that the horse remains on a straight line. In so doing, the horse is prepared for being ridden out in the open. In order to make the horse even better at this, one can repeat this exercise frequently on a small square and let the rider make it more sharply defined. From this, he goes back to the large rectangle, i. e. the whole arena, and tries to keep the horse bent-straight on the line as much as possible and with a lightened forehand to further a lively gait. As he did on a circle, the rider must lift the forehand and arch the head and neck with quick half-halts on the reins in such rapid succession that they seem to almost flow together.

During this exercise, it is very advantageous if, when the horse is halted, the rider and trainer with the lunge line have it reinback a few steps, as was done in the earlier lessons on the lunge. Now, however, it should feel the effect of the lunge line very little, and should step backward mainly due to the pressure on the reins.

The support with the lunge must finally cease and only the trainer with the whip in conjunction with the rider's legs makes sure that the horse halts straight. For this, the rider should not half-halt on the reins in such quick succession, but rather hold and tighten only on one rein for a longer period. This will cause the horse to want to stray from the line. The trainer has to work patiently and judge how much he should demand of the horse according to its conformation and ability. He must be satisfied with a few steps on a straight line if they are obedient and not too hurried. Mainly, he prevents the horse from rushing backwards, which the trainer and the rider must counteract with the use of leg aids and measured half-halts. The horse should neither rush backward nor lose its position and creep behind the bit. Instead, it must bend the hind leg and step backward when the individual rein on that side is tightened. Thus, the horse should not only become more obedient to the reins, but also become more flexible in the haunches. The reinback can be practiced at the end of every session just as the flexions are. More and more precision can be gradually demanded. The following conditions relating to the horse's conformation can make it necessary for the trainer to be more cautious in this work:

Horses with weak hindquarters — identified by the fact that they step forward — cannot reinback as properly and steadily as can horses with strong hindquarters. The horses with weak hindquarters are those that displayed a dragging motion with the hind legs during the previous lessons. Furthermore, great care must be taken in this exercise with horses that take steps that are too long, as well as those that have hocks that are bent at too great of an angle. With all horses that have these characteristics, all work that causes flexion in the hind legs must be done with great care if they are not to result in harmful consequences.

The horse should decrease the angles equally when bending its hind legs. If the angle is already very acute by nature, then too much weight is put on it in the flexion, which will cause much suffering. Horses that have very straight hind legs can flex very little. Therefore, they like to rush backwards or resist stepping backward. If the latter occurs and the horse plants all four feet stiffly on the ground, then the best way to force it to step back is as follows: The trainer allows the horse to step forward, and while it is stepping forward, just as a hind leg is being lifted, give all of the aids to step backward. First, the rider should tighten on the rein that is on the same side as the hind leg that is being lifted up. Horses with a weak back that have similar symptoms as those with weak hind legs must not carry their heads too high in the reinback. This would burden the hindquarters too much, strain the back excessively, and the horse, seeking to avoid the pain, would rush backwards or even rear up.

As the horse moves forward, the weight of the forehand is transferred onto the hindquarters. This is done by lifting the forehand. Thus, in reinback, the forehand must carry itself since the hind legs require a lot of freedom to step backwards, and for this purpose, the horse should be in the bridle. Only very strong horses are able to step backwards with a high head carriage. Weaker ones will resist, but will acquiesce as soon as their heads and necks are lowered.

The trainer with the whip should position himself at the center of the horse in order to keep the horse straight, where he not only can support the reinback, but also prevent the horse from rushing backwards. One must not be abrupt when driving the horse forward again with the whip, which should only be used with vigor if the horse betrays a propensity to halt at short intervals.

These are the main rules for the reinback. The more correctly it is executed, the more obedient and flexible the horse will become. The actual movement in the reinback is the exact opposite of the forward movement. The horse sets its legs down in the regular order, except that a hind foot is the first one to step back. This is followed by the diagonal forefoot. The straighter the horse is and the steadier the tempo is in the reinback, the more perfect the movement is.

If the trainer is successful in his efforts, then he can let the horse be ridden out more freely. For this purpose, he detaches the lunge line and walks either next to the horse or lets the trainer with the whip follow behind. If the horse has been correctly worked on a small square or on a circle in the foregoing lessons, then the horse will obey the rider's aids and can be guided by the rider alone. It is necessary for the rider to keep the horse in a purposeful, brisk walk, but not hurried. The horse must also be made willing to walk forward with the whip and the line and to gladly submit to these demands.

At the beginning of this exercise, the rider must round the corners and take care that this occurs in accordance with his will. He must also make sure that the croup does not fall out.

A few comments about the actual work on a square in contrast to a small circle are in order.

For as long as the horse is unfamiliar with the rider's aids, as already mentioned, it cannot be under our control on any line other than on a circle. If the horse shows the desire to go forward, however, then the exercise on a square is more beneficial for our purposes. It is, nevertheless, necessary to know the difference between the movement on a circle and on a square. It will often be more useful, for example, to perform the exercise of bringing the head and neck in with the inside rein on a square rather than on a circle. This is because, in normal riding on a circle, which consists of nothing but turns, the inside legs are already burdened more than the outside legs. This is increased even more when the head and neck are bent to the inside. The horse that is still rather inflexible cannot use its inside legs very well under such conditions, so then it no longer moves freely on the circle, leans on the reins, and falls out with the croup. On a straight line, in contrast, where one side of the horse is just as free as the other, it can carry itself in the correct position while bending the head and neck, because it is supported on the outside.

The horse is lunged at the beginning with a straight body position to preserve the desire to go forward with a light forehand before one teaches the horse the individual reins by turning his head and neck to the inside, and before the inside hind leg begins to bend. If the situation arises that the horse's desire to move forward at a good and purposeful pace suffers due to the bent position, then the bend must be decreased or given up all together. A good-natured horse should be ridden out in the open from time to time.

The choice between the two gaits — walk or trot, and the transitions between the two — depends upon the legs maintaining good movement. It is left to the rider's or trainer's discretion.

The main purpose of the work out in the open or in the large arena is so that the rider can teach the horse to take a good contact on the bit. In order to clearly understand what this type of work entails, "contact" must first be explained.

One understands the word, "contact," in equestrian parlance to mean the steady pressure that the rider's hand communicates to the horse's mouth via the use of the reins on the bit. This contact may be of three types: Firm, soft, and light. The contact is stronger or weaker accordingly. The horse is not allowed to evade the contact, i. e. creep behind the bit, lean on the reins, or pull against them. The horse's mouth must be in such harmony with the rest of its body that every sensation the rider's use of the reins causes on the horse's mouth will immediately determine the horse's position and direction. If this is the case, then the horse has a good contact.

It follows from this definition of contact that the horse is in balance when it maintains the best possible contact. It is fitting to refer back to what has already been said about the horse's balance, because the horse must be as flexible as possible in order to carry itself in balance. Therefore, the expression, "To give the horse the proper contact," can only be understood to mean that it is put in balance in this work more than in the previous work and is made more flexible.

The horse, which has a good understanding of the previous lessons, cannot possibly keep both its balance and perfect flexibility. This is because it is not quite properly positioned, in that it is mostly worked on a circle and is not yet straightened by the use of both reins. The latter is the purpose of the beginning work on a square. This can also be viewed as the preparation for the later and greater bending of the inside hind leg.

The horse, which is now being ridden freely in the large arena must be kept in a lively, purposeful walk in an upright or collected position. The rider should enliven the gait from time to time by using his legs. He should continue to pay attention to how he holds the reins and guides the horse as was done in the previous lesson. The lively, purposeful walk will awaken in the horse a tendency to transition into trot, especially when the rider increases the leg aids and yields on the reins to give the horse more freedom. The trot is maintained in the same position in which the walk was executed by using the previous aids, but now more strongly. If it is possible for the rider to keep the horse in a purposeful trot by using the driving aids, then he should drive it forward on a straight line from time to time at a faster tempo without giving or taking on the reins (this has been described as "holding.") A quicker movement will originate from the horse's hips without the entire weight of the body falling onto the forehand. This will result in the collection or the "putting together" of the horse. When alternating and stronger leg pressure is used, the horse's stomach muscles will quickly contract and the hind legs will step toward the direction of the line under the center of its mass. This exercise, which can be supported with the whip or riding crop if necessary, will lead to a determined and purposeful gait. One should proceed with vigilance because the hocks are worked more, and the horse loses any tendency to drag its hind legs. Naturally, this exercise is to be done equally in both directions as are all of the others.

If the horse gradually develops a more definite movement in a steady trot and keeps a lively gait and the proper carriage, then it will be advisable to let it lengthen the trot, and to transition from shortened to lengthened strides and vice versa. In so doing, the tempo will become steadier and careless movements can be thwarted. When the horse is strung-out, it does not support its entire weight properly by stepping under correctly with its hind legs. Because the four legs are farther apart, i. e. its balance points are farther apart, the load becomes heavier, and, therefore, the horse's back suffers. If one also takes into consideration how much the rider's weight adds to this as one returns to the saddle during the trot's powerful motion, then it is clear how harmful a very extended trot can be, especially for horses that are not strong.

The rider should always round off the corners in all tempos. If in lengthened trot, then shorten the gait before the corner. However, the horse may not suck back in so doing, but rather must maintain the purposeful, collected gait that was brought about by the rider's leg aids. The change of direction should be carried out as soon as the trot stride is no longer shortened. In the best case scenario, this would be done across the diagonal of the whole arena.

These exercises on a straight line with the horse in a straight position work both hind legs equally and enliven the gait. Therefore, these exercises must be considered to be preparation for greater bend in the individual hind leg on a circle. Switching between the trot on a circle and on a straight line is practiced, because the hind legs are driven under and the horse is put in balance more. In this way, the trot on a circle makes the horse more flexible in its haunches and more agile in the turns.

When halting the horse up to now, either on a circle or on a straight line, pressure was put on one rein and then the other in an alternating fashion until the horse either transitioned from trot to walk or stood still. The horse usually leaned on the reins more and loaded the forehand an inordinate amount with the hind legs neither under it nor flexed. Now that it has learned to bend its hind legs and step under itself in collected trot by heeding the leg aids with contact on the reins, the halt must be performed keeping the same position it had in motion. That is, it must be taught the full halt.

In order to describe to the rider the effect of the halt, one must remember the actual mechanism of motion, and in sum, the most essential is repeated. Upon closer inspection of the movement, one sees that the hind legs usually initiate the forward motion, and the hock's spring-like action is mainly credited with this. The hock lifts most of the horse's weight after the hind leg steps under the body and transfers it onto the corresponding foreleg. It does this by compressing and expanding in proportion to the other angles of the hind leg. The less the hind leg is flexed, the more the horse's weight is put onto the forehand. The more it carries itself on its forelegs, the less it is in balance. The more flexion the hindquarters assume, however, and the longer they carry the weight, the more the horse moves in balance and the less it goes on the forehand.

In the first gaits, walk and trot, the hind legs alternate between flexing and carrying the weight. The horse throws its weight, which is resting on the forehand, back onto the hind leg that is on the ground at the moment. It does this by switching one hind leg with the other to carry the entire load. In so doing, it tenses its back muscles and lifts the forelegs in an alternating fashion.

It follows that the rider must induce this if he wants to put the horse — along with his weight — in balance. For this purpose, he must put his and the horse's weight onto the leg that is on the ground. This occurs if he works on the individual reins in an alternating manner, and in such a way that he affects the hind leg that is on the ground with his weight as well as with the rein, while the other rein controls the movement of the other hind leg. This work, which demands a very keen sensitivity on the part of the rider, causes the horse to be in the best carriage, if not done too hurriedly. It also makes it most obedient to the reins. The horse learns to step forward and bend each hind leg according to the rider's will. This will be the result if he knows how to support the half-halts on the reins with the legs. So, for example, when the horse steps down with the right hind leg and lifts the left hind leg, the rider holds against the right rein more strongly, puts more weight on his right hip, and using the combined weight of horse and rider, causes the right hind leg to bend. Now, he drives the left hind leg under the horse, holds against it in the same way as the right when it is set down, and then lets it step forward again. This is called the half-halt, in which the rider only holds against one hind leg at a time. It will lead to a full halt, as soon as one wishes to execute it.

Although the half-halt does not demand as much obedience on the part of the horse as it requires the correct feel from the rider, the objection cannot be made that the average rider cannot do it, but only perfect riders can. Even the less experienced rider can do it, although not as well. He can use it to his advantage if the instructor makes him properly observant, supports him with increased intermittent pressure on the lunge line, and lets him work on alternating hand and leg aids. The horse will then obey the rider on its own, in that it will lead with the free hind leg, which is made lighter by the fact that the other hind leg that is on the ground is held back. If the horse is put back on its hindquarters more and its carriage is more regulated during the course of this work, then the full halt is easy to execute via increased rein pressure. The full halt consists of the horse — as it held one of its hind legs back in the half-halt in its steady position — now holding back both hind legs, and then coming to a stand still while maintaining the best carriage. Obviously, the full halt is a consequence of the half-halt, if one imagines the transition from one to the other.

When the rider has held one of the horse's hind legs back with the half-halt, then he drives the other forward and lets it move forward freely. If he holds against the other hind leg that is lifted up and that is about to be set down at the same time as the one on the ground, then the horse will halt on both hind legs. That is why the rider must play with the reins by tightening on each in an alternating fashion even with the horse's first halts. In this way, the horse that is not yet well-trained will be prepared for the correct halt. If the rider were to halt his horse in the first halt exercises right from the beginning with both reins without first preparing it for the even pressure on both reins by playfully increased tightening on alternating reins, then disadvantages could result that are not so easy to correct. It is usually the case that, when taking on both reins at the same time, the rider pulls too hard and too strongly. In most cases, the rider will also lean back with his upper body, especially with horses that still have little training. This overburdens the horse's hindquarters. Because of this, the horse stiffens its haunches and goes against the bit. This leads to a second significant mistake: The rider loses his upper body posture because the horse's resistance to his pulling on the reins negatively affects the upper body. In order to counter such mistakes, the rider's leg aids must be used before the hand until the horse has successfully stepped under with the hind legs. Every futile tug on the reins against a stiff hind leg makes the horse more resistant.

The trainer should never forget how little ability the horse has to obey during the first exercises under the rider. Therefore, he must not always suspect that the horse is naturally rebellious when things do not go as he wishes. Horses often refuse to be obedient because they do not know what is expected of them.

Chapter III

On flexing the inside hind leg (on two tracks)
or on the shoulder-in

From the beginning of the dressage training, the inside hind leg is worked more than the outside one partly by shortening the inside rein and partly by the work under the rider on a circle and on a square, whereby the hind legs are going in the same direction as the forelegs. In other words, they follow on the same track. It is possible to not only give the horse the proper carriage for balance and prepare it for flexibility while maintaining the desire to go forward, but to also achieve submission to the rider's will.

If the rider has achieved this via the previous exercises, then the horse must be taught to obey a single leg. It should learn to move sideways with one hind leg away from the increased pressure of one of the rider's legs, and not just forwards as it has up to now. This is done in order to burden it more, which results in increased flexion. The simplest exercise that can bring about the desired perfection in any horse is the shoulder-in. This lesson is also the best method to correct horses that have an uneven rhythm or that constantly break into canter. Only when the trot rhythm remains the same in the shoulder-in exercise is it time to prepare for the canter via flexion in the outside hind leg and to sufficiently confirm the horse in leg yield.

There are riders who are against this lesson and are more partial to the head-in/croup-out exercise. One reason is that the outside hind leg in the shoulder-in has too much freedom, and the head-in/croup-out exercise teaches the horse to yield to the leg more quickly. Another reason is that it takes too long to teach the horse the shoulder-in. Therefore, it is only used in riding schools where one can spend months on a lesson. The last objection is justified, if one wanted to demand of every campaign horse the same precision and perfection in the execution of this lesson as horses that are chosen for this work, which is why one spends a lot of time on this exercise. This perfection should never be demanded of the ordinary campaign horse. Therefore, the shoulder-in lesson can be used to teach the horse to yield to the leg in the allotted time, just as the head-in/croup-out exercise. It also has the advantage that the horse can never go on the forehand in the correct shoulder-in as it can in the head-in/croup-out exercise. The beginning of this lesson is the same as shoulder-in, even if not perfect, and only turns into the head-in/croup-out exercise, or an incorrect shoulder-in, when the croup comes around farther.

It is impossible for the latter-named exercise to free the shoulders. This is because it puts the horse more on its outside hind leg. The shoulders can only become freer when the forehand is set back more on the inside hind leg than on the outside hind leg. This burdening and flexing in the inside hind leg cannot occur to the required degree, because it is set down over or even next to the outside leg rather than in front of it. This exercise may be used in order to teach stubborn horses to respect the spur, yet only with care and temperance. This is because the legs cross, which hinders their movement. This exercise often results in shoulder lameness, tendinitis, injury to the coronary band, swelling in the knee, etc.

In order to clarify how the shoulder-in lesson affects the horse and how it is to be executed, the entire exercise must be broken down into its individual parts.

It should be noted from the beginning that every exercise, as simple as it may be, may only be carried out according to the skill and ability that the horse has developed, and only the proportionate perfection may be demanded in the exercise. If one tries to demand perfection of the normal campaign horse in the simple movements of walk, trot, and canter the same way one would demand of the School horse, then one would be demanding that every horse be the most highly skilled without exception.

To explain the procedure in the shoulder-in lesson, one must first describe how the horse's legs move. The natural order remains the same, namely alternating diagonal legs, but the position that the horse is to assume requires that the inside hind leg step straight in front of the outside hind leg. Think of the horse going to the right. At first, only its head and neck are bent to the inside. Then the horse's body is bent more to the inside, whereby the left feet step on a line that is about a half-foot to a foot away from the wall. The forehand is now brought farther away from the wall, whereby the outside hind foot may not leave the line under any condition. The farther away from the wall the forehand is, the greater the horse is bent to the inside. The horse may only be brought to the inside so far that it goes on two tracks or sideways, and this positioning to the inside is in accordance with its length. The lateral flexion to the inside and the forward and stepping-under of the inside hind foot can only be demanded to the extent that it does not become too difficult for the horse. Horses with long bodies can be positioned more sideways and bend more than horses with a more compact build.

By exact observation on the right hand, one sees that the left foreleg steps first, whereupon the right hind leg steps under the body and steps in front of the left in the natural sequence. The horse remains on the inside hind leg until it steps with the right foreleg forward and over the left one, whereby the left hind leg, following sideways, assumes the weight.

The greatest part of the horse's body weight is suspended this entire time. The right foreleg is not only raised and set down, but also steps over the left, and in so doing, describes an arc around the right hind leg. The horse must remain on the right hind leg longer, because it can only position itself on it as it sets the left leg down sideways.

This shows clearly that the inside hind hoof is worked the most in this shoulder-in lesson, assuming that the horse's training has progressed to the point that it no longer goes totally on the forehand. However, working the inside hind leg is not the only purpose of this exercise. It is also the most suited to teaching the horse the leg yield and to prepare it for the canter at the same time.

The reason for the various opinions about this can be found in the actual effect of the shoulder-in lesson as it is presented: "The inside shoulder is worked more in this exercise, in that it does not have to do a third of the movement as was required in the previous lesson; it is not only lifted up and set down, but also moved sideways at the same time as the inside foreleg crosses over the outside foreleg." This movement of stepping sideways occurs not from a sideways positioning of the shoulders, but rather from the rotation of the humerus, in that it is turned out and extended at the elbow. The shoulder only moves up and down, and the movement only becomes freer insofar as the lifting is not forced. What has been said about the horse's balance is evident, i. e. only the increased flexion in the haunches can make the shoulder movement freer, and this flexion is determined by the movement and loading of the hind legs. Thus, one must determine how the hind legs must step and how the rider should proceed in order to free up the shoulders using the shoulder-in lesson.

The process arises almost on its own out of the movement and positioning of the horse that has already been presented. In order to correctly execute the shoulder-in on the right hand, the horse should be bent in the neck such that the inner orbital arch can be seen. Then, the rider puts pressure on both reins with the right one working alternately on the right hind leg. This brings the forehand in away from the wall. Placing the right leg flat and close behind the girth, with the left on the flank, will create the required bend in the horse's ribs.

If the leg aids position the horse in this way along the wall, then the left forefoot will step forward first, and the right hind foot will follow it in a diagonal direction. As a result, it steps more under the center of the horse, thereby marking the suitable moment to burden it. It is difficult to recognize this by feel at first. However, the rider can identify it because the left forefoot is set down at the same time that the right hind foot steps forward. At this point, he is in the position to transfer the necessary weight onto this hind leg by putting pressure on the reins. This involves not only the weight of the forehand, but also the weight of the rider, whose weight is more on the right seat bone in the described moment. He does this by setting his inner side back more and, at the same time, uses his left leg to prevent the outside hind leg from moving sideways too much. Keeping this hind leg in place puts it in a position to act like a spring when the inside hind leg is burdened and flexed (in this case, the right one). The horse can only resist this if it transfers most of its body weight from the inside hind leg onto the outside one, and thereby evades by going sideways too much. This sideways-stepping may only be allowed to the extent that it does not hinder the proper bending in the inside hind leg. At the moment that the inside hind foot is loaded, the inside forefoot is in the air and is ready to cross over the outside forefoot. This is called "crossing." The reins must be held against the left hind foot for this purpose, whereby it is fixed to the ground. As soon as the inside forefoot touches the ground and the outside foreleg is lifted, the left rein is yielded so that this foot has the freedom to step forward again. Immediately thereafter, the rider holds against the right rein with it out to the right more so as to burden the right hind leg. If the rider uses the left rein to maintain the lightened position of the forehand, then he may never move his hand away from the horse. Instead, he may only move it back towards himself. Otherwise, he would work against the horse's proper carriage.

This explanation will be enough to understand the effect of the School shoulder-in. Executed properly, it will correspond to the purpose of dressage. However, if it is done indiscriminately and without moderation, it can be detrimental.

The rider who wishes to work his horse with care and keep it agile should never introduce it to going on two tracks, such as shoulder-in or half-pass, before it is put in balance in the walk and trot and goes at the correct tempo and with gusto in these gaits. Otherwise, he will never get the horse to willingly use its power.

Chapter IV

On flexing the outside hind leg (on one track)
or on the canter-position

One can hardly believe how difficult the movements on two tracks, i. e. renvers and travers, are for the horse if done before they are properly prepared for them. This is because they demand increased flexion in the outside haunch if done correctly by the rider, which corresponds to the purpose of dressage.

Just as the perfect School shoulder-in cannot be required in the campaign-horse's training, so too should renvers and travers be omitted from such a horse's training. Untimely use of these School movements can ruin the horse and confuse the rider. This will occur even sooner if combined with tight turns on two tracks. These can only be performed correctly by very skilled riders and by strong and well-schooled horses. In order to keep the horse on the hand and to keep good contact via flexion in its stiff hind legs, it is better to practice the School shoulder-in on two tracks gradually and to avoid any crossing over of the inside hind foot over the outside one, as this can cause the horse to go behind the bit. In renvers and travers, a horse that is not perfectly prepared is more inclined to cross over. As a result, it is more difficult to direct the forehand back onto the haunches.

In this way, incorrectly trained horses do not go in the correct tempo either in the walk or in the trot. Their movement is dragging, their canter is sluggish, also when jumping over fences, and the rider sits there in obvious embarrassment. Even the turns made by such horses are clumsy, because the inside feet usually get in the way of the outside feet. This is because the horse cannot move them freely enough. Injury to the coronet band, tendinitis, ringbone, even swollen hocks are the result. Above all, the shoulders suffer when going forward more quickly. One may ask how the campaign horse should learn the so-called half-pass? The horse is prepared for the leg yield via the shoulder-in. It must move its inside leg diagonally, i. e. sideways and forward. If it is properly obedient in this exercise, then it gladly obeys the demands for half-pass, that is, to step more sideways than forwards, especially if a straight head position is allowed. In order to sufficiently confirm the horse in leg yield, one should put it on its outside hind leg in the gaits on one track, in that this leg is more heavily burdened when it is placed forward and sideways under the horse.

As this exercise prepares the horse for the canter at the same time, it is also called the canter-position. If one rides the horse in this bent position in turns opposite to its bend, then it is called the counter-position. The latter is harder for the horse. Therefore, the easier one must be practiced first.

The main purpose of this lesson is to put the horse on the outside hind foot. The same rules apply as in the shoulder-in, but opposite. This is because, in the latter School movement, the horse is put on its inside hind foot. One must pay attention in this preparatory exercise for the canter-position that the inside hind foot does not evade, i. e. does not step sideways, but rather forward, and that the outside hind foot does not cross over it, but rather in front of or next to the inside hind foot.

If the inside hind foot steps into the foot print of the forefoot and follows it in a diagonal direction, then the movement is correct in this lesson. As a result, it is easy to give the horse the proper contact on the bit with arched head and neck and flexion in the back of the jaw. One should keep in mind the explanation of the straight and crooked positions of the horse in the General Section.

It is a very common mistake when horses are worked in this lesson that most are bent crookedly or go behind the bit in all three gaits. The inside hind foot does not step straight forward then, but rather too far in and sideways. The outside hind foot, which cannot step forward as far now, does not reach the point under the horse where it should be at the moment when it is set down. This is a problem if the rider wants to transfer the weight of the overly heavy forehand to the back and, thereby, make the hind foot more flexible. The result is that this leg stiffens or resists when it is set down. When this occurs, the tendons, ligaments, joints, etc. suffer considerably, especially in the canter, which is very similar to a buck and is very well-suited to awakening a predisposition for spavin, capped hocks, wind puffs, etc. This canter will convince the rider that he has not worked the horse correctly. Most riders blame the horse if they are jolted in the saddle in this incorrect canter and are even thrown when halting. However, the cause is not a back that is too stiff, but rather it is often weak hindquarters. Instead of collecting them via the correct forward movement, they are overburdened when the horse is pulled back violently, whereby the haunches either give out to the point of collapse, or as is more often the case, they stiffen to the point of rearing.

Many horses are ridden badly in this way and are even ruined. It may even be the case that the advantages that were gained by correct shoulder-in exercises were destroyed by a crooked position and cannot be regained by either the School renvers or travers.

In order to retrain horses that have become accustomed to these crooked positions, one should choose the previous lessons. In particular, one should practice the shoulder-in first at the walk, then in the collected trot, and even in canter on the circle, or on a small or large square, in which the inside hind leg that has become accustomed to pushing too much and resisting will soon be corrected. First, one should start over with the correct exercises in the canter-position at the walk and trot. One will soon be convinced that this alone will be enough to adequately prepare each and every campaign horse for the canter as well as for half-pass. Such schooling on two tracks, i. e. renvers, travers and especially very taxing pirouettes, only belong to the finer training, i. e. the School-riding. One spares campaign horses such training altogether, so as to create and maintain more serviceable horses.

Chapter V

On the Canter

The appropriate time to introduce the horse to the canter is when it is trained by means of the correct work in the previous lessons to the point where it can trot in the proper tempo both in the shortened trot and the collected trot, and can maintain it while going straight or bent in the shoulder-in position. Certainly, this trot is the indicator of the horse's good position. It is at least proof that the rider has it sufficiently under control to be able to canter at will.

The rules that govern all of the horse's training up to now can only be derived from the correct assessment of the mechanism of the gaits of walk and trot, just as the rules that have been presented for the canter derive from the theory of the movement of the canter. This movement occurs in the following manner:

The canter, depending on its perfection and speed, has two, three, or four beats. Strong carrière-horses and skilled gallopers allow only two to be observed. In the first beat, they lift the forelegs; in the second, the hind legs. The ordinary or campaign-canter has three beats. The collected or School canter executed by strong horses has four beats.

Because the ordinary canter with three beats is the only one that most horses are capable of, especially at the beginning of their training, it is described by the following observations.

So as to be able to explain the leg sequence and determine the moments the legs are lifted up and lowered back down, one should imagine the horse cantering to the right, whereby the legs on the right side step forward farther than the legs on the left.

Consider first the moments when they are lifted up. One notices that, in the first beat, the horse raises its right foreleg, in the second, the left foreleg and right hind leg at the same time, then in the third, the left hind leg, whereby the horse's entire body is lifted up off of the ground.

The feet are set down again in the reverse order. The left hind leg, which was raised last, is set down first, and the right foreleg that was the first to be lifted touches the ground last, the middle beat is comprised of the two other diagonal legs being set down simultaneously.

The forehand lifts when the forelegs touch the ground. Because the right one is the first to leave the ground in this process, the left hind leg is set on the ground via the diagonal movement of the weight, whereby the right hind leg is freed up and steps forward along with the left forefoot at the same time. Via the hock's spring-action, namely the left one in right lead canter, the horse propels its entire body up off of the ground. It catches it again with the left hind leg, and gradually supports it with the other three feet. From this comes the moment when the left hind leg supports the body weight. This does not occur, however, in the four-beat canter to the same extent. This is because the body, before it is propelled up, also rests on the inside hind foot during the time between the second and third beats, i. e. when the left forefoot and right hind leg are being set down.

When the horse canters in this way with even and observable beats, it is more perfect than the three-beat canter. It is also rarer, because it requires a great deal of skill and strength. This canter should not be confused with the canter of a weak horse that has four beats that can be heard in quick succession.

After this explanation of how the horse and its four legs move, one should discuss the rider's method of introducing the horse to the canter. It will usually be best in the beginning to do it on a circle on the lunge line (however, this is not necessary with horses that have a quiet temperament), in order to transition from the shortened trot to the canter. The reason is that horses are put on their hindquarters more in the collected gaits than in the walk. Thus, the hind legs are compressed more and are more suited to a springing action. In addition, there is the advantage for the rider that he can more easily act upon the hind leg that is to be burdened. This is because there are always two legs on the ground. The horse's sensitivity will determine how strong the aids will be to ask for the canter. It will also determine the choice of gait out of which the horse will transition into canter. There is a difference in how the aids are to be used on a horse that is already well-positioned and familiar with all of the gaits versus a horse that is not familiar with the canter. The former will work with the rider, while the latter must first feel all of the aids that cue the canter, in order to understand what is being asked of it. One sees clearly that the most essential preparation for the canter on the right lead is that, before the forehand is lifted up, first the left hind leg is placed under the body while the other three legs are still on the ground. They cannot be lifted up before this hind leg steps under. It will first be lifted up when the other feet are off of the ground and right after they are set down and under to begin the next stride.

The rider must handle his horse in accordance with this natural preparation for the canter, collect it first, and restrict the outside shoulder more, indeed the horse's entire outer side. When the left foreleg and right hind leg are set down, then he gives the aid. The trainer with the whip can support him for as long as the horse is to be kept in canter-position so that it can make the correct first stride in canter. The trainer with the lunge line can also be helpful, in that he can mark the moment for the rider when the left foreleg and right hind leg touch the ground. By using both legs together with the reins, mainly the left rein to restrict the left hind leg, the legs on the right side will most assuredly step forward more and the horse will canter on the right lead. In the first canter strides, one can allow the horse to be a little crooked, because it makes it easier for it to execute the movement. Positioning the croup to the inside too much makes it more difficult, because the inside hind leg is restricted in it forward motion.

In such situations, only the use of the inside leg is called for.

Should the horse not begin with the correct lead, then the blame lies either on the incorrect position or on the improper timing of the aids. If the horse bounds forward incorrectly, normally the left hind leg follows the right foreleg earlier than the right hind leg. The canter is then incorrect, i. e. a cross-canter. It can also be that it canters on the left lead instead of cantering on the right lead as it should. The horse should not be halted out of the canter, but rather should first be transitioned to the halt through the walk or trot.

It goes without saying that, just as with every new lesson, the rider must not lose his patience and mistreat the horse as soon as it cannot correctly guess what he wants. The more the horse is upset and confused, the less it will learn to understand the aids. Lazy and phlegmatic horses must be encouraged so that they can collect themselves better. At the same time, if the horse transitions off of the canter aids from the collected trot to an extended trot, then either its position was incorrect from the beginning, or the outside rein was not held tightly enough. To correct this, one should switch from the lengthened trot back to the collected trot, then ask for the canter again using harmonious aids.

If the horse does canter, then the rider must use the aids appropriately to keep it going. This is especially true because the horse, not being used to the movement, will easily fall back into trot.

The aids are repeated shortly before the completion of the third beat, whereby the horse is being lifted up into a new canter stride. In the same manner as the horse was collected in the trot, the rider should shorten the canter stride to a greater or lesser degree. The canter should not be maintained for too long. It is a highly incorrect and damaging opinion to believe that one will acquire more skill in a gait via a long exercise in that gait. The exercise will perfect its skill for only as long as the horse does not tire from the effort. As soon as the horse begins to tire, it loses the will to work. Any more effort will only weaken it. If the horse has achieved some degree of carriage in the canter, then one can transition to the walk as the best preparation for the halt.

If the horse learns canter-right properly, then it is time to also practice it on the left lead. Because cantering continuously on one lead makes the outside legs stiff due to the greater effort, diseases of the hind legs can often result. In addition, one should take care that the horse is worked the same to the right as to the left from the beginning of its dressage training, so that the necessary evenness on both sides is achieved.

The aids, i. e. the cue to canter left, are the same as they were in canter right as they relate to the different leg order. Just as these aids were given on the left more, now they must be used more on the right. This is explained more clearly if one describes the movement in canter left. The left legs step farther ahead of the right legs, and indeed in this way:

The horse first lifts the left foreleg, then the right foreleg and left hind leg simultaneously, and finally, the right hind foot. The feet are set down in the reverse order.

The horse is first introduced to this canter from the collected trot.

If the horse is now sufficiently confirmed in the canter on both leads, then it is time to demand greater perfection in this gait. This perfection consists of the horse cantering with the same tempo and the same carriage in three beats, which can be heard at equal intervals. The more it can carry itself on its hindquarters, the better it can maintain its carriage. Only through this proper carriage can it achieve an even tempo in its movement.

Because the horse easily loses the proper flexibility in the haunches in the canter exercises, one should finish each stint in canter with a proper reinback. This is due to the gait's bounding characteristic, which is unlike the other gaits, in that the hind legs do not bend to the same degree.

The young horses should only be asked to canter in balance, but never on the haunches. It is left to the rider's discretion how far he may go with this. It is the general rule that every campaign horse without exception should neither be too collected nor too extended. In the first case, the horse will tire too easily, and in the second, the hind legs cannot step under properly.

It would not be incorrect to mention something about the various deficiencies in the canter here, and especially about these mistakes as they relate to the rider's sense of feel. In order to be able to differentiate between the horse's movements, it is necessary that one knows the mechanism of it exactly, and learns to feel the correct setting down of the individual feet in every gait. In walk and trot, faults arise because the legs follow each other too quickly or in the incorrect order. This occurs most often in the canter.

When the horse is supposed to canter right, it can bound to the left, and vice versa. This is the easiest for the rider to feel, if he pays attention to the outside. This is always positioned more deeply in the correct canter, and at the same time, the inside legs move with more freedom.

With this, the rider can easily determine either canter lead by feel. He can also differentiate and correct faulty movements.

Another type of incorrect canter arises when the horse comes behind the movement in the trot. This is easy to feel because this movement is very different from the true canter. The horse is inclined to assume this gait if one tries to collect it out of the extended canter by using only the reins and not the legs. The inside hind leg fails to properly step under, whereby this trot-like movement arises.

One only undertakes greater collection in canter with a horse that is either very strong in the haunches or is more flexible in them, and never prepares the horse for the halt without preparing it properly with the legs. This can be considered the proper procedure.

In order to transition the horse from the walk, trot or halt to canter right or left at will, and with or without it changing the movement of the legs, it is best to ride it in the open where it can become familiar with strange objects that it may fear at first.

How the rider proceeds with the horse that is now trained, to transition to canter out of the halt, to canter on straight lines and to change hand in turns and to go in counter-bend, is explained in depth in the ninth chapter under "Rider Training." To properly counter the horse's shy nature if it refuses to obey the leg and rein aids out of fear by either rushing away from them or pulling back, spinning around, or even rearing up, see the seventh chapter on resistance.

The 8th chapter, "The Double Bridle," discusses the bridle with the curb bit that is necessary for the perfect training of the campaign horse, mainly in the canter, and its effect in comparison to the underlying snaffle. It also recommends which of the most common auxiliary reins, etc, to use should neither the curb bit nor the working snaffle suffice.

Chapter VI

On the simultaneous flexion of both hind legs
Jumping
Carrière

After the three gaits, walk, trot and canter are dealt with, a fourth natural movement of the horse finally receives mention, namely jumping.

Because the entire training relies upon finding and developing the horse's good characteristics, jumping may not be neglected and only considered to be a superfluous add-on to dressage. It is not to be practiced on its own, even if it is useful in certain cases, for example, to go over obstacles. In it lies something that is ideally suited to perfect the dressage training and to make the gaits that have been practiced even more regular. Furthermore, because jumping is an innate characteristic of the horse and it constantly finds reasons to use it despite all of the security measures, the rider is not in a position to properly resist a strong horse if it has not undergone previous jumping training and has been completely trained in it. In the horse's previous training, it was constrained in a suitable manner to put it in an artistic position so it could go well in the natural gaits, that is, in balance. Now, it will suddenly feel free of such constraint and will fall back into all of the errors that were done away with by a most arduous dressage training.

It is a famous rule of thumb that the rider of the as yet untrained horse has more control over the horse in the gaits that have more legs on the ground than are in the air. The reason is that the horse's training begins with walk and trot, only later is it cantered, and finally jumped. The last has consistently proven itself to be the most difficult in the training.

The canter, which is an unbroken sequence of bounds, is as related to jumping as walk and trot are to each other. Just as a good walk can only result from correct trot exercises, so too is jumping necessary for the development and maintenance of a good canter. The above sentence is true for a horse that is already trained in the reverse sense, namely, "The fewer legs on the ground, the more the rider can control the horse." Horses that are totally on the haunches in the School jumps prove this principle perfectly.

The disproportionate weight of the forehand inclines the horse to land with the forefeet first after jumping up off of the ground. This causes the front legs to suffer too much, especially if the rider's weight is added to them. It is then more difficult to collect the horse that is to be in balance. Its stamina is also impaired. If the horse remains in the position such that it will land with all four legs at the same time while jumping, that is, the weight distribution is the same as it was before the jump, then the horse jumps either in balance or collected. Being well positioned, it can then be ridden forward in any gait the rider chooses, and it will not tire as quickly. It is not to be expected of the ordinary campaign horse to land first with the hind legs after jumping over an obstacle. The rider must even prevent this, especially if the jump is high and wide, and the horse is supposed to immediately take off again. Only horses with the best dressage training and with the strongest hindquarters are in a position to execute these jumps on the haunches, which are not as high as those in balance, and are almost always performed on the spot. These are called the School jumps.

Controlling the horse under the rider such that it decisively jumps any obstacle with all four feet and without losing its balance while clearing it, depends on the breadth of the obstacles and the weight of the rider being in proportion to the strength and the agility that the horse has developed, and that the rider is capable of using the necessary methods quickly and effectively.

The rules to which the rider must pay attention to train a campaign horse that has been trained up to the canter and which is to be trained in jumping can be presented the most clearly after contemplating the mechanics of the jump.

If the green horse wants to jump over an obstacle on its own, whether it is high or wide, it collects itself and pushes the weight of its forehand off of the ground with its forelegs first, then transfers it to the hindquarters with the joints of the hind legs flexing more. The hind legs then launch the horse up off of the ground by extending suddenly. While the horse is in the air, it usually remains in a stretched-out frame. It first tucks its hind legs in when the forelegs hit the ground and have taken the weight. Most horses jump on the forehand, i. e. in the so-called deer jump, when they are at liberty. In this case, this may not be detrimental, but it is when the rider's weight is added. How the combined weight of horse and rider is evenly distributed and absorbed on all four legs is now easy to explain. It is necessary for the rider to collect the horse after it has propelled itself over the obstacle and is still in the air. Few riders will succeed in correctly collecting the horse as it takes off if it does not take a determined approach, i. e., if its thoughts, rather than being completely focused on clearing the obstacle are also partly on refusal due to a lack of confidence in its own strength or ability. In such cases, if the rider forces the horse to jump, the take-off is crooked and collecting the horse at the end of the jump is much more difficult. Therefore, campaign horses should not be schooled over ditches and barrier-obstacles as long as they can still assume a crooked position in their natural gaits under the rider. To avoid these is the rule. In the beginning, choose obstacles that are not very high or wide. They should be approached at the walk or trot. The rider must also leave it to the horse to collect itself in the beginning jumping exercises and be satisfied if it stays straight, regardless of whether it carries out the jump on its forehand. If the horse approaches the jump straight and with determination, then the rider can support it through collection in the take-off, as well as in the landing. The canter is the most suitable gait for jumping, because in its bounding movement, the rider can more easily determine the timing of the collecting or driving aids for executing the jump. This is because it can be clearly felt how the horse alternates between pulling itself together and stretching itself out. It is the horse's nature to be more inclined to stretching out, and even more so due to the rider's weight. For this reason, the drawing together deserves the most attention.

One can recognize the horse's good will to earnestly want to undertake a jump by the fact that the horse goes toward the jump on its own, or if this is not possible due to space constraints, then it will collect on its own. It is up to the rider to further one or the other; the methods for carrying them out are different for both. The horse puts most of its weight onto the forehand during the approach when it lengthens. Preparing for the take-off, it unburdens it and collects itself. The first is facilitated by yielding on the reins, pushing forward with the hips, and using leg pressure; the latter by half-halting on the reins, setting the hips back, and using spur aids. When using the spurs to collect, the heels are raised, and thereby, the calf muscles are relaxed. The leg pressure is decreased after that and it is easier to put the horse together.

It is difficult for a rider who has not practiced it to alternate between the partly driving and partly restraining aids in a timely fashion so as to control the horse in the approach to the jump. This will vanish as soon as he correctly understands his horse's thoughts and actions. He must give the aids to approach and those that prepare for the jump only when the horse is inclined to do so. This can only happen if it is going straight. With respect to the approach, if a horse has assumed a crooked position in front of an obstacle over which it is to jump, and the rider uses predominantly driving aids instead of straightening it, for example, then it could refuse. If it is not allowed to refuse and is forced to jump, then the jump will be executed in a crooked and unsafe manner. In such a case, it is the rule to not allow the jump to occur. Instead, one should counter this refusal by halting, and if the horse sucks back or goes backward, then counter that with the strongest forward-driving aids until the horse is left with only one path to choose, which is the one directly ahead, or in other words, the correct approach to the jump. As soon as it decides to do this, the horse's rump becomes narrower between the hind legs as opposed to wider, and neither side is bent. The rider's seat feels the hind legs decisively pushing, and the hands feel equal contact on both reins. The reins must be yielded a bit, if the horse appears to want to push its head forward. This is the moment to use the driving aids that have been described. Only when the horse has approached correctly can the rider's collecting aids be used at the correct moment to lift the forehand. In the contrasting case, however, when the crooked approach cannot be prevented, then the deer jump is necessary, and must be allowed. However, it will make it more difficult to clear the obstacle.

In the situation that contrasts to the one above, the rider will feel the horse collect itself in the correct approach to the jump. By pulling its forehand and hindquarters together, it gains in volume. The pushing action of its hind legs changes quickly into one of carrying, and the head and neck are both brought back into the bridle, so to speak.

This situation corresponds to the following: First, the rider must facilitate the widening of the ribcage with appropriate leg pressure, demand that the hind legs step under and carry the forehand via calf or spur aids, and finally, cause the horse to come into the bridle by using each rein equally and by putting measured pressure on each rein or by half-halting.

All of these aids are to be used to the degree suited to the individual horse. They should be used until the forehand leaves the ground.

The horse repeats these actions from take-off until the end of the jump, namely extending and then pulling itself together. The rider should repeat the aids accordingly.

The same means that were used in the approach, i. e. yielding on the reins, stronger leg pressure, etc., must be used from the time the hind legs leave the ground until the horse has cleared the obstacle. The rider has to decisively resist the horse's tendency to land with its forelegs first. He does this via the swift and purposeful use of the collecting aids, which must begin when the horse is still in the air. While the spur aids encourage the horse to tuck its hind legs in, the reins can easily maintain the position of the forehand, provided that the rider's upper body remains back. This directs his weight toward the hindquarters. As a result of these aids, the horse will pull all four legs in to itself at the same time and then stretch them out at the moment it lands, so that the weight is supported evenly on all four legs upon landing.

If the rider wants to halt after jumping, or perhaps turn, then he must maintain the collecting aids, otherwise switch to the driving aids.

From this description, it is easy to see when the rider must interfere when jumping, and when it becomes unnecessary and even detrimental. The driving leg aids inspire decisiveness and are only used in jumping when the hind legs are about to leave the ground. In contrast, the collecting aids, which only allow for a light leg contact, are used twice, namely at the beginning of the jump and at the end. Continuous clinging makes it impossible for the horse to remain in balance while jumping. In this case, the rider can only swing forward and up, in order to go with the motion.

Only very talented horses, of which there are few, will be able to collect themselves on their own while in the air. These horses will not require the rider's aids during the approach to the jump and subsequent take-off. Such naturally gifted horses are the most preferable and most suitable for every use. Their value will only be correctly recognized by their achievements in daily practice in jumping insofar as this serves as a touchstone for horse and rider.

On the Carrière

The training of the campaign horse can only be considered complete when it is able to extend itself and gallop tirelessly for as long as the rider wants without disturbing the required balance. An exercise is necessary for this that is essentially different from the previous lessons only in that it, while strictly preserving the balance that has been achieved, uses the extensor muscles more and stresses the respiratory organs, which have not been strained very much up to this point.

One should not confuse the carrière with the gallop. In the gallop, the horse goes on the forehand and not in balance. Neither should one consider it to be impossible for a horse to remain in balance in a faster than normal canter. Should the carrière become a method of training for the campaign horse, then the properly guided exercises described above will be required, as well as a good hand. Without these prerequisites, it is better not to practice it. However, if the rider has these assets, then there is no exercise more suited to waking up lazy or timid horses, to bringing ticklish horses that suck back onto the hand, and to making angry and hot horses that defend themselves by leaping sideways obedient.

The canter earns the name, "carrière," when the three beats flow into two. The forelegs hit the ground at the same time in the first beat. This puts the weight of the body onto the two hind feet, which then together lift the body and propel it forward in the second beat. Setting the legs down happens again in two beats. In the first, the forelegs touch the ground; in the second, the hind legs do.

The horse's balance and endurance are developed as a result of the hind legs simultaneously advancing and being set down, which carry the burden equally. This is because a greater power, namely both hind legs, simultaneously propel the body forward in the carrière.

As far as speed is concerned, it does not equal that of the racing gallop. Although the gallop strides do not follow one another as quickly as in the carrière, the ground covered by each stride is greater in the gallop. This is because the pairs of feet are not set down as closely to each other.

In the carrière, one foot does not step ahead of the other. This can best be seen, if not by the movement of the legs, by the footprints that are left by the hooves.

Only horses with a good conformation and very strong and supple haunches are naturally suited to the regularity of the carrière. Such horses require only very little support from the rider. However, it is necessary for the rider to have ridden such naturally gifted horses in this, their fastest gait, in order to feel the difference between the carrière and the ordinary extended canter. The movement that the rider feels in the saddle when both hind legs reach forward equally, and thus both equally support and advance the body, is quite different from how it feels if one of the legs is dominant.

It is assumed that the horse is sufficiently prepared for the carrière training, i. e. that it already collects itself with increased pressure from both spurs and with equal restriction on both reins. In the beginning, choose an area that is as flat as possible, avoid turns, and always transition out of the ordinary canter into the carrière by collecting the horse. Whether the horse starts with the right or left lead is not important; only the cross-canter should not be allowed. The horse, positioned straight between the equally restrictive reins and the legs, must constantly feel a steady and soft contact on the bit. If this contact becomes too hard as a result of the hind legs pushing too much, then the rein hand should not yield. Instead, it holds more firmly and is supported by measured spur aids until the hind legs step under more. The horse will then yield to the hand and return to a good contact. If the contact is hard because of one of the hind legs, for example, the right one, then the horse is leaning more on the right rein and is positioning its head and neck in a crooked manner towards the left. In this case, the left leg must first be made to step into action, the left rein must keep a steady contact, the right rein must be held against the right hind foot, and the right spur must be used.

If the horse refuses to obey these aids and transition into the faster gait, then one should not practice the carrière yet. Instead, return to the preparatory exercises.

It is usually difficult to resist the horse's natural inclination to extend into the gallop because it is easier to encourage it. If one wants to do that, then use the driving aids, which have already been introduced when jumping. However, if one wishes to temper a too great extension, then use the collecting aids in this case. The rider will develop the carrière out of the ordinary canter with three beats, in which two feet on one side step in front of the other, after which they will step freely, The rider will get equal control over all four feet. If, for example, the horse is cantering right, then use the aids to canter left so carefully that it does not cause a flying change. In the process, the left legs are given more freedom, and the right legs take shorter yet quicker steps. If a flying change occurs, the rider must pretend as though he meant to do it, but then by using aids that make the left canter more difficult, he tries to get the hind legs to step forward and down equally as required in the carrière. Once this is achieved, the driving and collecting aids must be used equally and simultaneously on both sides of the horse to accelerate and maintain the gait. Because the carrière is a series of successively wider bounds, whereby the horse, as described when jumping, stretches out and then pulls itself together, the aids that further this task are also to be used here, and a repetition is not required.

How long this exercise can be carried out depends on the individual horse. Horses with short, strong backs and firm tendons first obey the leg pressure and the spurs and assume the extension and rein contact necessary for the carrière when a small amount of fatigue sets in. In contrast, horses with long and weak backs that go too strung-out and with firm contact will not collect until the continuous use of the spurs begins to become intolerable.

The result, the collection, is the goal. This should determine the length of each individual exercise.

The horse should never be halted directly out of the carrière. It should be collected to the canter, then transitioned into the walk.

In order to more easily shorten the canter to a collected canter, it is necessary to work with the curb bit. The curb is indispensable because of its lever action. In the exercises in jumping and in the carrière, it should be considered a hindrance in the former, but the foundation in the latter.

The bridling with the curb along with its effect and use has been discussed partly in one of the chapters devoted to it, partly in the chapter about teaching riding, after that in the chapter on the resistance of the horse and how it can be countered.

Chapter VII

On the resistance of the horse and rider feel

During the course of the previous training, the rider has encountered occasional resistance from the horse. This was expressed in different ways depending on the horse's character and conformation, but mostly by too little or too much forward motion. If one knows exactly how to judge the essence of the resistance, then it will be easy to find the method to counter it. This will be either driving or collecting aids depending on the nature of the resistance.

Horses try to resist the rider's demands by using four types of disobedience. These are by

1) Bolting;

2) Bucking;

3) Going behind the bit, spinning around, rearing, and rolling;

4) Finally, by standing still, refusing to move forward, and even lying down.

Depending on the conformation, temperament, and sensitivity, horses choose one of these methods to resist. It is less common for them to pick more than one, and seldom does one choose all of them to resist the rider. If the horse defends itself in several ways, then it knows to quickly change the various methods of resistance. Much skill and careful thought are required of the rider who wishes to retain mastery over a horse by using his aids.

The last of the bad habits described above is the worst of all. As long as the horses keep moving, whether forward too much, on the spot or backwards, we still have control over them. The easiest to correct is bolting.

It has already been determined in the General Section that the horse's movements can only be organized if the position of the two connected arms of the front and rear double-armed levers, i. e. the spine, is in balance. This position is possible for every horse via both of the other lever arms. Up to now, significant resistance from the young horse has not been anticipated. Now, however, it is assumed that the horse is already fairly old and has been spoiled by incorrect handling, i. e. its rider has not succeeded in gaining control by correctly positioning the rear lever arm (the pelvis) or the foremost lever arm (the neck). Therefore, the correct positioning of the spine has failed, and the horse is not under control.

The resistance is a consequence of this (if it is not due to physical defects). As a result, it is easy to find the means to change the position of the connected lever arms. These consist mainly of the following:

When a horse goes in balance under the rider, then the power of the forehand and hindquarters meet at one point, namely, where both double-armed levers are connected. At this point, their effects are either cancelled out, or they can be used by the rider as he wishes.

On a horse that bolts, the opposite condition can be found. The power of the forehand and hindquarters do not cancel each other out. Instead, their power is combined and expressed in one direction. The collecting aids that were discussed under half-halts and halts are suited to this type of resistance. However, they only serve to completely overcome the pushing power of the hindquarters if used when the hind legs are stepping forward and down, either at the same time or, if this is not possible, one after the other.

When bolting, the horse abuses the pushing characteristic of its hindquarters, in that it uses the extensor muscles of the hindquarters along with those of the neck to oppose the rein hand. It goes against the reins with a stiff poll, and ignores the rider's collecting aids. Whether the horse goes forward or sideways in a jumping-motion or in trot, or even in walk, the regular alternating action of both of the double-armed levers is always interrupted. This will continue to occur for as long as the forefeet and hind feet step too far apart, and especially if the hind feet remain behind the line of the haunches.

When a bolting horse is positioned straight and refuses to bring its hind legs in front of or at least to the line of the haunches due to insensitivity to the spurs, and will not allow itself to be halted despite all of the efforts of the rein hand, then one should resort to using the underlying bridoon. With this, one can affect the individual hind leg with intermittent increased rein pressure, after which the corresponding spur drives the hind leg forward and under. This is easier to do if there is enough room and the horse is still manageable enough to be ridden on a circle. In this case, one must first try to bend the inside hind leg by the means previously indicated, after which the horse, if it is cantering, must transition to walk or trot. However, if it is necessary to remain on a straight line, one should try to bend an individual hind leg with the position and the aids that were given for the canter position. The rider can tell whether the loading and flexing of one leg has been achieved by the rein contact becoming less hard. He should not hesitate to use the curb and both spurs then, in order to give the horse a good position via half-halts and halts.

Horses that are given wrong or unsteady aids will usually assume a crooked position by bending their necks incorrectly. This makes it impossible for the rider to burden the hind legs. Therefore, one must first straighten the neck to achieve the desired effect via the collecting aids. If an unsteady neck is attached to a weak or even concave back, then it is more difficult for the horse to collect. Horses with convex backs and steady yet flexible necks are easy to halt with the spur. Their backs connect the forelegs and haunches better and the neck furthers the effect of the curb's shanks. To counter the inflexibility in the hind legs, the rein back is recommended after halting from the walk. This very effective correction must be carried out with much careful thought, and indeed with similar aids as were described when collecting the horse. The legs and the spurs must be used before the rein. This rule is especially valid here, because the horse, in order to step backwards, must first lift a hind foot. Short, quick spur aids are the most suitable to use here. When the right spur prompts the right hind foot to leave the ground, for example, the reins are used to burden the left foot, and the right hind leg is set down and back.

The right spur must prevent this foot from stepping back too far from the other hind foot. This is because it is a main objective that the hind feet remain close to each other both in forward motion as well as in backward motion in order to burden the haunches. In rein back, the rider must put his body weight on the hind leg that is carrying at the moment, in order to increase its flexion and, at the same time, allow the other foot to lift up and move.

By carrying out the procedure in reverse, one will try to bend the right haunch. In so doing, if one of the haunches feels as though it is more inflexible than the other, then it must be worked primarily. This occurs via rein back in the shoulder-in or in the canter-position, as well as on a circle and on straight lines. If both haunches can stiffen in this because the rider reverses the order of the aids described above, then he should be prepared for the horse to rear, whereby the horse will come behind the bit.

Ad II. The second of the resistances presented, the buck, is usually suited to green horses. It was already mentioned in the section on first mounting and riding. Here it deserves special mention regarding the horses that make a false jump on the spot, and usually kick out behind before they touch the ground with the forefeet. Horses that have this bad habit are always the ones with strong backs, but often also have weak hind limbs. One may not demand balance from them before they have "given their backs" as one says, i. e. before the visibly convex line of the back has become straight.

The lever action must be pointed to here again, as it was explained in the General Section. The foremost double-armed lever becomes one when the horse bucks, or its position becomes so incorrect that it cannot be used to restore the horse's good position before it has been re-positioned so as to be functional again. The method for handling green horses that buck is mainly to lift the head and neck. Our control over the front lever depends on how we position the hind lever. In the natural condition, the first arm of the lever (the lumbar vertebrae) is horizontal, and the second (the pelvis) sits at an obtuse angle to it. When bucking, the horse positions its pelvis almost perpendicularly, in that it brings its four legs as close to each other as possible and then raises its back. In this case, one must use all means available to restore this lever's natural position, because it will be easy to lift the foremost arm of the front lever (the neck) as much as necessary to regain control of the horse's back.

This is often not achieved. Many equestrians ride horses with hard backs from front to back too much and too early, and rob them of the desire to go forward rather than awakening the desire to go forward by riding the horse from back to front. For this purpose, the pushing characteristic of the hind legs, that is their movement behind, must first be furthered as much as possible via extended trot and canter. Even if the horse kicks out behind in the beginning, it should be forgiven. This can only be countered by gradually lifting the head and neck during the most extended gait possible. This is because the more the hind legs step behind the line of the haunches, the more the pelvis is lifted, and the more the rear part of the spine (lumbar) will lower. This presses down on the vertebrae and makes it easier for the rider's hand to lift the head and neck, thereby restoring a good position of the back. The process to make horses go smoothly and extended the gait was already mentioned in the first and second chapters of this section.

Ad III. Creeping behind the bit, etc. A horse comes behind the bit, i. e. it drops the contact on one or both reins and loses its tempo.

Just as the predominantly pushing activity of the hind legs caused it to bolt, so too will too little pushing action lead it to first come behind the bit, and consequently cause it to spin around, rear, and so forth.

The hind legs step too far in front of the line of the haunches, whereby the horses either set their head and neck up and back in an exaggerated manner, or arch their necks too much. In another case, they remain behind the bit, whereby the horse generally goes against the hand, tosses its head, and takes steps that are too short.

In these cases, using the reins effectively is not possible because there is no contact.

Other means to achieve contact must be chosen depending on how the hind legs are moving.

In the first case, when the hind legs step too far forward and under, the horse must be collected via the half-halts that have already been mentioned and worked in shortened gaits.

In the second case, when the hind legs do not step forward and under enough, one drives the horse forward and makes use of extended gaits. One spares such horses full halts for as long as is necessary for them to take a firm contact on the reins.

The horse will always come behind one rein before it spins around. The horse throws its weight onto the legs on one side, drops one rein by bending its neck incorrectly, and then spins around. This can be prevented if one restores contact on both reins quickly, then disciplines the horse so firmly with the spur on the side towards which it turns or drops contact that it is persuaded to go forward again. A few strong spur aids afterward will prevent any further attempt.

Before a horse spins around, it will pause in its motion and thereby betray its intention. There is often time for the observant rider to restore the forward motion via leg and rein aids, because it is always better to prevent problems than to have to punish afterward.

Before the horse can rear, it must first stop moving forward. Therefore, it is advisable for one who fears that the horse is about to rear to not let it come to a standstill. The horse's haunches are stiff rather than bent when rearing. When flexed haunches are burdened, they propel the horse's forehand forward, but stiff haunches throw the weight backwards. The horse may fall down, if the rider pulls on the reins and uses his weight at the wrong moment. It is for skilled riders to counter and use the initial raising of the forehand in rearing, in order to break this bad habit, i. e. those who have skills at their disposal that were gained partly from a long experience in riding resistant horses and partly from the higher School.

In general, one should fear that the horse will fall down more than one should fear falling off. For this reason, there are more good hunt riders than School riders. Only through School exercises can the rider attain the following stratagems, the quick and decisive use of which will remove the danger that the horse will rear and fall down.

As long as the rearing horse does not throw its nose up in the air and cannot drop the contact, i. e. it is still correctly in the bridle, one need not fear that it will fall down. However, if the horse stiffens its hind legs and assumes the incorrect head position, then the rider must quickly prevent the horse from rearing up higher than a 45° angle from the ground in order to not fall down. If the angle is more acute than this, the haunches must bend under the weight, and then every horse is more inclined to lower the forehand and rush forward, rather than to rear higher or to throw itself over backwards. If this burdening is not possible, then the rider must hold the reins with determination, lean backwards, and spur the horse strongly in the sides. It will then hop with the hind legs and leave the ground. Now that it is in the air, it is under the complete control of the skilled rider. In order to lower the forehand, the rider must hold the reins more strongly, so that it either reaches the ground at the same time as the hindquarters, or even better, a moment later. If the latter is the case, then the horse has been so thoroughly punished for its misbehavior that it will gladly go forward upon the rider's urging. Punishing the horse via the halt from the jump is considered to be a universal method to use against resistant horses. The only difficulty in this lies in bringing the horse to rear, which is made easier by lifting and then taking back on the reins at the ideal moment and holding against the forehand. With horses that quickly rear up, this is most difficult and demands much quiet consideration on the part of the rider, which is not for those who let fear get the better of them.

If the horse has already reared up higher than the given angle, then the rider must yield on the reins and help to unburden the hind legs by leaning forward. Because the hind legs stiffen here, the smallest amount of weight on them will encourage the rear and help make it fall down. The rider can almost always prevent the horse from falling down by giving on the reins at the correct moment. If not, he must dismount as the horse's neck is coming towards him. In the case that he does not land on his feet, then he must roll to the side, so that the horse does not fall on him. This will only be necessary in the most infrequent of cases. It is better if the rider stays in the saddle and quietly waits for the forehand to lower again. Then he holds the reins with firm contact when the horse reaches the ground again, and lets the horse feel the spurs so intensely that it will hop forward and under with the hind legs. Now the courageous rider will not hesitate to cause his horse to rear, and this time, give the appropriate aids at the right moment to halt out of the jump. It is to be wished that at least the riders that mount a horse in order to break it, and that possess a proud spirit, could use their spurs for this universal method — the halt out of the jump. Well begun is half done! Danger and fear disappear with the advantages that are gained. Only then does riding gain the highest and ever increasing appeal.

Ad IV. The rider is confronted with many difficulties when the horse resists the leg aids to move forward, and despite all driving aids and punishments, it either stands stock still or leans on some object, such as a wall, fence, etc, and thereby makes the rider's legs, which are indispensable, ineffective.

The worst bad habit, however, is when the horse throws itself and the rider down, and then remains lying down. In this way, it robs the rider of the only tool at his disposal, namely, the forward motion. In such cases, all skill comes to an end, and the rider must dismount when the horse remains lying on its side or even tries to roll. Such extreme cases are, thankfully, rare. They are the result of previous unreasonable torment and counterproductive treatment. Such ill treatment can cause horses to become so hostile towards humans that they can free themselves of the bridle by throwing themselves down and then attack the rider with their teeth and hooves.

One should protect oneself from making horses this angry and putting themselves in an impossible position as a result of this powerlessness.

When we know how to use the aids that have been described to prepare the horse for the forward motion, that is, to keep the horse in collection, then the horse cannot creep behind the bit. This is the beginning of all disobediences discussed here except for bolting. However, should this preventative measure have been neglected, driving the horse forward will correct the fault shortly after it occurs.

However, if standing still has become rooted as a misbehavior, and if it is not enough to drive the horse forward and to punish it, then one can make use of one of the most effective methods, the rein back, which was discussed in the resistance of bolting. It must be done until the horse is motivated by the bending in the haunches to move forward again. Only horses that stiffen the haunches and step behind the line of the haunches are inclined to resort to this bad habit. All methods that lead to the loading of the hind legs, mainly the rein back, are to be used.

When a horse sticks to the wall or leans against it, then one must bend the neck in such a way that it runs into the wall with its nose before the rest of its body. At the same time, use the spur on the side that is in danger of being made unusable by the horse's misbehavior. If the horse has already reached the wall and the neck can no longer be bent, then the rider's leg is at risk of being made useless. To deal with this bad situation, the rider uses the spur of the free leg to make the horse pick its hind leg up on that side and step backward. Without making the hind leg mobile, it will be difficult to get the horse to step back or to bring the forehand away from the wall. If he succeeds, then a continuous rein back on a circle in the middle of the arena is the best corrective measure.

In order to not put oneself in such a bad situation, one should work such horses out in the open, ride them in extended gaits, straight at the beginning, no matter which gait, and then only go on circles and squares. One should not bring them back into the arena until they no longer creep behind the bit, because this is the cause of this obstinacy.

Horses that show so little forward drive that they throw themselves down under the rider and out of stubbornness remain lying down are extremely rare. This is because their training and education is now much better understood and conducted.

However, if this case arises, then the horse's training is best started over from the beginning. Lunge line and a trainer with a whip are needed again, and one goes through the process that was taught in the first chapter.

From what has been said up to now about the horses' resistance, it is evident that its origin is always a disturbance in the correct relationship between the carrying and pushing force of the horse's hind legs. The extremes are expressed in only two ways — by bolting or by lying down.

The experienced rider never lets it come to one of these extremes, such that the horse can use its entire weight against him. He immediately senses any deviation from the correct relationship, i. e. from the good movement, because he knows how to recognize the emergence of resistance. He knows how to cleverly prevent it, and one says of him that he has the correct

Rider Feel.

The opinion, "A good rider can guess his horse's thoughts," is correct in so far that the horse's will induces certain muscular activity, depending on the horse's energy, that is always the same. It can be partly seen and partly felt by the attentive rider. The rider can draw a correct conclusion from it with regard to the next voluntary acts of his horse, as well as the state of the internal organism from its breath, pulse, etc. The visible, although not reliable, features consist of the pointing and laying back of the ears, raising the head and sticking the nose out, pushing the head sideways with an incorrect bend in the neck, tossing, shaking and throwing the head and neck, etc. Most riders know how to correctly interpret these expressions of their horses, perhaps only because they are visible. The foregoing, not emphasized as essential, require no further mention here. They deserve less attention than the characteristics that are only perceptible by feel. These always appear one moment before the visible ones do. Not only are they more reliable, they never lie.

The correct assessment of the visible manifestations has nothing to do with rider feel, which only refers to the rider's sense of feel. This occurs by correctly distinguishing and interpreting how the horse moves those parts with which the rider is connected through the natural points of contact.

These parts are the horse's spine and ribs. Only from their movements can the rider deduce correctly by feel what the hind legs are doing, from which alone the impulse to move forward can be awakened and upon which everything depends in riding.

The rider feels the movement of the spine mainly with his seat. He feels the horse's ribs with the flat part of the inner thigh.

The main difficulty in dressage, recognizing the correct moment to give the aids and corrections using the hand and leg, is made easier when, apart from the seat, one is also able to use one's legs to feel how the horse's hind legs are moving. Here, the rider is more surely guided by feeling the movement of the horse's ribs with his thighs than by feeling the movements of its backbone. This is because the seat is less sensitive by nature than the inner surface of the thighs. However, this ability to feel the horse's movements is only developed by the rider if he practices riding in every respect so as to learn to determine the position of the seat and thighs such that he can use them to either precisely follow or counter the horse's movements in any situation. Furthermore, he knows how to use other parts of his body to support this sense of feel.

The campaign rider, the School rider, the hunt rider, and the jockey all ride differently, both in terms of their position and that of the horse. Even their aids and the horses' gaits are not the same, in that every one of them requires a different tempo. Accordingly, every one of these more accomplished riders has a special sensitivity, commensurate with his individual circumstances. Consequently, he who would be equal in all of these types of equitation would be the most educated. It has already been explained to the campaign rider in this section how he can achieve sufficient rider feel. For him, the previous explanation is enough. Trainers and School riders encounter greater difficulties in this. If they consider it to be their duty to give an honest account of their actions, then they need a fine sensitivity. This has already been indicated here, but can only be more fully explained in the following section on the School.

In order to be able to fully perceive the change in the shape of the horse's rump, which is a subject of particular concern, the rider must first have acquired this skill via School exercises, namely by riding without stirrups, such that one can close the trapezoid of one's thighs around the horse's ribs. The movement of the ribs can be most clearly felt towards the middle of the horse. If the base of his upper body is positioned in that location, then he will be able to most accurately tell how the hind legs are stepping: Whether too much in front of or behind the line of the haunches, whether they push too much or too little, whether they bend or not, and whether one or both hind legs is or are most suited for being loaded.

By riding difficult horses, especially those that defend themselves with the most extreme measures that have already been mentioned, the rider can learn to clearly perceive and interpret the change in the shape of their rumps. So, for example, the horse that bolts has a rump that is longer and narrower, while the hind legs step too far behind the line of the haunches, i. e. they stiffen and push too much. With the horse that wants to lie down, the hind legs are too far in front of the line of the haunches. In the first case, one feels too little between the legs; in the second, the rib cage has too much volume.

This widening and lengthening of the rump occurs before the various tendencies of the horse to resist appear. It may vary in degree, but otherwise, always remains the same.

If the rider has first gained the skill to make it more difficult for horses to abuse these characteristics, then he will gradually succeed in using them to his advantage: The widening for collection and the lengthening for the extended gaits. The place, position, and degree of leg pressure will become the main subject of his consideration. He no longer uses crude leg contact, but rather the correct School leg contact or leg position from which alone all degrees of the aids can be given. The individuality of the horse, not the arbitrariness of the rider, will determine the use of this or that leg aid, as well as the distribution of his weight, which is almost as important as the aids. Precision in the use of the aids has reached its peak when they no longer appear to be coming from the rider but actually arise from the movement itself, that is, they are communicated through the horse's movement. The rider can only reach this perfection if he makes the flexion in the haunches the main goal of the dressage training, whereas those who worry too much about the bending of the head and neck will never reach that goal. It is clear from what has already been said, and it will later be proven even more, that those riders who prefer to focus their attention on the hind legs and work on their stepping, bending, and loading act more according to nature, because the engine is in the hindquarters. The unforced and yet strong position of the rider is then ascribable not to his anatomy, but to the proper movement of the horse, which hardly allows for a different position. Such riders are correct in the saddle on such horses, and soon feel what is missing in the training. They quickly discover every deviation from the rule, and their methods are targeted at doing away with these mistakes. It is only they who possess true rider feel.

Chapter VIII

On the curb bit and the most common auxiliary devices

It is up to the rider's previous experience to determine the correct time to introduce the horse to the curb bit. The following can be established only in general terms.

As far as the time for introducing the double bridle is concerned, a horse that is well-prepared by the lessons that are described above will gladly accept the curb. It will become all the sooner accustomed to it, because the particular lever-action makes it easier for it to go forward. Horses that already go naturally in balance under the rider also allow themselves to be ridden with the curb, if they are properly obedient to the leg aids. A primary requirement is that the rider has a skilled hand. Otherwise, the horse will have good cause to resist.

If the horse is not in balance because of various defects in its conformation, or because it is still green and ignorant of the aids, then it will be assessed during a proper workout before it is ridden with the curb bit. This is not always the most suitable bridle for the beginning training of the green horse under the rider. This is assuming that time and opportunity allow a systematic training, that is, allow for a training process of the basics from the ground up. Only in an emergency can working the green horse in the curb appear to be expedient, as soon as it willingly goes under the rider. Such a case would be in war, for example, where it is important to put the cavalryman quickly in line without consideration for how much the horse suffers or how much it is ruined. In any other circumstances, experience shows that such quick dressage training methods are reprehensible.

As far as the choice of curb is concerned, it is necessary for horses that are almost built in balance, and for those that are less favored by nature in their conformation but have become receptive due to their previous dressage training, to be given a curb in which the individual parts are always the same in relation to each other, but vary in other respects due to the different construction of the horses' jaws.

Depending on the degree of the horse's predisposition to go in balance, one uses curb bits that have countless differences in their shape. Thus, no rules can be established for their greater or lesser effectiveness. New ones are invented on a daily basis, especially in England, which can be quite expedient for those who ride their horses almost always in the natural position, as will be discussed at greater length in the third part.

A curb consists of three parts,

1) The bit or mouthpiece;
2) The shanks;
3) The curb chain.

The curb bit muss give the tongue room to move freely, because it is through this freedom of movement that the horse's mouth stays fresh. Thus, a port is absolutely necessary. It should be at least one inch wide, because the palate is about 1 1/2 inches wide at the point where the bit has effect. The height of the port depends on the thickness of the tongue, and can vary from one inch to 1 1/2. A joint on the port is not necessary. Both sides of the mouthpiece, which make contact with the bars of the mouth, must be equal in height and have a circumference of at least two inches.

Hollow bits are preferable only because they are light in weight. If the horse cannot be stopped from tossing its head, then a hollow bit can prevent injury to the bars. Most important is the width of the bit, which as already mentioned, must be determined according to the horse's mouth. Usually with horses of average height, it varies between 4 1/4 to 4 3/8 or 4 1/2 inches.

Every curb bit consists of a cheekpiece, and is divided into upper cheek bar and shank. The shank is connected to the cheekpiece of the main bridle via the headstall ring, which incidentally, must be round. The curb chain is attached to the headstall rings with curb hooks. At the bottom of the lower shanks, there is a rein ring to which the reins are attached. An inch or so above and behind it is the lip strap ring through which the lip strap goes, after it has been run through a small ring in the middle of the curb chain. This strap prevents the horse from grabbing the bit with its teeth. It also prevents the bit from injuring the palate if the horse tosses its head severely. When it is used, the lower shanks can have a straight position.

In the cavalry, this strap is not recommended due to the time-consuming bridling. Therefore, the rounded shanks are the most suitable.

There is no definite length that can be assumed for the upper cheek bar. This is because the cleft under the jaw above the groove for the curb chain begins lower on some horses and higher on others. If it is low, then the normal measurement of 1 3/4 inches for the length of the upper cheek bar will be too high, and the curb chain will lie on that point where the cleft begins or over it, which can be identified by two sharp ridges. The horse is much more sensitive to the pressure of the curb chain on this point than to the pressure of the bit on the bars. The effect of the curb is then reversed. Instead of the horse coming into the bridle, it goes against it and tosses its head. Under these circumstances, the length of the upper cheek bar may often be only one inch. In the other case, when the curb-chain groove is wider because the cleft of the lower jaw begins higher, the usual length of 1 3/4 to 2 inches may be kept, and then the generally assumed length of the lower cheek bar, namely twice the length of the upper cheek bar, may remain the same. The length of the entire curb from cheek ring to rein ring would thus amount to being about six inches. If the upper cheek bar is only one inch long, then the lower cheek bar can be up to three inches long.

The curb chain should only be regarded as a counterpoint, or the support point, of the shank, which acts as a lever, and should cause no pain. Accordingly, the more it covers the whole chin, and the flatter and closer the links are joined together, the less sensitivity the pressure will cause. Since the individual links of the ordinary curb chain are shaped so that they fit together exactly by twisting them far enough to the right, they will be able to form a flat surface. Their pressure will cause less pain the stronger the individual links are. However, they may not be so big that they extend beyond the curb chain groove. The double reinforced curb chain is the best.

The correct position of the bit is usually a thumb's width above the lower canine teeth. However, this provision is relative, since the position of the lower canines is not the same for all horses. They are higher for some, and lower for others. With some, they are high in the mandible and low in the lower jaw, so that when the position of the bit is assumed by the canines in the lower jaw, the canines of the mandible hit it. Mares generally have no canines. Therefore, the position of the bit is better to determine according to the curb chain groove, and indeed in the way that, when one sets the bit in use with a correctly attached curb chain by taking back on the reins, it rests directly over the middle of the curb chain groove on the bars. With horses that have no perceptible groove, which often occurs, one must determine it according to the cleft in the lower jaw, under which the curb chain should lie when the reins are taken up.

On the effect of the curb on a horse that has been made receptive to it

In order to be able to clearly explain how the curb brings about perfect balance in a horse that has been prepared for it, think of the curb as a lever of the second kind (see General Section) acting on a lever of the first kind, namely on a horse that is so far along that it deserves this designation. Only when the horse has assumed an artistic and deliberate position rather that its natural position does the curb work in the intended way in accordance with the demands that are made on it. For example, if one allows the fully bridled horse to stretch out in a state of rest such that the hind legs remain behind the line of the haunches rather than being over or in front of it, pressure on even the best curb only affects the foremost double-armed lever of the horse. The rear lever remains free, because the hind legs cannot be flexed. The hind legs are easier to burden the farther in front of the line of the haunches they step when the horse is moving forward. Therefore, it is easier when moving forward than in a lateral movement, if the hind feet do not track over the hoof prints of the forefeet. The horse's balance cannot be separated from how the hind legs move. Thus, the curb can only have the desired effect on a horse that is in balance.

In order to explain the effect of the curb as a lever, one thinks of the force working on the rein rings, the resting point on the cheek rings via the curb chain, and the weight of the mouth piece on the lower jawbone. If these follow the direction of the pressure, then the condition for the lever of the second kind is fulfilled, namely, that the force and the load move in the same direction. The curb acts incorrectly or as a lever of the first kind, if the horse goes against the hand, pulls against the reins, and tosses its head. This is often blamed on an incorrectly placed curb chain, or that the curb is too high, and the horse is trying to escape the pain caused by the curb chain by tossing its head. Usually, however, it is insufficient preparatory work for the double bridle that is the cause.

It is often said that the correct effect of the curb will depend less on the shape of the curb than on the horse's conformation and proper preparation to accept it. Quite erroneous is the view that the pain caused by the bit can replace the rider's skill.

Furthermore, the direction of the force has an effect on the influence of the curb. This follows from the fact that the rider can increase or decrease it by moving his rein hand, i. e. by raising or lowering it.

If right angles with the curb shanks are formed when equal pressure is put on the reins, then this position of the hand from which the pressure originated is correct. This is because the greatest strength and precision can be developed from it. According to the laws of jointed levers, its greatest effectiveness is expressed in a right angle (see General Section).

On a horse that has been positioned straight and has already been put in balance, the force acts via pressure on equally taut reins. It first presses on the lower jaw and then on the two joint surfaces of the first cervical vertebra at the back of the head. In the same way, this pressure continues along the entire spine to the sacrum, where it separates to go to the joints of both haunches from hip to patella (see the skeleton), and causes all joints in the hind legs to bend.

If the force is stronger on one hand than on the other because one has put more pressure on one rein, it will continue to propagate as before along the spine, but with the difference that it will have a greater effect on that side and cause a greater flexion in the joints on that side.

As described above, the curb works on the skeletal system, which on a well-trained horse is to be regarded as a system of levers upon which the muscles only act as subordinate conductors. If these soft structures dominate, that is, if the horse is green or badly positioned due to its training, then the bones are the subordinate conductors, and the goal has failed.

Even the best curb in this case cannot work as described. The rider becomes a plaything for his horse. Countless diseases arise due to the misuse of the untamed strength of the muscles and tendons. Even the bones become diseased because of the tremendous strain and resulting inflammation of the soft tissues that are attached to them.

The rule that was stated in the General Section that the rider must work most on the skeletal system in order to gain control over the forces of the soft tissue and especially of the muscles with certainty, will be understood more clearly hereinafter. One will also be convinced of the truth of this via the correct use of the curb in the case of a horse that has been prepared according to this principle with the use of a snaffle bit.

The preparatory work with the snaffle bit is necessary and, even if one bridles young horses with the curb from the beginning, one should always use the underlying bridoon to prepare for the bending in the hind legs, and through that the lower jaw. Only after this preparation is it possible to work directly on the haunches with the curb. A main requirement for this is a steady neck position. Wobbly necks easily evade the curb's effect. Thus, the initial flexions of the entire neck should not be continued for too long with green horses, and should no longer be used when fully bridled. As long as the horse can evade the load by bending its neck incorrectly, there will be as little flexion in the haunches (the point of resistance) as with a horse that is still not correctly trained to the leg aids. At the moment when the flexion in the haunches is to be maintained, it falls out with the croup.

Riders who work their horses in these incorrect neck bends misjudge the purpose of the curb, and in general, that of dressage. They work primarily on the soft tissue structures, and therefore, fail to succeed with their training.

First bridling and riding with the curb bit

In order to bridle the horse that is not yet acquainted with the curb bit, the following rules apply:

First, one stands at the horse's left shoulder, places both reins over the neck, holds both bits with the left hand, and holds the crown piece of the bridle with the right, and at the same time holds the horse's head on the forelock or upper jaw firmly with this hand. Before the mouth has opened to accept the bits, which is easily induced by lightly tickling the horse's upper gums with the tip of the thumb, the right hand may not release the head, but rather at the moment the horse opens its mouth, insert the bits into the mouth as quickly as is safe and slips the bridle over the back of the head, whereby the left hand keeps holding the horse's head while the right lets go. The position of the curb can be set by adjusting the cheekpieces. The throatlatch should not be too tight, unless necessary because the horse has the habit of removing the bridle when it stands tied up. The noseband is to be attached under the cheekpieces of the snaffle bit so snugly that, when the horse opens its mouth, the distance to the incisors of the upper and lower jaw is at most a half inch. This is because the horse cannot so easily evade the effect of the bits by incorrect movements of the lower jaw. When attaching the curb chain, the hooks must remain under the bridoon. One fastens it with the index finger and thumb of the left hand from the front of the upper part of the left shank, places the hook under it, while the right hand goes under the horse's chin and lays the links flat from left to right starting from the headstall ring all the way to the link that is to be attached to the hook. In this, the fingertips that hold the link are positioned to the outside and place it on the hook from above to below, so that it lies flat against the chin along with the hook.

The curb chain strap may not be attached so tightly that the curb chain is pinched under it when the reins are used, nor so long that the horse can grab the chain with its lips and teeth. The strap is only used to prevent this from happening, and should not determine the position of the curb chain.

When removing the bridle, one first removes the curb chain, then grasps the curb chain hook as described, unhooks it, then unbuckles the noseband and, finally, the throatlatch.

The reins are then taken onto the left arm, and while clasping the horse's head with the left hand, just as when bridling, slips the bridle off and then onto the left arm with the right hand. While the right hand holds the horse's head firmly, take the halter with the left hand, and just the same as before with the headstall of the bridle, slip it on. The throatlatch of the halter should not be attached too loosely.

When first riding the horse in the curb bit, the rider may not let the horse feel the curb, but must rather use the snaffle as before and keep the curb reins loose and just use the snaffle. However, when using the bridoon, take care because the horse is far more sensitive to it due to its small circumference than it was to the working snaffle that has been used up to now. The use of the curb chain strap will make itself clear right from the start, in that it holds the curb in place even if the horse moves its head a lot. It is not uncommon for the horse to toss its head before it has become accustomed to the curb.

When first riding with the curb, it does not matter if the rider leaves the curb reins lying on the neck or sticks them between the ring finger and pinky of the left hand. He uses the bridoon to lead the horse through the previously described lessons, in order to prepare it for accepting contact on the curb bit. The curb reins are gradually shortened until they are eventually the same length as the bridoon reins, but the contact on the bridoon must always be dominant.

It has become more common to see the double bridle misused by working with equal contact on both the curb and the bridoon reins, as well as working the horse with a bridoon rein and curb rein in each hand. The latter would be expedient if the curb bit had the same joint as the snaffle, but this, of course, would no longer have the same effect and thus, could no longer be called a "curb." If this were the case, then one could use it to affect one side of the lower jaw just the same as with the snaffle. Putting pressure on the snaffle would bend the horse's haunches just as little as it would if one held the snaffle reins the same as those of the curb, i. e. only with the ring finger of the left hand. Similarly, the effect of the curb reins would hardly approximate those of the snaffle if one held one rein in each hand.

Each of these bits has an entirely different effect. The snaffle serves to work on the individual hind legs alternately, to bring the horse under control, and to prepare for the curb. This can only be successfully done if both curb reins control both haunches from one point, even if one more so than the other. The joint on the jointed curb, therefore, can be completely done away with because it serves no purpose.

When one can ride the horse with full contact on the curb reins, one must nevertheless keep ahold of both bridoon reins without using them to the same degree as the curb reins. As has already been described, the snaffle must be used by means of repeated half-halts on one rein and not by a continuous pressure on the corners of the mouth, which is how the curb works on the bars of the mouth. These individual half-halts serve to prevent the head and neck from bending incorrectly. This is the job of the bridoon. It is used to restore contact on the individual curb reins that have lost their effect due to such incorrect bending. In such cases, it is not a mistake to combine the steady contact on both curb reins with the individual snaffle rein.

On the correct and incorrect head and neck position
in the double bridle

It has already been stated that the position of the hand is correct when the reins make a right angle to the curb shanks. However, there are circumstances in which the horse does not want to accept the position created by the curb, or even the curb itself, even when the horse is bridled and ridden correctly. The various reasons for this, which lie either in parts of the horse's conformation or in its entirety, must be considered here more closely, since these cases now become more apparent when the horse is ridden with the curb.

Establishing the correct position of the horse in general, as already stated, is done by comparing the positions of the individual parts along with their faults and deficiencies. The causes are then easy to discover. The rules to improve them can be just as easily determined.

In general, the position in which the horse is most in balance and obedient to the rider can be called "correct." This is the position in which the horse carries its head and neck raised and arched at an angle from the poll and slightly in front of the vertical. A horse can seldom carry its head on the vertical without losing the raised position of the neck. This is also because the curb affects the second or third vertebra rather than the first. With horses that have a tendency to carry the head on the vertical, it is usually the case that the poll and first vertebra are too deep. This often causes the curb's effect to be incorrect. When pressure is put on the reins, the horse assumes a head-set that is too deep.

In general, this would be the head and neck position that would correspond entirely to the established requirements for a correct position. This lifting of the head and neck furthers the horse's balance the most. If the head is slightly in front of the vertical, then the horse is most easily put under the rider's control.

The various deviations from this position are more or less incorrect. They can be reduced to the following three.

The first incorrect position is the one that one usually encounters with green horses. Namely, the horse sticks its head and neck out in front without keeping them steady.

The second incorrect position is when the horse's neck is too far back with its nose in the air, and the upper part of the head is thrown back, as with the so-called ewe-neck or upside-down neck.

Finally, the third incorrect position is the one in which the horse bends its neck so much that it almost hits its chin on its chest. The horse rounds it rather than lifts it, and indeed so much, that the upper part of the head goes down with it.

If one also includes the lateral bending of the neck, then all of the individual deviations are likely to fall under these three incorrect positions to a greater or lesser extent.

The methods for improving these incorrect positions are already largely indicated in the preceding lessons. They mainly concern the bending in the hind legs. Applying them to position the horse in balance can be much easier in the training of the campaign horse, as it should be guided with one hand as soon as possible. Thus, many auxiliary devices, which in individual cases would be very helpful, are not generally suited for the military.

As always, the main point here is that the trainer has to assess how far the horse's conformation, both its individual parts and as a whole, allows for the more or less correct position.

He will not choose to give horses that are too badly built, have defective hind legs, or mares that are especially ticklish a higher value via a continuing fine dressage training, namely via the School. He will put them in service as campaign horses, and choose the well-built and strong horses for the School dressage.

On the Auxiliary Reins

When first riding young horses and ones that have been ruined from work, the rider will often encounter traits that he is not able to overcome with the simple snaffle. In this case, if one fears that a young horse, due to mistrust, or an old and badly ridden horse due to obstinacy, could rid itself of the rider by bucking or rearing, then one would use bucking reins for the bad habit of bucking and a martingale for rearing.

Bucking reins are two long, rounded straps that are attached to each side of the pommel, first through two side rings on the headstall near the browband, and then pulled through the snaffle rings. The ends of the reins are fastened either directly to the pommel or held in the hands. The latter affords greater security, in that one can hold them fast or yield on them depending on the circumstances.

The running rein also consists of a long strap, with one end attached to the saddle girth on the left side. It then runs through a ring on the breast plate, which is attached to the girth underneath the horse with the other end where the ring is located, until it reaches the tip of the breastbone and is put through a neck strap. From there, the martingale goes through a free-running ring on the chin piece or a second or underlying snaffle, then back through the first ring on the breastplate, and finally, into the rider's hand. The rider will then either hold it or attach it to the pommel.

The effect of this rein has some similarities to the curb bit, in that the bit does not press on the corners of the mouth as with the ordinary snaffle, but rather on the ramus of the lower jaw.

Because the running rein does not cause any sideways bending, but rather is meant to prevent the horse from tossing its head up, in order to facilitate the flexion in the hind legs, the use of a simple martingale rein as described is sufficient. It simplifies not only the ordinary work in the snaffle, but also has the benefit that it is comfortable and can be used with the curb bit.

These two auxiliary devices will suffice for the rider who is training the horse.

Running martingales are also used to put the horse into the bridle. These are breast straps that are divided in half and that have rings on both ends through which the reins run. However, because the degree of their effect cannot be determined as precisely as with the running rein, they are less recommended as auxiliary devices in dressage training as for horses that are already trained or for horses that are ridden in their natural position.

These, like so many other auxiliary devices meant to put the horse into the bridle and lift it, are only useful in the horse's further training when they are used in combination with the rider's hand, leg, and spur at the correct moment. However, any rider who is capable of this simultaneous action will most certainly be able to do entirely without such devices.

The best methods to use in the dressage training of such unruly horses are always a good lunge line trainer and whip trainer. They assist the skilled and brave rider to soon be in the position to break the horse's stubbornness and willfulness.

Unfortunately, it is rare for harmony to exist amongst these three people. The result is that the horses become even more willful and mistrustful. Therefore, it is necessary at the beginning of the green horse's training to divide the process to achieve a rapport between the trainers. If this takes place, then it will not be difficult to win over even the worst behaved horse.

On the Cavesson

The most solid tool for the horse's dressage training is the cavesson, which can be used from the beginning to the higher levels. Unfortunately, it is not used enough nowadays. Up to the present time, there has been no better instrument than the cavesson with which to bend a stiff haunch on one side as determinedly and persistently by using one rein without holding against it with the other. Wobbly necks are set straight with the cavesson. Tender mouths take contact after preparatory work with it, and indeed in a shorter amount of time than can be done working with the snaffle.

The use of the cavesson requires arm strength that not everyone possesses. Therefore, it is generally recommended to use the snaffle bit with the auxiliary reins. One can compensate for deficient arm strength by attaching the single cavesson rein, but the horse must be completely obedient to the spur. The rider must also know how to use it precisely, otherwise this tool could be dangerous.

One usually places the cavesson a thumb's width below the cheek bone, and firmly attaches the noseband under the cheek pieces and over the snaffle bits. If the horse is less sensitive in this area, then one can place it lower, and indeed so low that the chin strap can be fastened under the snaffle bit.

In order to avoid injuries, one should rarely jerk on the cavesson, but rather use pressure to achieve one's goal. The nasal bones only have a thin layer of skin covering them. Jerking and yanking can easily cause injury. This can lead to rheumatic disease that causes swelling that disfigures the nose.

On the Pillars

The pillars, considered to be a training tool, do not correspond to the actual purpose of dressage. This is because they cannot replace the calculated use of our arms. Therefore, their use is only recommended here to make the already trained horse more suitable for the instructor to use for teaching. To put a young, untrained horse between the pillars is of no use.

The work between the pillars must begin without the rider, and is comparable to work in-hand. Just as force is to be avoided in-hand, so, too, must there be no force in this work. Therefore, it is best to exclude horses from this exercise that have violent temperaments and that object to being tied to the pillars and desperately fight back right from the beginning.

Before one puts a horse between the pillars, it should at least be able to go perfectly in the campaign-gaits, namely the collected trot and shoulder-in. Then, at the beginning, one should not demand any artificial steps, but rather just let them occur naturally in an uncontrolled fashion.

For the work between the pillars, the horse should be outfitted with a strong working halter with thick leather and flannel, which, in addition to the throatlatch, has another appropriate neck strap next to it that prevents it from slipping off. Each rein on the halter must be three cubits long, and made of strong leather or thick cord. They will not be attached immediately, but rather drawn through the pillar rings and simply held by two assistants, so that they can be quickly shortened or lengthened in an emergency.

The horse can be bridled with a snaffle with a strong bit under the halter. The bridle reins are fastened to the girth and have no effect.

At first, one puts the horse between the pillars such that the forefeet come to the point where the lead lines are connected to each pillar. Use the crop, or better yet, the whip, to drive the hind feet to step right and left as far as possible while keeping the forefeet on the same spot. Horses will very willingly carry out these first movements that do not involve flexion in the hind legs. Only later does one demand that the horse step straight into the reins with the croup remaining fixed at the center of the pillars by softly tapping it with the whip. When it does this, praise it and end the lesson. Repeating these careful exercises a few times will remove the initial fear that the horse felt, because the whip, the immobile pillars, and the presence of indispensable assistants at the beginning aroused its mistrust. To do away with this fear is the sole purpose of the lesson that is described above.

One must be satisfied with the beginning uncertain pitter-pattering leg movements, if the horse steps straight into the lines. Gradually, one can touch the croup with the whip an imperceptible amount to drive the haunches under more. At the same time, the assistants can encourage the horse to lift its forelegs by touching the knees softly with a crop.

If the horse begins to work more willingly and collects itself when it is driven with the whip rather than leaning on the reins, then one makes the reins so long that the middle of the horse's body comes over the line of the pillars. Greater flexion in the haunches is gradually induced in more definite steps until it finally results in piaffé. (See the 2nd section, "Piaffe.")

It is dangerous for the rider and difficult for the horse if one tries to bring the horse to piaffé under the rider without having done this exercise first. It should only be done mounted after the horse has been properly exercised in it.

At the beginning, it is sufficient if the horse positions itself straight upon the leg aids and takes contact on the reins. These should have the same tension as the halter. In the case that the horse does not step into the halter, then they should have either no effect or only very little. If the reins can be held with firm contact, then the tension on the halter must decrease, so that it can gradually be dispensed with. Only then may the haunches be more heavily loaded and the half and full halts be used.

Tapping with the tip of the whip and the rider's clucking with the tongue should make the assistants superfluous. They often make it more difficult to gauge the correct aids. The assistant with the whip should be directed to touch the horse only on the croup and on the rump, but never on the cannon bones, and to measure these aids exactly according to the horse's willingness to perform.

When the horse exhibits such a collected trot-like movement between the pillars that it deserves to be called the piaffé, it energetically lifts one foreleg at the same time as the diagonal hind leg and as high as the latter at first. Both are held in the air for a moment, and then they are placed back into their hoof prints. Then the other legs do the same.

If one wants to perfect the piaffé between the pillars, and likewise the canter, the flying change, the levade, and teach the School jumps, then follow the instructions given in the next section. After the piaffé-exercises between the pillars, let the horse trot on the spot in a collected manner. Let it canter on after the levade and the School jumps. It will be easy for the riding instructor to fulfill his difficult obligations with a horse that has been worked in this way. It will be especially pleasant, if he knows how to combine it with a systematic pedagogy.

With the exception of lunging, training-gadgets and other work in-hand are not recommended. They would have to be aimed only at preparing the horse for flexing the inside hind leg. This flexion cannot be achieved using them, because it is impossible without the rider. These devices are more expendable than the pillars, because the horse can be worked between the pillars with or without the rider. It is only possible for the rider to quickly counter resistance and to impress the horse with quick and decisive handling because of his connection to the horse via his legs. The trainer can never have as much success with the horse in the work in-hand. It is not just the legs and spurs alone that give the rider this superiority, in that they support him with their powerful, pain-inducing qualities. It is much more his sense of feel that he has to thank for this superiority. Using this, he can correctly guess the horse's negative inclinations before they occur, and can prevent them by milder means and, if necessary, counter them.

Despite what has been said to recommend these gadgets for the horse's dressage training, they will never be able to replace the rider.

The reproach that the burden becomes too arduous and detrimental for young horses deserves no consideration, provided that crippled horses are not meant to be trained, and that there is no excessive weight disparity between horse and rider. This is because, if the weight is correctly and evenly distributed on the legs, then the horses will suffer no harm.

The gadgets will never be able to replace the hand and leg aids, and if the trainer wants to represent the legs with the whip, it will still not be able to fully replace them. The gadget will always be a dead instrument. It does not deserve to be suggested as a substitute for a light, sensitive hand. Likewise, the whip cannot replace the rider's legs, since the degree of their use cannot be precisely measured. Moreover, the whip aids are used only when they are needed. They are, therefore, not comparable to the leg aids, which are given before the eye even notices them (see the chapter, "Rider Feel.")

If the systematic order set up here is followed during the horse's training under the rider, then it is so simple that the work in-hand becomes superfluous. One can do without assistants sooner, and the delusion that the neck is the seat of resistance is not promoted. It is not possible to acquire the training gadgets everywhere, and they are useless expenses, anyway. However, they can be useful to prepare the young horse for the flexion in the hind legs

Why would anyone want to use such instruments to achieve a goal that can be obtained with simpler and more natural methods? Of course, if the desire or the ability to think is lacking, then one ought to go ahead and use them. The rider then becomes a gadget himself, which only keeps going for as long as his balance is not disturbed by some unusual event.

Experience shows that there are few good riders where the horses are worked in-hand a lot.

In Russia, where a great deal of training is done with devices similar to the Spanish Rider, no luminaries of horsemanship have come to the fore.

In England, by contrast, where gadgets are used only for the training of the carriage horses and for exercising the foals, but other work in-hand is almost unheard of, there are the most determined and reputable riders. Although they often do not achieve the purpose of dressage, i. e. the attainment of balance in the horse, they achieve another, which is reaching the greatest speed.

In France, where they used to excel in School riding, good riders have become rarer and rarer. This is all the more worrisome because they have recently taken up the work in-hand, which threatens to destroy the rest of the good Old School bit by bit.

In Germany, despite some challenges, the School has still retained its characteristics. It will continue to do so for as long as one remains true to its old principles.

The horse's dressage training in-hand is to be secondary to any work under the rider. It is only recommended for the circus, where it can be used successfully. Usually, only canter is required, which the horses, going on a circle, easily accept. Unfortunately, since it is not connected with the balanced position, it can never be executed without detriment to the good walk and trot. However, this does not matter, because those gaits are not used in the circus, anyway.

The Spurs

Spurs have always been the most useful means of training the horse. Those who are still in doubt have never recognized their power.

The spurs belong to the leg aids. Therefore, if one speaks of the leg aids without specifically mentioning the spurs, then this does not mean that they are just to be used for punishment. The skilled rider, on the other hand, uses them as an aid rather than as a punishment, and regards them in this case as the most potent stimulus that the legs can bring to the horse's abdominal muscles.

It is generally as difficult to determine the degree to which the spurs are to be used as it is where on the horse's sides they are to be applied. However, both are geared toward the incorrect movements of the hind legs. If the hind legs step too far under, then the spurs are used on the flanks to awaken the pushing power of the hindquarters. However, if the hind legs lag too far behind, then the spurs are used just behind the girth, where they urge the hind legs to carry.

Since the only intention of the horse's dressage training is to subordinate these two forces to the rider's will, and as proven, it is mainly the spurs that can do this, their great benefit is beyond doubt. However, it is true that using them properly is the greatest difficulty in equitation. Even applying the spurs as an aid or as a punishment requires a lot of rider feel.

As for the spurs themselves, the length of the neck should correspond to the length of the rider's legs in such a way that short legs receive short spurs, while long legs receive long spurs. Using short-necked spurs on long legs would delay the effect and bring the legs out of their proper position, while in the reverse case, the opposite occurs. In the first case, therefore, the spur neck should be at least two inches long, which may be reduced to one inch, depending on the rider's legs.

The five-pointed spur rowels are the most useful when the tines are broad at the bottom and more pointed at the top rather than too dull, so that a vigorous poke with the spur leaves a wound that is long and bleeding. This type of injury does not cause swelling, which always takes longer to heal.

The eight to ten-pointed, sharp, needle-pointed spur rowels are not recommended for dressage. They are overly irritating and make the horses ill-tempered and angry. On the other hand, in cases in which it is important to drive horses to the greatest speed using the most violent pain, their use may be allowed.

Riders who cannot yet use their spurs to master the movements of the horse's hind legs do better to choose blunt spur rowels rather than sharp ones.

Training in Campaign Riding

To be able to teach the student in the simplest and, at the same time, most thorough way, the teacher must have his own pedagogy that he developed from his own experience, in addition to knowledge of scientific principles. This is so that he will be able to better communicate abstract theories and not just regurgitate established rules that he has memorized.

Everyone, especially the educated, should be able to give an account of his training process. It will give him comfort, and even great pleasure, if he can defend it with good reasons. The good rider must be able to appeal to education, but he may also feel the need to explain his actions. He seeks to ground it in nature in a scientific way, and thus, forms a system upon which to base each individual action. Even if his views are not correct, he will be more useful to the subject than harmful. New experiences may cause the earlier theories to be discarded and perhaps lay the groundwork for more correct ones. It is undeniable that, if the rider shapes himself in this way, then he will reach his goal more quickly than the crude empiricist, whose experience only comes to the fore with age.

The riding instructor is required to teach using scientific methods. This is because, even if the majority of students are content to learn the practical and artistic skills to show a certain mastery on horseback, there will be others who are not content with that. These students will want to delve deeper into the matter, and ask the trainer's advice. If the latter cannot give the desired information, the inquisitive student will be dissatisfied. He will be forced to view the teachings as empirical, reject them as being worthless, or will at least regard them with contempt.

The disciples of such a noble art cannot allow it to be degraded, but rather it is their duty to elevate it and promote it in every possible way.

After the best experiential instruction, the student will encounter cases in his later training that are new to him and for which he knows no means to combat them. He will find himself greatly embarrassed, and will seek refuge in aids that may be the least suitable for his purpose. The consequence of this is that he loses control of his horse, or else his incorrect handling leads to its detriment. On the other hand, if the student has enjoyed systematic instruction, then it will be easy for him to discover the cause of unusual situations and to correctly choose from the available means with which to address it.

As for the riding instruction itself, every student who wants to practice horseback-riding, or who wants to learn it as a hobby or as his future profession, must be informed of the same beginning principles, so that it is possible for everyone to attain greater or lesser perfection depending on the circumstances.

Just as with the horse's position, the laws of balance can be applied to the rider's posture. They are considered to be general principles of horsemanship. These principles must be universal if they deserve to be called "general."

The basic principles that follow and the principles that have already been discussed are based on a general theory. Therefore, repetitions are often unavoidable.

On the Rider's Seat

The normal position of the person on a horse, like that of the horse itself, requires balance. For the purpose of explaining this, the same principles of structural engineering apply to horsemanship, which were already discussed in the General Section with respect to the horse's balance. There is a point on every solid body that, if it is supported, then all of its surrounding parts are in equilibrium. This point is called the body's center of gravity. The lower the center of gravity is, or the shorter the directional line is in the ratio to the diameter of the base, the more stable the body is. Also, the larger the base area, the more secure it is.

Applying these principles to the rider and his body must determine a method of teaching for the rider's seat. This base area of the upper body is formed by the seat muscles and is bordered by three fixed points of the skeleton. These three points lift the hips. These are the two seat bones and the coccyx. Although the latter is not as close to the saddle when riding as the two seat bones, because it is higher than they are, it is indirectly connected to the saddle by the underlying seat muscles.

If the body is in balance, the line of its center of gravity falls in the middle of these three points. It is, therefore, necessary for the upper body to assume such a posture that the position of all of its individual parts favors the fulfillment of this requirement.

The supporting surface of the upper body can be enlarged if the legs are turned so that they lie flat on the saddle and the hips are positioned vertically. The seat then widens around the two thighs and the body becomes more balanced. Accordingly, the rider's good posture depends on the correct hip position. This is clearly indicated by the fact that one has to pull one's body in, round the back and pull the thighs up when the hips are down and back, for example. As one straightens them, however, the back is pulled into the natural position and the thighs are lowered. Earlier, it was stated that the hips must be placed vertically in order to meet these requirements, and even the mechanics prove that the vertical position of an upright body on a horizontal one gives it the most secure position. This is because every other horizontal position is inclined to fall. In this position, the lumbar vertebrae are straightened at the same time, whereby the spine, which has to determine the body's posture, acquires a quieter and more secure position.

Therefore, the vertical position of the hips is the first rule for the rider's seat on a horse.

The lesson begins with mounting and dismounting. It is true that saddling is also explained at the beginning of the first part on starting the green horse, and therefore, needs no repetition here. However, there could not be any talk of using the curb reins before mounting and dismounting, so it is appropriate to discuss it here for the first time. As far as bridling is concerned, the proper placement of the curb chain, as well as the curb's position, is the main issue, as was already mentioned in the chapter on the curb bit.

In general, the effect of the reins was explained in the same chapter. It can be seen how the direction of the rein pressure determines the horse's position and direction.

To mount from standing at the horse's left shoulder, the student first grasps the curb and bridoon reins with the right hand. This is so that the left hand can be placed in front of them on the withers, with the nails vertically oriented. From now on, the right hand will serve the left. That is why it is called the "helping hand," this rein hand. Using the right hand, the bridoon reins are first placed in the whole rein hand, then the curb reins are placed on the rein finger, i. e. the fourth finger of this hand, to divide the reins. After the right hand has shortened the reins until there is contact and the ends of the reins are between the thumb and the index finger of the left hand, with the end of the curb reins hanging on the right side of the neck, grasp some mane hair with the left hand and wrap it around the left thumb. Now make a fist with the left hand, which remains gently closed even when it leaves the mane. It should only open again when dismounting, in order to create, as before, a support point on the withers via the mane, whereby the right hand is again the helping hand.

When mounted, the student first positions the hips vertically so that the coccyx comes to rest on the middle of the saddle. The thighs must lie flat so that the base of the body is widened, as explained above. How much this happens is determined by the hip position. The knees are slightly forward. Any other position of the thighs will either cause the hips to be tilted back or lifted up off of the saddle. The former arises because of stretching forward too much; the latter occurs because the thighs are pulled back too far. However, the thighs can only lie flat to a certain degree, and only to the point that part of the inner surface of the knee touches the saddle, leaving the thigh without any tension in the muscles. The upper body is positioned so that the back vertebrae come forward, while the lumbar vertebrae go back, without, however, disturbing the position of the hips and taking away from the natural suppleness of the spine. By lifting the chest, the shoulder blades come closer together and lower slightly. It is possible to tilt the lumbar vertebrae towards the back by tightening the abdominal muscles.

The head must be carried with a steady but not stiff neck. It is not possible, then, for the rider to look down at his hands or any other part of his body. His sense of feel should guide every adjustment.

The upper arm should hang from the shoulder so that the elbow is neither pulled in close to the body nor held out away from it. The forearm is carried without effort, so that the hand is held in a relaxed manner at the middle of the body.

The thighs must lie flat on the saddle with the lower legs hanging down vertically without being stiff. The foot should be held straight at the ankle, so that the sole touches the stirrup tread from the ball of the foot to the pinkie toe. The heel should be lowered to stretch the muscles of the upper thigh, but only so far that no tension arises in the calf or in the ankle. Keeping one's stirrups depends on the mobility of this joint, as does being able to regain the previous leg position if the horse jumps around. In general, the entire lower leg must be held so that the calf is flat and the inner edge of the shin hugs the horse without moving noticeably. Only then is the securest seat possible. Any other leg position raises the thigh, lifts it away from the saddle, or makes it unsteady. This makes the horse's movement all the more jarring.

In this regard, the horse can be viewed as an oval body around which the rider's legs wrap. If the jolt of the horse's movements is not to disturb the legs, then it must be absorbed below the middle of the oval. It also offers the greatest advantage that the leg aids can be given immediately, and they do not have to be brought closer from a position that is farther away.

With this, the seat on a balanced horse has been sufficiently described. Deviations, as they can come about in various circumstances, can be easily dealt with, relatively speaking, and one will often later return to this seat.

As for controlling the horse, the rein hand should assume a certain position. This is because every direction, and every turn of the horse is brought about by moving it. It will be easier and shorter to describe it, if one assumes a certain or normal position, such as the one described below.

The left hand, called the rein hand, is held at about the middle of the body above the pommel. It should be held in a straight line with the forearm in such a way that the thumb is on the same line with the fingernail is on top. It is most expedient to divide the reins with the fourth ring finger. The fingers, bent most at the middle joints, close the fist without boring into the palm of the hand. This is because any rigidity must be avoided.

————————

The rider must pay attention to the position of all of his individual parts. This position will be easier for him to assume the less he tries to force his posture. In order to most quickly train the student, it is advantageous to first let him ride on the lunge line without having to control the horse. The trainer uses the lunge line to guide the horse, which makes it possible for the student to put all of his attention on his hip and leg position, which is mainly what is demanded of him in the beginning.

The student will soon acquire the prescribed correct seat even without previous riding experience. It will be more difficult for those who have already grown accustomed to an incorrect, faulty seat. In order to improve it and to reach the goal more quickly, the trainer must often deviate from the established rules. For example, if the rider is used to sitting with his hips back and his knees drawn up, then it is wise to have him put his legs back farther than is recommended. On the other hand, if he has his hips too far forward and stretches his legs down so much that the seat bones almost do not touch the saddle, have him put the hips back more than prescribed until the hips and legs gradually come into the proper position.

It is to be noted in general that the better the horse is trained upon which he receives his first instruction, the easier and faster the pupil will learn. He should, therefore, never be put on a horse that is difficult to ride in the beginning.

In order to acquaint the pupil most easily with the use of legs, stirrups, and whip, and to confirm his posture, the instructor chooses an exercise for which a suitably bridled and, as previously mentioned, well-trained horse is necessary.

It is saddled with an English saddle, which can be upholstered a little on the front of the flaps. On the saddle pommel, there is an upright ring through which, as will be mentioned later, run the snaffle reins. In addition, the horse is bridled with a curb that has a second snaffle rein. This rein runs through the throatlatch, and goes through the ring on the saddle pommel. It is loose enough to allow the horse to bend laterally.

A martingale, which prevents the horse from tossing its head, and a ring on the noseband to attach the lunge line, complete the equipment. Finally, there are straps on each stirrup bar onto which the student can initially hold tight, so that there is less danger of falling off. It is a misconception that the beginner should be thrown often to acquire the proper posture in the saddle.

Now that the rider has developed the seat described above while the horse is standing still, and is also familiar with the position of the hand and how to hold the reins, let the horse first proceed at a walk. Allow the student to grasp the straps on each side of the saddle as he does the snaffle reins. The curb reins are placed on the neck and the slider gives them some contact. After the exercise in walk has been properly mastered, carefully drive the horse into a trot. Make sure that the rider maintains the correct position. Have him drop the stirrups so that he acquires the proper skills without them. Should this be too difficult, then let him drop one stirrup at a time until he can finally do without both of them. To recover the stirrups, the rider opens the knee, which gives the stirrups freedom to swing back and forth. The heels are pulled up and the toes are pointed in and down to where they can catch the stirrup, if this has not already occurred while searching for them. If the knee does not open, the stirrups are held tightly toward the back, which makes it much more difficult to recover them.

Just as with the stirrups, the straps on the sides of the saddle must also become dispensable. This can be achieved by alternately releasing one and then the other.

The same exercises are to be carried out in the lengthened gaits (however, still without the rider guiding the horse), and in the same order as with those just described.

Some ways to hold the reins and other stratagems, the knowledge of which is of great importance to the rider, are to be explained during the periods of rest.

Every rider must strive to be as independent as possible on his horse, and to not need others to help him. This concerns in particular lengthening and shortening the stirrups, which the rider can do on his own in any movement of the horse, if he learns the hand movements for it. Everyone knows how often it is necessary to adjust the stirrup length. It would be superfluous and time-consuming to cite individual cases that make it necessary to do so.

So that one may lengthen or shorten the stirrups at will, the stirrup leathers must be positioned such that the buckles are on the outside at the top of the saddle flaps.

To adjust the right stirrup, the rider grasps the end of the stirrup leather close to the buckle with his right hand, removes it by pulling the prong out of the hole, and then presses it down with the index finger. The thumb then slides the buckle up or down, depending on how long or short the stirrup is supposed to be. The rider can make this easier by stepping more forcefully or more softly on the stirrup tread.

The thumb finds the new hole into which the bolt is to be inserted, and at the same time, pushes the buckle over it. Then, the index finger directs the bolt into the hole.

To adjust the left stirrup, the left hand does the same thing. The right hand grasps the reins (curb reins) from above so that they are in the hand without being divided. The thumb, resting on the left reins, closes around them. If the horse has a snaffle bit, the reins should be taken into the hand in such a way that they cross each other.

When adjusting the stirrups, the rider may not change his upper body position under any circumstance, neither may he look down at his hands. This not only allows him to determine the length of the stirrups, but also because situations often occur in which he cannot sacrifice the proper upper body posture to adjust the stirrups.

Since no exercise is more suitable to acquainting the student with these hand movements than those described above, they should be taught in all gaits.

If the beginner is confirmed in all of these exercises, then it is time to learn how to use the driving aids. As his legs will at first be very unhelpful, and he may lose the good posture of his upper body when they are used, allow him to cluck with the tongue and to use the riding whip in the beginning. Make him acquainted with the whip as follows: The whip is held in the rider's right hand. It may either be pointed up or down towards the ground. It is assumed that it is held pointed upwards vertically next to the rein hand. It is often sufficient to swish the tip to drive the horse forward. However, if this is not enough, then it may be necessary to drive the horse forward by using it to tap on the same spot where the spur is normally used. The whip must be held pointed down for this purpose. However, the horse must not see it, as it could easily become frightened. Therefore, put the shaft of the whip into the rein hand (which must not be opened), turn the right hand so that the thumbs come together, and move the whip past the right ear down along the right side toward the ground. If one needs the right hand for some reason, then bring the whip to its upright position in the same way, pass it over the left hand with the right hand, stick it under the upper arm and forearm, whereby the elbow can be at a slight distance from the body, and position the whip so that it can be firmly held to the body with just the upper arm.

If the whip is to be used again, then the right hand pulls it down to the underarm, grasps the whip underneath, and brings it back into its initial position. During all of these movements, the left hand should not change its position or lose contact on the reins.

This simple procedure has been described in a somewhat complex manner for various reasons. The beginner will, upon closely following these procedures, become accustomed to a certain degree of accuracy in all of his actions on horseback. The horses will not be frightened or become mistrustful by being threatened carelessly with the whip. Finally, the rider, who has become familiar with these hand movements, will be prepared for his erstwhile soldier training and will become skilled in the use of the saber and other weapons.

If the beginner is familiar with what has been practiced so far, i. e. mainly the correct seat on a horse, then it is time to get busy with teaching him how to guide the horse.

This should not be done sooner, because that would be fruitless. As long as the student struggles with his seat, it is impossible for him to pay proper attention to his hands. Now would be the time to teach him to control the horse himself. However, this is preceded by various explanations.

The reins, with which the rider became acquainted in the first exercises on the lunge line, were given to him for no other purpose than to convince him that it was necessary to keep a steady rein hand, and that using the left arm to balance the body disturbs the horse's gait and his seat. Before the student uses the reins and legs to guide the horse, it is necessary for him to first be acquainted with the length of the reins and to correctly judge the use and effect of the legs and spurs, as well as the rein hand and helping hand. The rein ends are generally attached to each other in one of two ways. Either this is done using a button with a leather wedge placed between them, or they are stitched together flat. In the first case, the reins are usually provided with a slider, which is missing in the latter. This slider helps the campaign rider maintain the necessary rein length, since it is rarely necessary for him to adjust it. There is also the advantage for the rider that, if he drops the reins, he can immediately pick them up again with the correct contact. Should it be necessary to frequently change the rein length, then the slider is more of a hindrance, and, therefore, should be slid to the ends of the reins.

Since both reins are equal in length, it is generally believed that they must also work uniformly when pressure is put on them without taking into account the various positions of the hand and forearm, which are to be regarded as weak, normal, and strong. In the weak position, the back of the hand is pointing up. In the normal and strong positions, the fingernails are vertical and the thumb is on top. Rotating the elbow joint results in one position or the other. In most cases, the normal and strong positions are used. From these arise the proper hand motions to halt and to restrain the horse in various ways.

If the rein hand is held in the weak position just over the middle of the horse's body, and both reins are held by the rein finger in the same way with the horse's head and neck straight, then one can clearly feel the pressure that both reins put on the rein finger when the hand is rotated to the normal position. One can also feel that the contact on the right rein has decreased notably compared to the left, even though both exerted the same pressure before. Only by shortening the right rein about half an inch will one again have the same contact.

The circumstance is rarely taken into account that, when the rein hand is rotated from the weak position in which there is equal contact on both reins to the normal, the little finger describes a larger arc, whereby the left curb rein, which is either above or below it, has a much stronger contact, and as a result, has more effect than the right. This inequality cannot be seen at the ends of the reins, but rather can only be felt by the rein finger, be it the pinkie or fourth finger. This is assuming that one does not have an iron fist that has become insensitive.

There are various disadvantages that arise for both horse and rider due to this unequal effect on the reins. For example, restricting with the hand will not lift the horse, but rather will make the head and neck crooked, usually to the left. Restraining on the right rein will not turn the horse to the right, but rather will throw it around to the right, if it does not actually turn to the left because the tension on the left rein is stronger than on the right one. Only when restraining left do both reins have the same effect, making it easy for the rider to turn left and to canter to the right. For these reasons, horses are easier to handle on the left than the right. If one were to hold the reins in the right hand, then the reverse would result. Older texts have given us the idea that the horse is easier to handle on the left than right because it is fed on the left, saddled on the left, bridled on the left, and also lies bent to the left as an embryo in its mother's womb. That is why they recommended that we work the horse more to the right than to the left in its dressage training. Of course, this is not necessary if the rider knows how to use the aids as well on the right as he does on the left. This also explains why even well-trained horses bend their head and neck to the left upon incorrect, uneven reins, and make it impossible for the rider to straighten the head and neck or turn the horse to the right without the help of the right snaffle rein.

In order to make the reins even, either the right rein must be shortened or even cut by about half an inch. The latter would be less advisable, because if one wanted to ride in the weak hand position with the horse in its natural position, then the reins would be uneven again. It would be best to stitch the rein ends together flat. If one wanted to lengthen the left rein with the two reins stitched together, then one could just let that part of the left rein be, so that in the normal position and when the hand applies momentary pressure on the reins, the effect is equal on each side of the horse's jaw.

Since it is often necessary to adjust the length of the reins by shortening or lengthening one or both of them, the hand grips for this purpose are briefly mentioned.

If both reins are to be shortened, then the rider grasps both curb reins tightly with a closed right hand above the left hand, and using the thumb and index finger, pulls them through with some force as far as is necessary. The left hand may not be opened under any circumstances. Do the same thing to shorten the individual reins. However, it should be noted that the left hand is then the upper hand, while the right is the lower hand.

Since the reins are yielded when they are lengthened, it is not necessary for the rein hand to be closed so tightly. Therefore, the reins can either be pushed from above through the opened hand, or if one does not want to lose the position of the rein hand, they can be pulled through.

If the reins are to be made even, or if the rein length is to be tested, then grasp the rein end with the thumb and index finger of the right hand and lift it vertically into the air. The unevenness of the reins will become more pronounced. This can be easily corrected by shortening the longer rein.

Before the rider can guide the horse, it is necessary for it to move forward. The legs have to be used before the hand is able to do anything. The whip and clucking with the tongue should gradually be dispensed with, and the finer aids alone should get the horse's attention. The leg aids are divided into visible and invisible, and their use depends on the perfection of the horse's dressage training. Only very well-trained School horses that are on the haunches make the visible or crude driving aids superfluous, and then only if their riders commit no offense against the rules for its carriage. In the case of the lesser trained or campaign horses, it is necessary to use these aids, since the finer ones can only be used if they have been prepared via the visible ones. The latter relate more to the punishments, and must precede those so that the horse sufficiently recognizes the rider's superiority and gladly submits to the slightest demand, assuming that it has been given to him in a way that it can understand. The principle that every animal evades pain and that it alone makes is possible to keep the horse under control is not the most correct, if one does not add that there is a proper time and place to give the driving aids. According to the theory of the lever, this principle cannot apply to the effect of the bit, which is why the earlier bits that caused great pain have been completely rejected in modern times. Neither will spurs nor whips be able to control the horse even if used in the most painful of ways but in the incorrect places.

The leg aids can only serve two purposes. Either they serve to collect by achieving a shortened gait, or to drive forward to lengthen the gait. If they are used just behind the girth, they stimulate the abdominal muscles, which contract as a result. In order to facilitate this contraction, the hind legs step forward and under farther, and the horse naturally increases in volume. This is because the leg pressure acts on the true or fixed ribs, which the horse cannot compress together.

By pulling itself together, the horse's power is concentrated. This is referred to as collection. These aids are to be used in various ways. Either they are given only with the leg, by pressure or nudging, or with the spurs. The leg pressure can be produced by the inner surface of the whole leg, while the nudge is commonly given with the lower leg, whereby the leg lies firmly on the saddle from thigh to knee, and the lower leg prods the horse with a hard calf by quickly rotating the heel one-half of a turn. Although this movement occurs from the hip joint, it must not result in an open knee. It is easy to explain why the beginner can easily lose the correct upper body posture. This is why he should first practice using these leg aids with one of his legs while supporting his upper body with the other one by stepping on the stirrup.

The campaign rider should only use quick jabs of the spur behind the girth. One should not show the student this prickling with the spurs, because it is not to be used on a well-trained horse.

If the legs exert pressure on the false or mobile ribs, the same stimulus is produced, but manifests itself in a different way. The rump is not pulled together, but rather stretches out. This is why the hind legs cannot step under, but rather push forward more.

Both types of leg aids are used at different times and for different purposes.

The hand requires only three positions to guide the horse, which always start from the normal position. These are called restraining, right-restraining and left-restraining. Before any of these actions occur, the hand must be held steady with contact on the reins. The hind legs are then driven under the horse. The hand is used only after this occurs.

To restrain, the rein finger is brought back to the middle of the body with the wrists extended. The reins are tightened evenly on the neck, and there will be equal pressure on both at the same time, as well as on and under the ring finger. Skin wrinkles will also form on the inside of the carpus.

When restraining right, the middle joint of the rein finger must be turned toward the right hip with the thumb on top. The pressure of the right rein on the ring finger becomes palpable first, then the pressure of the left rein on the pinky does. The skin wrinkles remain on the inner surface of the wrist, but are pulled upwards more.

To restrain left, the hand is bent toward the left hip, and the rein finger is directed back toward it and downward. The effect of the reins is opposite from restraining right. First, the pressure on the left rein is caused by the ring finger, then the third finger puts pressure on the right rein. The skin wrinkles can be seen on the inner surface of the wrist, but form farther down.

If the hand is returned to its normal position from one of these three rotated positions, but the rein contact is not visibly decreased, this is called yielding. It will be used after each of the other three actions, as soon as the intended purpose is achieved.

A total yielding on the reins may only be permitted in order to check to see if a trained horse can carry itself without the rider doing anything.

On the Turns

Explaining how the horse moves forward will further the correct procedure that the rider should use to turn the horse.

If one watches the horse in walk, one can see that the four legs are moved diagonally one after the other. The front right leg is raised and then set down at the same time as the left hind leg, followed by the other two legs in the same way.

The horse always keeps its weight on the legs that are on the ground, and takes the weight completely off of those that are in the air. If it is going on a straight line in a correct walk, then one leg is not allowed to carry more than the other, nor remain on the ground longer. However, if one leaves the straight line, this equality is disrupted. If, for example, the horse transitions from a straight line to a right circle, then not every leg steps forward as far. The left legs step farther forward than the right ones, which remain on the ground for a longer time, and are, therefore, burdened by more weight than the others. The size of the turn is determined by how far forward the outer (left) legs step.

It can be concluded from this what the rider must do to guide the horse as he wishes. The less he works against the natural motion and the more he encourages it, the easier it will be to make the turns. Before the rider is able to navigate through the turns, however, he must be able to direct the horse on a straight line. The driving aids will be limited to gradually increasing the leg pressure on both of the horse's sides, while the rein hand stays in its normal position. If the horse walks straight ahead, both reins have the same contact, i. e. one does not work more than the other. It is necessary for the hand to restrain to shorten the stride. Because the rider restrains on both reins equally, they restrict the movement of both hind legs, i. e. each rein affects each individual hind leg in the same manner. If the right rein is tightened such that the counteraction of the left prevents the neck from bending, then it restricts the right hind leg, just as the left hind leg is restricted if the left rein is used before the right rein.

If the horse is to be turned off of a straight line, then the rider does not go against the natural movement. Instead, he causes the inner side of the horse to contract, the inside hind leg to stay back, and the outside to step farther forward.

For this purpose, the inside rein is tightened while the outside is held against it, so that it can give the necessary counteraction. This will vary in degree, depending on whether the turn should be tight or wide. The inside rein induces the turn, while the outside rein defines it.

The leg aids are used mainly on the outside, but the rider must never allow his upper body to follow them while using them, but rather he must keep his position on the inside.

To make a right turn, it is necessary to restrain right. This is because, in this case, the reins act on the corresponding legs in the specified manner. At the same time, the rider should burden the horse's inside feet more heavily with his weight by putting his inside shoulder and hip back on the inside hind leg; how far back will depend on how tight or wide the turn should be. In the same way, the rider's outside leg must drive the outside hind leg forward. Just as the horse held back each individual hind leg when there was a half-halt on an individual rein, it also moves the hind leg forward when the rider applies leg pressure on that side.

The left turn is executed in a similar manner by restraining left, while the right leg does the same thing that the left leg did to turn right.

The same aids that have been given here for the walk are the same for the trot, but they are used in quicker succession. This is because the aids must always correspond to how the legs are stepping, and the trot is a faster gait.

It is more difficult to collect the horse in trot before the turns, as the aids must follow each other more quickly. However, it is done in the same way as in the walk, but is adapted to the speed of the trot. As even trained horses frequently evade the even pressure on both curb reins by assuming a crooked neck position, it is necessary to use the underlying bridoon to keep the neck straight, as well as to be able to immediately regain the straight position. If, for example, a crooked neck position to the left has made the left curb rein slack, then there is no better means of regaining the proper contact than to use the right snaffle rein. It is not necessary to counteract with the left one, as it is replaced by the curb rein.

The snaffle reins can also help attain the proper head position, which even shortened curb reins cannot always achieve in the desired manner.

Because the snaffle reins only serve to support one curb rein or the other, the use of both at the same time is not only of no use, but also a hindrance. This is because it produces a counter effect on one of the curb reins, in that the curb reins cause the horse to come into the bridle, and the snaffle reins lift the head and neck up. If lifting the forehand is intended, then the snaffle reins are the most suitable means, but must be used without the curb reins.

In this preliminary teaching, the trainer explains how the arena is divided as follows.

The line along the four walls is called the whole arena. A second line, which connects the middle of the two long walls, divides them into two equal halves (the half arena). This is to distinguish them from the long half arenas, which are formed by a connecting line of short walls. Each half arena is divided into four equal parts — voltes — by a cross.

The rider is already familiar with the circle. It is located in each half arena, and has its center at the point where the crossing lines intersect.

The lines suitable for changing direction are the diagonal ones that go across the whole arena. They do not start at the corners, but rather connect the long walls a horse's length before and after the corner. The diagonal lines of the voltes can also be used to change direction. If both circles are connected by a change of direction, then they form the so-called figure eight.

After all of these explanations have been made, it is time to detach the lunge line and leave the rider to his own devices. One supports him only by repeating what has been said throughout the rest of the lesson.

It is less useful for the student and more difficult for him and the trainer, to proceed contrary to the process described here and to immediately have to guide the horse in a School saddle without stirrups, or begin the first ride with just the saddle pad. This is all the more true if the instructions given here are first communicated to the student while he is busy trying to guide the horse and maintain his seat.

This results in the following disadvantages:

1)   The lack of simplicity in teaching;

2)   The difficulty of thinking through the given instruction while struggling with the seat;

3)   The cantle of the School saddle and the lack of stirrups make it too difficult for the rider to have a good posture in the beginning. In fact, it is almost impossible.

The objection can be made that this teaching method means that the trainer can work less en masse, since only one student can ride the lesson horse at a time.

However, closer examination reveals that this is not the case. This is because, while the trainer is explaining something to one student or showing him hand grips, etc., the others can learn by observation. In this way, they can get a clear understanding of the matter, and since they are left to their own devices, they can think about it more easily and freely. They see all sorts of mistakes when others are practicing. They then think about how to correct them, and take precautions to prevent themselves from making the same errors. A few words will then be sufficient to correct the resulting mistakes.

Since only a few horses are required for these exercises and are always under the trainer's supervision, none of them can be ridden incorrectly. Therefore, as instruments for teaching, they remain unspoiled, and the trainer can teach with success. One should not expect that a trainer with many students will teach with the best results. As he corrects one, he will often notice different mistakes that others are making, but he must forbear on correcting them. The others continue to ride incorrectly, believing that, since they have not been corrected, that they are using correct aids.

Therefore, the lessons must be imparted to each student individually. This is because many are not in a position to draw a suitable conclusion for themselves from a general instruction.

Walk and Trot

In addition to the diagonal leg movement, these two gaits are related to each other in that the horse's forehand and hindquarters are supported at the same time. The trainer must explain the suitable aids, and explain how they are different from those of the canter. Only then will the student and the trained horse be able to understand the aids. The horse, continuing with the collection at the beginning of each ride, will step forward in walk or trot by lifting one of its forelegs and stepping forward in a collected manner, if it is supported by leg pressure that is weaker or stronger depending on the circumstances. If the horse steps forward without collecting beforehand, then it will proceed without the correct carriage, which will disturb the rider's good posture.

A sudden tug on the reins to collect usually results in the canter. The student should not be taught the canter before he has perfectly mastered the aids for walk and trot.

Before the rider transitions the horse from halt to walk, he must be made aware of one mistake that beginners often make: If the rider does not following the horse's motion, falls back and hangs on the reins, or even goes ahead of the horse by falling forward and dropping the rein contact, then he will lose the vertical position of his hips. The next consequence of this is that the horse will step incorrectly, and later the false gait or pace will develop. This arises because the timing between the hoofbeats becomes uneven and the diagonal sequence of the legs is disrupted to a greater or lesser degree. The instructor does not allow the student to become familiar with these erroneous movements of the horse in the beginning, so he often has him halt after a few steps and start over correctly from the beginning.

In the initially shortened trot, repeating these aids becomes even more necessary, and especially when riding into the corners, as in the case of the turns. Because the outside leg is the more active one in the turns, the student often makes the mistake of leaning with his upper body toward that side.

In order to maintain the correct walk and trot, the pupil must repeat the same aids after a few steps that he used to make the transition. This is because even the trained horse becomes insensitive to the effect of the legs and the bit if the pressure is always the same. Moreover, every animal strives to be free.

The first sessions should not be continued for too long, especially in trot. The student should be reminded that he should not forget the collecting aids in the transitions to the other gaits, and to maintain the proper position of his hips in particular. It is at first of no small difficulty for the budding rider to use the correct amount of leg and hand for collection, so that when the horse stops trotting, it will at once transition to walk, and neither cease to go forward on account of too little collection, nor break into canter as a consequence of too much. Of these untimely transitions, the latter rather than the former must be intended by the rider. By alternately delaying one front leg as it steps forward by restricting it, and by driving the diagonal hind leg forward by using leg aids, the feet can no longer step in time, and the walk is the result. In contrast, a sudden disturbance in the trot-tempo makes the horse want to canter.

The rider rounds the corners in lengthened trot and practices halting on the spot. Even greater collection and a stronger upper body position are required for this. However, this does not consist of leaning back with the entire upper body, but only in dropping the shoulders, which is facilitated by firmly setting the hips by stretching down with one or both legs. The so-called stirrup-stepping, which is done by extending the leg at the back of the knee, is one of the subtle aids that drives the hind legs under. It is done by stiffening the foot against the stirrup. When doing this, however, the leg does not become so elastic that the rider sits more deeply in the saddle when halting, but rather is jolted out of the saddle.

The rider goes into the corners in the walk. He keeps the horse on a straight line until its head gets to the edge of the corner. By restraining with the hands as specified, the forehand is led through the corner. The inside leg presses the hindquarters into the corner, and the outside leg prevents the croup from falling out. In a measured trot, the corners have to be ridden a bit more rounded, and even more so depending on how powerful the trot is. In all turns, whether in the corners or anywhere else in the arena, the horse should now be bent to the inside from head to croup in proportion to how tight or wide the turn is. In this position, the pupil practices the turns on many dividing lines, such as voltes, circles, etc, and makes sure that he always yields again after retraining with the hand, so that the horse does not become insensitive to the rein contact.

One should not expect that the beginner will always target the correct hind leg while restraining in the turns. This is because he could not yet have developed such a fine feel. He will be able to do so in walk and trot before he can do it in canter. This is because in canter, one must repeat the same aids after every stride, as will be explained later. Thus, the trainer must be content with the said restraining and yielding of the hand, if the aids are not too obvious, and the horse is prevented from going completely on the forehand.

To prepare for the caracoles, the student has to learn the changes of direction after the previous instruction. It is easiest to change direction on the diagonal lines across the whole arena at first. Just as with every turn, the horse must be collected for every change of direction. It is of great importance that this corresponds to the gait and occurs at the right moment. When the rider is changing direction from the right hand across the whole arena, he must make both reins even at the middle of the arena by lengthening the shortened right rein, straightening and collecting the horse, then shortening the left rein, and finally by positioning the horse left before the end of the diagonal. A faster sequence of these individual moments in the change of direction is required on shorter transition lines, but especially on the tight half voltes, and changes after a tight turn or on the spot.

The tight changes in the trot by means of semi-circular turns, i. e. the serpentine, are the most suitable exercises along with the figure eight to prepare the student for cantering. This is because he must pay attention to how the horse's hind legs are stepping, namely from right to left and vice versa. In order to further refine this feel, have him ride these turns without changing the horse's position, i. e. alternately making half a turn, and then making a counter-turn, and complete these walk and trot exercises with voltes or figure eights entirely in counter-position.

These turns are given the nickname "counter," because the horse is turned opposite to its head position. They could just as easily be called "throwing" rather than "turning."

In counter-turns, the student, if he wants to keep the correct position, must never make a tighter turn than his skill allows without being detrimental to the proper position of the horse in the normal turns. In general, beginner riders must practice changes of direction with precision more often to be able to turn rather than make the turns more difficult with positions that go against the rules. Counter-turns do not make skilled riders and will easily cause the horse to go behind the bit.

On the Reinback

After the student has acquired the necessary skills to correctly walk and trot at will, to maintain them, to turn and change direction, he must now be taught how to properly reinback, but not before. It is detrimental to the student and trainer to practice the reinback exercise prematurely before the student has learned to distinguish the incorrect steps from the correct ones using his sense of feel when the horse is moving forward. Because stepping backward is less natural for the horse than going forward, they seek to evade this compulsion by taking incorrect steps, which disturb not only the rider's seat, but also the rein contact. Further, even the best trained horse may creep backward incorrectly and lose its balance, which the student will not be able to correct. For the time being, the horse must be regarded as a ruined instrument that makes teaching impossible.

After a successful halt out of a strong trot, the student straightens and collects the horse with even reins. One of the hind legs begins the reinback, and the rider's legs or spurs give the aid for this. Before this movement of the hind legs is felt, his rein hand may not encourage the horse to step back by restraining more strongly, and especially not if the hindquarters evade out to the side. In that case, the horse has lost its correct position and must be collected again. The rider's hand can prevent this mistake from arising if, at that moment, it targets the hind foot that wants to step sideways. This will plant the foot on the ground, which can then easily be moved to the line of the horse's center of gravity by using the leg or spur. It is better still if the instructor prevents the hindquarters from evading by initially allowing the reinback to be practiced along the wall, and by using a riding whip to support the rider's deficient leg aids. It is most useful if the student is allowed to practice the exercise away from the wall without the trainer's help, because great hand and leg coordination is required to keep the horse straight.

In the correct reinback, the horse only covers half of the ground that it does while moving forward in a collected gait. This is because, as explained further in the School, the force that pushes the load forward outweighs the one that is used in the reinback. Both the rider's safety and the horse's proper carriage are at risk if the horse rushes back with long steps. Such cases also give the student the opportunity to learn to use the spurs as punishment. He will use both at the same time if the horse creeps back in a straight position, whereby the reins must be yielded. If, however, the horse goes back sideways, eg. to the right, then he must use only the right spur once the right rein hand has positioned the horse's head to the right by restraining on it.

This exercise is also the most suited, apart from making the student more familiar with how to use his legs and reins than the previous ones, to convince him how necessary a determined and steady posture is. As long as he still makes the usual mistake that most riders make of leaning forward when the horse steps backward instead of sitting on the coccyx, he can neither distinguish the movement of the horse's hind legs, nor the correct use of his legs and spurs to collect the horse if it rushes back in reinback.

Initially, it is necessary for the student, when riding forward as well as in the reinback, to keep his eyes fixed steadily upon a point that is in front of him to help him stay on a straight line. However, he is best led by his sense of feel, which, when well-developed, is his best and only guide in many circumstances, such as when riding in the dark.

On half-pass or riding on two tracks with
a straight position of the horse

If the rider intends to go sideways without first turning his horse via a half-pirouette, then he must know how to guide it on two tracks or half-pass. In so doing, the order of how the legs are lifted and lowered, as was previously explained for each of the three gaits on a single track, must not be disturbed. The pupil should, therefore, cause the horse's legs to move sideways such that the outside legs are placed in front of the inside in such a way that their movement is not impeded. To execute the right half-pass, for example, the rider must first position the lightened forehand a half a step sideways to the right by holding with the right hand and putting his weight on the right, and at the same time, using the left leg behind the girth to make the hindquarters step forward at the same time. During half-pass, the right leg must prevent the inside legs from going sideways too much. Otherwise, the horse will lose its balance and start to rush. In this case, especially when performing half-pass in the trot and canter, it will be difficult for the rider to follow the horse's motion. He can only avoid this mistake if he uses his inside leg correctly, and supports most of his weight on the inside stirrup. Via the dominant effect of this leg and by restraining with the hand against both hind legs, a halt must end the half-pass, but not a School halt. Just as with reinback, one leaves it to the student to practice at the end of the sessions, but only a few steps. In so doing, teach the rider that it behooves him to only work the horse in those difficult movements for which it is capable of being trained. In contrast, one looks ridiculous when one shows off in public places and promenades by performing reinback, flexions, and half-pass, when he was only asked to ride out.

So that the student does not confuse the half-pass with the difficult School travers, explain to him that in half-pass, the outside leg is dominant, while the inside leg is dominant in the travers. In accordance with the purpose of horsemanship, travers can only be executed with greater bending in the horse's haunches. (See the 2nd Section. Travers and Passage.)

On the Canter

One should never acquaint the budding rider with the canter until he can keep his upper body in balance in the walk, as well as in the collected and extended trot, and knows how to use the leg aids, especially soft and hard leg pressure.

Further, the pupil must be able to determine by feel which of the horse's individual legs is being picked up and set down, especially the hind legs, in walk and trot. This is so that he can determine the correct moment to give the aids to canter. One can see how the front legs are moving by the action of the shoulders. One can feel it by using one's legs, which embrace the forehand. It is very important to be able to distinguish this by feel, as the rider's gaze should be on the horse as seldom as possible.

It is to be regarded as a necessary preparatory exercise for cantering and for what is to follow to teach how to accurately distinguish the change in the movement of the hind legs. The rider can use his seat to identify this without disturbing his posture.

In walk and trot, the rider first observes the movements of the horse's shoulders; the upper parts move backwards when the legs are lifted and the lower ones move forward. The opposite is true when they are set down. He indicates that he correctly recognizes the movement of each foreleg by moving his hands visibly at first (for which he only uses the underlying snaffle) to imitate the action of the forelegs. He does this by alternately raising and lowering each hand a tiny amount. This practice not only encourages the lifting of the individual foreleg, it does not interfere when it is lowered, acts according to the nature of the movement, and as a result, also becomes more correct and easier to feel.

This method also has the advantage that it makes it easier to recognize how the hind legs are moving. At the same moment when the right foreleg is lifted, the right hind leg steps forward and down. A half-halt on the right rein that is directed toward the back and is aimed at lifting will encourage the right foreleg to lift. This furthers the increased loading of the right hind leg. As the right hind leg is compressed against the ground, the hip lowers. If the rider has a correct seat, then it is very easy to identify how the hind legs are stepping.

The right hind leg is lifted because of its pushing activity, in that the hip moves in an opposing manner. It is easier for the rider to recognize the movement if he yields on the right rein at that moment.

The obvious hand movements that were recommended in the beginning must gradually become so imperceptible that eventually only the rider is aware of them and they disappear into his and the horse's movement, as it were. These aids only become completely invisible with the double bridle.

The rider must also eventually refrain from watching the horse's shoulders, and use only his legs to feel how the forelegs are moving, and to try to figure out from that how the hind legs are moving. Finally, he will also lift his legs off of the horse and use only his seat to feel when the reins should be usedm which will depend on how the hind legs are moving. The more points of support he has, and the more skillfully and steadier he carries his body on them, the more accurately he will feel how the hind legs are stepping. For riders who can accurately feel their horse's gaits, they may be successful in using the following procedure.

The rules for the rider's procedure to canter an already trained horse, and to keep it in balance, must be taken from the canter movement already described above (see "On the Canter" in the first part), which will be explained as follows.

Since this instruction concerns the campaign rider, only the ordinary canter with three beats, or the canter in balance, will be discussed. So that the rider becomes aware of his actions using his own sense of feel, which is more difficult the faster the horse is going, it is most useful to transition from the collected walk to the canter. The procedure to canter right will be discussed here first. Only in the event that the trainer is in the unfortunate position of not having a perfectly trained horse for the student to ride can he allow it to transition to canter from the shortened trot, which is actually only allowed in dressage.

The trained horse will already anticipate the canter when the rider collects it in the walk. The hind legs, which are close together, step under more quickly. Before the beginner canters his horse to the right, he must feel this moment for several steps, so that he can develop the right feel. He must then change the position of the horse's hindquarters. The hand takes a stronger rein contact, and he uses his left leg to encourage the left hind leg to step under more quickly. In this way, in the canter right position, many horses will fall into canter on their own. This can easily become detrimental for their carriage, and the rider develops a feel for this incorrect transition. Therefore, it may not be permitted. The rider's hand is to give the aid to canter by restraining on the left rein and transferring the necessary amount of the extra weight of the forehand onto the left hind leg. This awakens the springing force, and results in the bounding canter stride. The canter is maintained if the left hand restrains at the moment when the left hind leg is set down, and if it returns to the holding or normal position as soon as the foot begins to push again.

Restraining on the left rein is then the natural aid to transition into the right lead canter. The rider has to not only determine whether the left hind foot is pushing or carrying, but also to judge how much it is stepping under.

If this process has been presented to the rider and the reasons for it have been clearly stated, then the trainer must have him collect the horse in the walk and organize the movement of the hind legs into a canter on the right lead. This will be referred to as "canter right" in the future. For this, the trainer must tell him the correct measure, and if it has been achieved, do not forget to tell him to restrain left and to encourage him to canter with the voice command, "Canter," at the moment when the left hind leg steps forward and down.

If the horse assumes a crooked position when these aids are given, then it must be overlooked in the beginning. This is because it would be too difficult for the beginner rider to think about the horse's straightness along with so many new responsibilities. It is sufficient, for the time being, that he experiences how, by doing what has been said, the left legs are hindered in lifting up and stepping forward and the right ones are supported in this, and that repeating these aids after the first canter stride to a lesser degree maintains the canter.

The aids are to be given to a lesser degree in each subsequent stride, because the horse, which already knows what the rider wants, does not need the same aid. In addition, giving the same strong aids over and over again can disrupt the proper canter very easily if they are used on the wrong hind leg. In such a case, a lesser disruption would have insignificant consequences.

In the beginning, it is only necessary for the instructor to tell the student when it is the appropriate moment to restrain. The burdening is then caused not only by the rein hand, but also by the rider's weight, which is directed onto its rearmost supporting point and onto the left seat bone at the moment when the left hind leg steps forward and down.

If the rider has learned these aids well, then he will be able to canter any trained horse. However, if he does not combine them with his right leg and momentarily restrain with his right hand, he will make a very significant mistake. This is with respect to his good posture and the position of his horse, which is still crooked. He will now have to begin to prevent the latter.

The horse shares with all four-legged animals the tendency to go crooked. It is more inclined to do so in canter than in any other gait. The rider can best nip this disadvantageous position in the bud when it arises in canter right by placing his inside leg flat and extending it in a vertical direction, thereby forming a counterpoint, and at the same time, bringing himself into a good position suitable for the canter. This is called the canter-right seat. This canter-right seat is only easy if the horse canters straight. Only then can the rider use his right leg without great stiffening and hard pressure on the stirrup to achieve and maintain the strongest upper body position, even when the hindquarters are moving powerfully.

The canter-right seat, the use of the hand and leg to canter the horse straight, and the strongest position of the rider require more thorough explanations that will be more comprehensible to the beginner rider the simpler they are, i. e. the more they take from the horse's movement and position in canter and are presented accordingly.

First. Concerning the canter-right seat.

When cantering right and in the right-lead canter, one restricts the horse's hips and shoulders along with the legs on the left side, but gives those on the right freedom to step ahead of those on the left. The rider does the same. He puts his hip and shoulder back more on the left than on the right, thus fulfilling the requirements of the canter-right seat. When the left hip is back, the left leg also comes in contact with the horse's abdomen, where it can easily get the left hind leg to step under. The rein hand follows the position of the shoulders, from which the first degree of restraining left results.

Second. How can the horse be straightened in canter?

If the horse is crooked, then the right feet step too far apart from the left (the disadvantages for this as they relate to the horse have already been explained in the first section on the canter position). As a consequence, the rider is prevented from having a good posture; he hangs either towards the left leg or right leg, whichever one is working more. This will not be the case if the feet stay as close together as possible. To achieve this, the rider must also bring his feet closer together by lowering the right heel and bringing it flat against the left at the moment when the right hind foot leaves the ground. In this way, the hind legs are prevented from too much canter-right, and it will be easy to straighten the horse if the hand restricts on the right while the forefeet are still in the air. As a result, both hind legs are more connected to each other, in that the right is now more apt to support the left in carrying the load. The hand can still act more forcefully for this purpose by restraining, and will only restrict with the left if the horse tries to break from the canter.

The more the horse lowers its hips due to the restriction on the hand, or the more it puts itself on the hand, the easier it is for the student to improve his posture. This is because he can set his hips and distribute the weight of his upper body evenly on the three supporting points. Only then will he be able to regulate the horse's movement at will. With this, the third condition is fulfilled, namely, the strongest position of the rider.

From the discussion of these three requirements for the proper canter position of the horse and rider, it is shown that this good seat can be acquired only by the skillful use of legs and hand, and not vice versa. In other words. the seat alone will not lead to the proper handling of the horse. It was necessary to refute this fairly common belief, so please excuse the clumsiness of this explanation.

Before the student ends the canter, he must know how to transition the horse back into the gait from which it had transitioned into canter. This is because halting on the spot will be too difficult for him, as the necessary coordination between the leg and hand aids is still lacking.

In order to transition the horse from canter to walk, the rider should let the left hind foot step forward more freely, but in contrast, hinder the forward movement of the right, as with the position of the hindquarters to the right in general. If the aids that maintain the canter are no longer given, the right leg is pressed against the flank, the hand is held against the right hind leg as it steps down, and finally the canter-right seat is stopped. Then the canter right will also stop. So that the horse does not come abruptly to a full halt, but rather continues immediately in walk, both legs must press firmly at the same time and the strong posture of the upper body must be maintained.

To canter left, it is necessary for the student to carry out the same procedure, but in reverse. To mention the details would be a superfluous repetition, since they can be inferred from what has already been said.

When the rider is properly practiced in cantering on both leads, begin to have him canter in small voltes, as in the trot, but ones that are not too tight in the beginning. The rules for turning that have already been explained apply here as well. At the moment when the horse begins the stride, that is, when it sets down its outside hind leg, the rider's outside leg must prevent the hindquarters from falling out while the hand executes the turn by restricting on the inside rein.

Depending on the horse's conformation and dressage training, as well as the student's skill, the instructor has to determine how large the voltes should be.

In order to teach the rider how to caracole in half-voltes with flying changes, or to transition from one canter lead to the other, further preparation is required. Following from the canter movement that has already been explained, the flying change from one canter lead to the other involves the horse suddenly changing the entire order of its legs. The rider's aids must be changed just as quickly. This presupposes an exact sense of feel, and cannot be demanded in the beginning. The following movements are most suitable for preparing the pupil for the flying changes. For example, if he is cantering the straightened horse to the right, a few steps before the spot where he should switch to the left lead, let him first transition to walk, then at the desired location, while he changes all of his aids in the proper order, and by using his hand in a particular way, i. e. by restraining right, have him transition to canter. After some practice, the rider reduces the number of walk steps between the changes, so that in the end, there is only one step to make the transition from canter right to canter left.

The rider, thus accustomed to changing his aids more and more quickly, has to make sure that the horse does not falter when halting, that the horse takes calm steps between the changes, that he does not hesitate to give the horse the correct position, and finally, that the transition to the left-lead canter is as calm as possible. This is because both horse and rider can easily be mistaken about the aids.

The procedure for a flying change without walking steps in between is explained and executed in the following manner:

Since the outside hind leg starts the canter stride, as stated, and the continuation of these strides also determines the canter, the horse must, therefore, be on this leg the most. Thus, it is easy to conclude what the rider has to do in a flying change. Only a quiet transition from one canter lead to the other is allowed here, and not violently throwing the horse to one side, forcing it to change at least in front so as not to fall down.

A few canter strides before the spot where the horse is supposed to change from right lead to left lead, the rider switches from restraining with the left hand to holding. This allows the outside hind leg to step forward and farther under when the rider uses his right leg more, and transition to canter left at the same time, if the right hand restricts on the right rein at that moment. While the horse's left shoulder and left hind leg become freer, the right shoulder is held back. Pressure from both legs will surely bring about the left-lead canter. Now the student, for which he was prepared in the walk and trot exercises, must canter the horse with the head to the inside, that is, with a shortened inside curb rein, and change the horse's head position when he executes the flying change.

It will be less difficult for the rider to change leads on strong horses, if he has sufficient feel and skill to give the aids at the right moment, i. e. when the horse sets the inside hind leg down. In contrast, it is better and safer to practice only the above preparatory exercises on weak horses, because it takes a lot of strength and good carriage on the part of the horse to execute these sudden changes while remaining appropriately calm.

It goes without saying that the rider also has to change the position of his weight at the moment the flying change is executed according to the rules that apply to the canter. The changes in the half voltes require even more accuracy, especially because the position of the horse's head must be positioned more to the inside than during the changes on the straight line, so much so that one can see the orbital arch from the side. However, this position will not be possible without shortening the inside rein by one to one and a half inches.

If the rider already perfectly understands the aids for a flying change on a straight line, then it is easier for him to cue for the change at the right moment in the half volte. By putting more weight on the inside hind leg, the horse is prepared for the flying change.

Moreover, in these flying changes in the half-voltes, the rider must pay more attention to the correct distribution of his weight than previously, if the horse is not to change before the correct moment.

The most difficult is reserved for the student for last — ending the canter with a full halt. In walk and trot, this was easy for him. In these gaits, the horse's weight was more evenly distributed, and was pushed from one hind foot to the other in a diagonal direction. In the canter, on the other hand, due to the bounding strides, the halt must be executed in a different way.

The horse, in order to halt properly, i. e. without losing its balance, must transfer the weight of the forehand, which is lifted by the hindquarters, and put it onto the hind legs for a moment so that the forehand can return quietly to the ground. For this purpose, a stronger flexion in the hindquarters is required than is necessary to halt from the walk or trot. In order to halt the horse from the canter in one beat, the rider must use the aids that he already knows to collect the horse in the last canter stride. The moment the outside hind leg steps down is the appropriate one to give the aid to halt. If the rider is not yet adept enough to feel it, then the moment must be marked by calling out, "Halt!"

Incorrect halts on the forehand out of the canter hurt the interest of the trainer, if he loves his horse, as well as being of no use to the student. This is because they give him an incorrect feel. The instructor and the student must do their best to prevent the horse from this abrupt halt, which can sometimes even be detrimental to the rider's health. It may be sufficient for the instructor to use the lunge whip shortly before the halt to drive the hind legs under the horse, if the student is not yet able to do this with his legs and spurs. Due to this support, the halts must initially be practiced along the wall. The wall, along with the whip, prevents the croup from failing out. One may not demand that the student halt in the middle of the arena before he has correctly felt it along the wall and knows how to use his legs to drive the hind legs under. Once they have practiced it, they can easily avoid the mistakes mentioned above. As in all cases, the hand should yield after if has caused one or both hind legs to bend as intended. It must also do so now after a successful full halt. However, the contact and the rider's strong posture must not be lost, if the horse is to retain the correct carriage. If this carriage could not be demanded of the horses while mounted, then it should be demanded after being dismounted following a correct halt. After the student has fastened his rein hand to the mane on the side at the withers, he must maintain the steady contact on the reins until he has completely dismounted, when the hand lets go of the mane and the reins. Such a proper ending will keep the horse correct under the rider, whereas it will be confused and dissatisfied after an incorrect halt when returning to the stable, if it has not been brought back into a somewhat proper carriage by means of a reinback beforehand. The trainer must also have the student use this method, the reinback, when the horse pulls hard against the hand when transitioning from the shortened canter to extended canter.

Before the student is able to keep the horse in the proper carriage as directed, he should not be allowed to ride tight turns, and especially not in counter-position. The counter-turns differ from the ordinary turns only in that the horse's outside hind foot serves as the pivot point for the turn. Therefore, it is strained more than the inside one, even in tighter turns. The aids for this are derived from the canter. The trainer is advised not to practice this exception to the rule with the student too early, because it can easily bring the horse out of the proper carriage, and the difficulty of riding this gait correctly does not make it obvious enough to him. The horses creep behind the bit as soon as they are allowed, even in the tightest counter-turns. The resulting incorrect trot, however, quickly reveals the pointlessness of such an exercise.

On Riding Out in the Open,
On the Carrière and Jumping

The time has now come for the student to learn to ride fast, even over obstacles, without his and the horse's carriage suffering as a result. Space in the riding arena is too limited for this purpose. Neither can it be expected that the rider has the skill yet to ride the horse in a carrière into the corners. To practice jumping in shortened gaits is at the heart of the matter. Therefore, it is advisable to have the jumping lessons in an open field, combined with lengthened gaits (even in the carrière), and later to practice jumping on the spot with those who have already prepared for this by jumping on straight lines and over natural obstacles.

The trainer accompanies the student, so that he can tell him the necessary rules. It inspires more confidence in the student and makes it more comprehensible for him, since he can see how the methods are applied. These exercises are more strenuous and demanding, and require great will power and attention from the student.

Short stirrups and reins are the first requirement. First, the rider judges the correct length in the carrière or after a jump. He decides for himself depending on the circumstances. He who rides with stirrups that are too long should fear the carrière and jumping, because maintaining one's balance in them is difficult for many riders. In the carrière, there is less of the horse's mass between the legs and more in the shortened canter. As a result, in the latter case, there are more points of contact or connecting points and fewer in the former case. If one wanted to stretch one's legs into long stirrups, the points of contact would be reduced even further, while they increase when riding with short stirrups. Short stirrups are even more necessary when jumping, because they make it easier for the rider to use the spurs. They should be used near the horse's girth. Their use becomes as necessary here as when collecting in the carrière if the horse gets too strung-out and threatens to get out of hand. By the way, it should be noted that long stirrups are easier to shorten than short ones are to lengthen.

It is a difficult task for the campaign rider to maintain a good contact in the carrière and jumping, i. e. soft and steady in the hand. It is futile to try to obtain this excellent advantage by riding long intervals in extended trot without stirrups, or by trying to put the horse on the haunches via shortened School exercises. A field with uneven footing, ditches, hedges, and hedge rows is the only suitable arena for this, and especially when hunting hounds are in the lead. Letting the horse run around with loose reins would risk an accident for both horse and rider. It has already been established that good contact is the main requirement. The reins must be as short as possible, so that the hand is almost at the middle of the horse's neck and almost touches the mane. Then, only the upper arm can come into contact with the upper body. The forearm is free, and the elbow is not bent as much. The hand, closed into a fist, keeps the snaffle reins short, but with less contact than on the curb reins. The right hand also holds the whip in the middle, so that the hand can be even more tightly closed in an emergency, if one needs to use the snaffle reins.

During this first time riding out, the instructor should not forget to acquaint the pupil with the few matters that have to now be observed before the beginning of the intended exercise and that remained unsaid during the instruction in the arena. For example:

The rider's attention, in addition to everything else, must be mainly on the points that the horse has to pass, even before the horse notices them. He should not ride the horse on stony ground unnecessarily, especially if it is unshod. He should refrain from clucking with the tongue and from using the whip too obviously when in the company of other riders, so as to not disturb the pace of the other horses. He should leave walkways, sowed fields, etc, undisturbed and avoid pedestrians. He should also not get in the way of other riders, which if intentional, is unforgivable.

When riding uphill, the rider leans forward a little so that he can better follow the horse's motion, yields on the reins, and leaves the horse to its own devices. When riding downhill, on the other hand, he should set himself in the strongest position against the horse, take a firmer rein contact, and not lead it down in a straight line, but rather in a zigzag, especially in lengthened gaits.

It has already been stated that riding in other people's way is a very great offense. One can avoid it when approaching other riders by always passing on the right, as is the custom. He who fails in this betrays little sense of decency when riding.

Since nothing should disturb the rider's upper body posture, the rider is permitted to greet others without bowing. It should be noted that the horse should not see the hat, and, therefore, it must be taken off to the side.

There are still many rules of behavior for the student to learn, but to detail them all here would be digressing too much. Therefore, it is left for the trainer to make the rider acquainted with them.

In walk, trot, and canter in a somewhat lengthened gait, the instructor chooses terrain suitable for the intended exercise, while teaching the student about the horse's idiosyncrasies. These may still be unknown to the student and may only show themselves in a fast gallop or while jumping. In the event that he is riding a horse that is strung-out, fast, and sensitive, then encourage him to avail himself of the collecting aids more than the driving aids. The student, however, initially remains more passive than active, especially when jumping.

On the approach to an obstacle in a lengthened canter, every horse must be collected in front of the jump. The aids for this depend on the horse's sensitivity. For the student, the rule is to start with the mildest. Therefore, he tries to collect with a few half halts or full halts, and induces the take-off with a quick squeeze of the legs. If the horse is insensitive and lazy, then the driving aids are prescribed, and the leg pressure is to increase until the spurs are used. However, this easily causes highly strung horses to lose the proper carriage.

During the whole duration of the carrière, the pupil should work almost exclusively on the horse's carriage and on how he is controlling it. This is because maintaining the carrière is wholly dependent on it. The aids to control the horse — the upper body posture and either firm or soft leg contact with legs that are extended to a greater or lesser degree — should be used gradually depending on the circumstances.

No exercise other than the carrière and jumping is able to more convincingly prove the statement made earlier, namely, that the good seat makes the rider more secure in the saddle than clinging does, which is generally popular but only makes it more difficult, if not impossible, to control the horse. The carrière compels even the laziest rider to think about how to control the horse, because the unfamiliar fast motion awakens in him the desire for self-preservation. It should be the trainer's intention to choose a horse whose speed suits the student's ability and timidity. So far, it has been easy for the student to tell whether the horse cantered on the forehand or in balance. It was harder to tell the difference in the trot, and the most difficult in the walk. Both conditions are the easiest to tell in the fastest movement and in jumping. The rider can comfortably follow the horse's gait when it is in balance, while a constant jolting and jarring characterizes being on the forehand. In addition, the student will notice that in the latter, it is difficult for him to keep his seat in the saddle, but it is not hard when going in balance. Without the horse being in balance, it is difficult to touch the necessary points of contact with the legs and knees, because the horse's barrel is long and narrow. In the other case, it is easy, since the chest is opened and expanded.

Therefore, the carrière exercise is extraordinarily advantageous to the student, because it gives him a more correct feel for balance. It also makes it possible for him to distinguish a correct walk and trot from incorrect ones. It will always remain unclear what a balanced horse in motion actually feels like if one never experiences it. Such a rider is as little able to control his horse as someone who rides with loose reins.

It is to be expected that the horse will go onto the forehand at the very beginning and when galloping. The trainer must notice it as soon as it occurs, and immediately remind the rider to use the collecting aids. This shows a hitherto unknown difficulty in the use of the spurs, which are absolutely necessary for collection, as has already been explained. To that end, the student has to lessen the leg grip. Therefore, he has a difficult internal struggle, because it seems unlikely to him that just the position of his hips alone without gripping strongly with the legs is sufficient to be able to follow the horse's motion. However, the longer he hesitates with the collection, and the longer he seeks to achieve this by just restraining on the reins alone, the more the pushing property of the hindquarters is stimulated, and the more ineffective the collecting aids will become. Since controlling the horse becomes too difficult for the pupil at this point, he must resort to using the snaffle reins and apply intermittent half-halts on them individually, as was taught in the chapter, "On the Resistances," when the horse bolts.

In such cases, such exercises cannot be of any use. One should not commence with jumping until the student has overcome his fear and knows how to use the spurs. One should not think that the spurs are to be used to poke the horse in the ribs or to cling on with them. One uses them in this way to drive obstinate horses forward, but not to collect horses from lengthened gaits. The spur aids can be considered a secret aid of horsemanship, because the degree of their use must be determined by the horse's actions, which are only perceived by the rider through his sense of feel. Accordingly, they cannot be told to the student, and are left to the rider's discretion. If he has learned them and made use of them in the carrière as well, then the instructor can combine them with the hand aids, and continue with them until he is able to execute a full halt.

The full halts, if they succeed, quickly convince the student that the spurs give him control over the horse, if used properly. They will also be the best preparation for him to acquire the posture in the saddle that is essential for jumping. In the halt, the horse flexes the hindquarters as though to jump, thereby bringing the rider's upper body into the strongest position in which he can follow the horse while jumping without losing his seat.

When the student is fully prepared, the trainer will seek out obstacles. At first, he should choose ditches that are not too wide or deep, low hedges or hedgerows. He reminds the student to collect the horse with a half-halt in front of the ditch.

However, if he sees that the student neglects to do so, then he should be satisfied if the student is still in the saddle after the jump. The same mistake that made collecting difficult in the carrière also makes half-halts impossible, i. e. clinging with the legs and failing to use the spurs. The horse will not execute a correct jump because of this. Instead, it will make a flying or deer jump. The rider loses his balance right away, and the horse must be collected again. This is done in the extended canter by working on the snaffle and the curb reins in an alternating fashion.

If the student has lost his initial uncertainty after several successful jumps over ditches, then one rides with him first over hedges, and then over solid obstacles. In all jumps over high obstacles, he has to collect the horse more than over ditches. To jump over obstacles that are higher than three feet, execute a full halt after several half-halts. To prevent the horse from stopping in front of the jumps, however, he should not neglect to encourage the horse to jump by using strong leg pressure or even a smack with the whip and to yield on the reins a bit. If the rider starts the jump well, then the trained horse will complete it well on its own. In other words, it will land with all four feet on the ground at the same time, and keep itself and the rider in balance. After the jump, depending on the command, it will continue in carrière, or stop and turn immediately. This is not so easy to execute after a jump on the forehand. The trainer concludes the lesson by acquainting the pupil with the few matters to which he must attend after dismounting, if he is obliged to tend to the horse himself. This includes first running the stirrups up. After the rider has taken the curb reins over the neck to lead the horse, it is most expedient to run up the stirrups as high as possible, because they stay there more securely and do not make the saddle dirty.

Running up the stirrups has a second advantage. First, they do not bother the horse by swinging back and forth, and second, it prevents them from getting stuck on something and causing damage to them or the saddle.

It is more expedient to lead the horse with the curb. This is because its reins are usually longer, and the horse respects them more. However, it is better to tie the horse with the snaffle reins, because they are stronger and less likely to hurt the horse's mouth than the curb bit. If the rider intends to leave the horse tied up and saddled for a while, then he should unfasten the curb chain, tighten the throatlatch, loosen the girth and air out the saddle. Do not forget to redo all of these things, however, when remounting.

If a horse suddenly goes lame, the rider should make sure that the horse has not stepped on some sharp object, and if it has, remove it. Stones often get between the horseshoe and the sole, which are easy to remove. In the worst case, however, they can cause severe damage to the hoof.

If the horse is in a sweat or very agitated by the ride, then it should be walked at a quick pace in a place where there is no draft so that it can cool down. It is better, of course, if one takes it back to the stable immediately, rubs it dry with straw, and covers it with a blanket.

The continuation of this teaching, which ends only for the campaign rider, is for those who intend to acquire a higher education in horsemanship, both in the first part on dressage training and in the second part on the School. Because they are one and the same, and in order to avoid unnecessary repetition, the terms, "teaching" and "training," are combined.

———————

The training of the campaign horse as well as the campaign rider is completed with the collection to the full halt in balance, both out of the collected and the extended canter, as well as after a jump and out of the carrière. In this regard, for the trained rider as well as for the budding rider, the necessary aids that are recommended are to "use the legs first, then the hand." Only by using the aids in this order, i. e. the restraining aids after the driving ones, the horse is taken out of its natural position on the forehand and put in balance. If this has come to pass, then the simultaneous use of hand and leg will keep it in balance.

If a fully bridled horse has been prepared for balance via a well-directed lesson in the campaign gaits that it is supposed to learn, and if it is to remain in a balanced position for a while after a full halt, then neither hand nor leg may be used before or more strongly than the other. Instead, they must both be used equally at the same time. With this, the campaign-training and the teaching on trained horses has reached their goal. It is not only more difficult to keep the horse in balance at rest than in motion, it is the most difficult. Therefore, it is the goal of every campaign rider.

Every full halt in balance serves to correct the horse in its training, especially if it is able to sustain it for a moment in the halt. In this way, the budding rider develops a feel for differentiating between balanced gaits and others. Whether the rider must use hand and leg simultaneously or must use the latter first in order to correctly control the horse's movements depends on whether he can correctly tell whether the horse is moving in balance.

The halts cause the horse's haunches to partially flex. The easier this becomes for the horse, the more comfortable and useful it is for use as a campaign horse. The more skillfully and greater the rider can bend the horse's haunches, the more control he has over it. Greater bending in the haunches until it is balanced sets the horse in an elevated and collected gait, which is called the School gait. It is not practical for campaign service, insofar as it takes too long to travel to different locations as is necessary. On the other hand, it is of extraordinary use for all other intended purposes. In regard to the already balanced horse, this makes it easier for it to flex the haunches as required, and to make it more obedient and give it greater endurance. As for the rider, however, it teaches him what flexion in the haunches is, so that he can more quickly and without mistake learn the concept of the balanced horse under the rider, and can obtain it in the most suitable manner.

Riders who always let their horses go in a natural position cannot possibly have any idea about a balanced horse in motion. Those who have never felt School movements and only aim to achieve balance in the horse are often at odds even with themselves about whether they have actually achieved it or not. The instruction that follows in the second part shows us the horse with more beautiful carriage and in nobler gaits. However, the hand and legs are used in the opposite order from before, with the hand being used first and the legs after, or the latter not even being used at all.

SECOND PART

The School, or on the movement of the horse with stronger flexion in the haunches

---

In recent times, riding in fast gaits is often regarded as the highest goal of horsemanship. This is partly due to the increased use of Oriental and English horses, or horses bred according to English principles, partly due to the increase in races and hunt riding, and the increased demand for speed, and partly due to other circumstances (eg. fashion, etc). Unfortunately, this has caused School riding to become neglected. However, it was not these circumstances alone that contributed to this deplorable condition. Other factors contributed, such as the noticeable lack of competent School riders who could serve as teachers and the pedantry that prevails at some riding barns. This is evidenced by the fact that some put too much stock in external appearances rather than the deep wisdom that lies in the School and the truth that it contains, which should lead to new prestige, respect, and cause it to become more widespread. Another principal cause of the neglect is the restless rush to strive for and attain instant gratification in a flash right away that is a characteristic of our time. The School requires a lot of time. This is because even the thinking and consistent rider, who has a systematic training technique, will succeed only slowly and gradually in achieving such a lofty goal.

It is generally enough for the campaign rider and the military if a horse can be ridden in balance in the various campaign gaits. However, for the latter, whose service often requires a higher education in equitation, the results obtained hitherto by the campaign dressage training are often insufficient, whether it be to keep the strong, older horse in constant submission, or to make ill-behaved horses that have been ridden badly serviceable again. For this, we are now to use the School gaits, or those movements of the horse that are caused by greater flexion in the haunches. If the pushing power of the hindquarters became resistant rather than activated by unsuccessful partial bending in the haunches, then it can only be remedied by its opposite, that is to say, by the carrying capacity over which the School has dominion. Once this has been done, the rider has complete control over the pushing power of the hindquarters, and thus over the entire horse. As a result, over-exertion of effort on either the part of the horse or rider no longer takes place.

Thus, the School rider can develop power in the horse's haunches and thereby affect the horse's disposition. Pacers and horses that have already been somewhat worn-out regain regular and confident gaits. The gaits of uncomfortable and jarring horses, after having been properly trained, become elastic, and lazy horses become hard-working. Mean and angry horses become mild and obedient again, the common ones refined, and the noble ones surpass all expectations.

As it relates to the rider, the School, in addition to his skill, completes the rider's knowledge of the horse. This is because the strength required of the haunches for the School is less obvious to him than in the balanced gaits. The greatest possible development of the springiness in the hock joints takes place only when the joints of the haunches are flexed in proportion to the latter. (See the General Section.)

The rider who has felt the power in these perfect School movements, which is caused by elasticity in the hindquarters, will also seek to discover how it is brought about. He will develop a sort of dynamometer that he can use to determine the ability of horses with various conformations to push and carry, which will depend on how their individual parts are put together. He will be able to do this without always needing to actually see how they move. There should be no doubt that these allow for the most infallible assessment and give one the surest gauge.

There are riding books that establish the purpose of the horse's finer training through School movements to not be for its greater utility in cavalry service. Instead, they recommend School gaits so as to be able to produce horses that are better for parades and other events. There are also many riders who are not convinced of the usefulness of the School work for the cavalry riding service or, because of their ignorance of it, are reluctant to retrain their horses through School exercises when they have lost their otherwise good carriage while in the service or on the hunt. One can also rarely explain to them that the trained School horse is also the perfect campaign horse. If this is not the result, then the School is not to blame, but rather the one who undertook it without knowing its requirements and levels.

The study of the School is as enjoyable as it is difficult. Many riders have sacrificed half of their lives to acquiring the secrets that are contained within this art. As with mathematics, and partly through it, it has been established as an irrefutable truth for centuries, but it is only clear to those who use natural methods and who practice it diligently and tirelessly. However, no one will succeed in transforming the hitherto almost imperceptible progress of equitation into a huge leap, neither through the greatest diligence of theoretical studies, nor through practical exercises in riding, just as is the case with the sciences, with which this art goes hand in hand.

———————

The halt and the reinback are also a method to collect in the School dressage, and cannot be regarded as individual movements here. In order to more easily understand the various rules for the halts, and to not confuse the School halt with the balanced halt or the incorrect halt, the School halt will be discussed in more detail.

All horses whose hind legs are free from defects and are correctly set naturally have so much strength in the haunches that they can carry the forehand on them for a greater or lesser amount of time. One can see this when jumping younger horses, for example. This means that they can be brought into greater balance at an older age by skilled riders who gradually increase the flexion in the haunches. Only a few horses are suited to the most perfect flexion in the haunches of the higher movements.

In the first part, it was proven that one prepared for the flexion in the hind legs, namely the hock, by first tightening on an individual rein and then by mainly using the half and full halts when first riding the horse. After the horse was prepared for collection by walk, trot, and canter exercises, the half and full halts eventually gave it the necessary balance by bending in the haunches. This is the difference between *arrêt* and halt. The former bends the hock joint, while the latter bends the haunches. If the latter is increased to the point of developing into a School movement, then it is called a School halt.

Each halt should either correspond to the gait out of which it was made, or pertain to the next intended School exercise. One must, therefore, distinguish between walk, trot, and canter halts, and know how to use them to transition from a lengthened gait to a collected or accelerated one, or even to suddenly take the horse from the liveliest motion to the most perfect stillness under the rider. It is important to note that every halt, regardless of which School movement out of which it is done, is performed on one track. In contrast, half-halts on two tracks can be useful if done correctly. The halts with a straight position are preferable to those with a degree of bend, especially for horses that are not very strong.

In the balanced halt, the rider still feels the counter-effect of the ground, upon which the weight of the horse's forehand is supported (the cause of all jolting and disturbances of the seat). In the School halt, this weight mostly rests on the haunches when the front hooves are on the ground. However, such perfection can only be the result of well-directed School work in all of its various lessons.

Many riders who engage in training their horses in dressage misjudge the School halt. Therefore, they avoid it because they fear that the flexing in the haunches will cause various diseases of the hind legs. Just how erroneous this view is will be shown as follows.

As is well known, too much stretching of the hock-capsular ligament can cause spavin and wind puffs, as can sudden pulling on its attachment points on the inner upper edge of the cannon bone, on the talus bone, the two navicular bones, and on the splint bones. Now the question arises: Does this over-extension and strain take place when the hock bends under the load or when it pushes off? In other words, is it the carrying or too much pushing action of the hock joint that causes these conditions?

In the artistic halt position, the loaded hock is compressed to a more acute angle than usual, whereby the attachment points of the capsular ligament, namely the lower end of the femur and the upper edge of the cannon bone (see the skeleton), come closer together. In this way, there is less strain on the capsule ligament in these places, and since the spavin is now seated on the inner, lower side of the joint, it is obvious that the bending of the hock is not the cause of the diseases mentioned.

Thus, proper halts not only do not harm the hocks, they become the means of maintaining the hock's natural strength. In the stiff, protective movement of the hind legs, the hocks form a more obtuse angle. As a result, the ligaments mentioned above are greatly stretched and strained on the front and on the inside, which can lead to diseases.

Similarly, joint diseases can arise due to impacts or incorrect jumping. This is because the joint surfaces collapse, which causes the periosteum to become inflamed. Exudation, adhesions, etc., are the result.

Even after this explanation, it is still necessary to clarify why horses that mainly use the pushing power of the hock joint, such as racehorses, for example, develop spavin and wind puffs less often than those that are incorrectly schooled. Those horses encounter either no or only very little resistance to the pushing action of the hock joints from the rider. Thus, the horses are subjected to less resistance than is the case with horses, even ones with strong hock joints, that are under an unskilled School rider.

Such a rider puts the pushing property of the hock in opposition to the ground without first having positioned it for the strike by lifting the horse's forehand an exaggerated amount and by the position of its weight. Thus, it is no longer possible to oppose the force. If the pushing power of the hocks is released in badly calculated strikes, the horse's body usually lifts up high above the ground in *Lanzaden*. The higher the horse lifts up off of the ground, the more the joint surfaces suffer from contusions. If, on the other hand, the carrying capacity of the hock joint is used to excess, often sickle hocks result. Therefore, if the hock is naturally too bent, then it can be regarded as an obstacle to School work.

The beginning of the School dressage develops the desired School position. This is done primarily by means of halts, out of which develop the School gaits.

If the horse obeys the rider's legs as a result of its previous dressage training and no longer evades them in the full halt, and if the hind legs step in front of the line of the haunches while the rein hand keeps restraining after the halt for a few moments, and if even greater pressure on the reins bends the haunches into the School position, then the hand alone, working before the legs, will be able to induce the horse to go forward. This movement is different from the previous one, and is called "School movement."

It is necessary to distinguish between movement and forward movement (see the end of the General Section). This is so that one can explain the development of the School movement that has been hinted at, and to not incorrectly use the means by which these natural characteristics of the horse can be subjugated to the purpose of dressage either individually or in combination. Forward movement refers to the action of the haunches, whereas movement refers to all parts of the horse's body. The horse can move its head, neck, one of its forelegs, or one around the other, without moving from its spot, but as soon as these movements are combined with the carrying and pushing power of the hind legs, there is forward motion. Consequently, as has already been explained, the artistically positioned horse under the rider, just as the naturally positioned horse without a rider, must first move in order to load the hind legs to perform artistic movements. This will lead to the development of spring in its forward motion. To that end, the rider's hand should first seek to set the horse's forehand on the hind legs on the ground before his legs prompt the horse to go forward. However, if the hind legs evade the effect of the reins, then the rider's legs must be used first. To carry out the School halt or the transition from the forward motion to rest via the initial use of the hand requires the hind legs to step completely under with greater flexion in the haunches to the line of the horse's center of gravity. If this does not take place, then the rider's legs must, as known, first energetically drive the hind legs forward and to step under. Then the rider's hand should be able to direct the weight of the forehand so that it is mostly supported on the hind legs in the halt.

If the halt position is maintained by the simultaneous use of hand and leg, and the use of the hand alone causes greater bending in the haunches, then the movement begins with the "School position." If the rein hand puts intermittent pressure on the curb with greater force, then forward motion must arise as a result, if the load — in this case, the horse's forehand — is on the hind legs, which have been transformed into springs. This creates "the School walk."

If this intermittent pressure on the reins loads the hind legs more and at a quicker pace, always alternates, and is used evenly on the hind leg that is stepping forward and under, then a swinging forward motion will develop. The horse will accelerate its steps, thus beginning the School trot.

If, in the School trot (on or moving off of the spot), the intermittent rein pressure is directed with increased strength at the hind leg that is stepping down, then an uneven motion of the hind legs will come about. This will be either right or left lead canter.

If the intermittent pressure is greater on the hind leg that is moving diagonally, i. e. the one more suited to carrying, then the horse develops a springy motion. This can be either right or left lead, and is called the School canter.

These various gaits have other names, depending on whether the horses go forward to a greater or lesser degree, sideways, or on the spot, namely "piaffé, passage, redopp," etc. These belong to the "Airs on the Ground."[3]

In the correct School position, the line of the horse's center of gravity can no longer be at its middle, but rather must be behind it. With perfect flexion in the haunches, it intersects the point where both levers of the horse connect, and it is labeled with GH on the skeleton. The line of the backbone can no longer be level as with the position of the horse in balance, but rather it will be lower behind. This is because the greater flexion in the joints of the haunches causes the croup to lower. Because the line of the center of gravity of the rider forms a right angle with the horse's spine when his upper body has the correct posture, he has a more or less diagonal position with the ground now, depending on how bent the haunches are. Because the line of the horse's center of gravity and that of the rider's meet at one point, the rider must not follow the horse's motion.

These are the general remarks to introduce the School. Before it is explained in detail, however, it should be repeated that the horse should never be started in the School too early. In any case, it must already be able to go in the campaign gaits with the utmost perfection possible. If one wanted to introduce

---

[3] Translator's Note: In the Complement, the author indicates that the following should be added here: "If these collecting aids work even more strongly and in a more sustained fashion on both haunches, then the courbette, croupade, balotade, and capriole are developed. These School jumps comprise the "'Airs Above the Ground.'"

it to the School too soon, then the greatest disadvantages would arise. When the time comes for the School exercises, results can be attained from the full halt out of any gait, and most certainly out of the carrière. If it is possible to keep the horse in the position given to it by the halt for a while without it falling out with the croup, that is, it obeys leg and spur completely, then one can begin with the School gaits. Therefore, the halts are to be regarded as a touchstone for whether the horse is suitable for the School or not.

If the rider has little regard for this rule, and despite it introduces the horse to the School gaits, he will bring it behind the bit. He will also ruin the good campaign gaits that it has already learned.

LOWER SCHOOL

Chapter 1

On the preparatory bending in the haunches via School walk
and School trot on one and two tracks
(Plié, Renvers, Doubliren, Travers)

The School gaits require that the horse's hind feet do not step under the line of the haunches but only up to the line of the horse's center of gravity because of the greater flexion in the haunches (see the skeleton). The more the line of the horse's and rider's center of gravity unite at the point of the horse's spine where the two levers connect, the more perfect the School movements become. The forelegs step higher, whereas the hind feet stay closer to the ground. They trail behind with shorter steps than in the balanced gaits, and do not reach the footprints of the front hooves.

In particular, for the sake of clarity, this School dressage is divided into lessons in the first chapter. Each lesson is divided into three sections, beginning, middle, and end, with each section explained and designated by School position, School gait, and School halt. The length and necessary repetition of the lessons and sessions cannot be pre-determined, but rather must be up to the rider's own discretion based on his experience.

In the second and in the following chapters, the division into lessons and sessions is not maintained. That is because it must be up to the rider to decide how to connect the canter exercises to those of the walk and trot. The canter exercises and those of the higher School always depend on how successfully the horse was prepared by the walk and trot exercises. They should be forborne in the case that they are not successful.

The beginning of the first session of the first lesson is comprised of the School position. This develops from the campaign halt, as has already been explained. The School position will be practiced in either the School walk or School trot depending on the horse's temperament. Excitable horses must be schooled in walk; in contrast, lazy horses in trot.

One cannot demand regularity in these gaits immediately. From the described School position, the horse will begin in a shortened walk with a straight position of its entire body, which is brought about by the use of the reins followed by the rider's legs. The School walk develops from this later, as soon as the increased pressure on the reins matches how the horse's hind legs are stepping forward more quickly and farther underneath.

The hand movements used to affect the reins will gradually become imperceptible to the eye of the observer. Now, the quickest squeeze and even just holding with the hand will almost be enough to load the haunches, if the hind legs step under. The loading that is necessary to develop the School walk or trot then happens on its own, as it were. If the School gait does not succeed, then the School position was not correct. The correct one must first be the goal, and is brought about by proper preparatory halts in balance. The good beginnings are followed by several good steps. However, these become more and more irregular depending on how much the horse loses the School position. If it is not possible to prevent this mistake while moving forward, then this first session must be completed without a School halt, which is actually supposed to end every session. One should then begin the second session by returning the horse to the School position by using the previous aids.

It is of substantial advantage in the School work that the horse remain in the School position whenever possible during the interim period between two sessions. This may only be a few minutes. If this can only be a tentative goal of the session, then it is advisable to halt the horse often to reestablish the position it has lost.

One can unmistakably recognize the regularity of the preserved School position by the fact that the horse is very willing to bend in the jaw at the slightest request. For this reason, one usually concludes each session with such flexions.

In the course of the exercises, the rider strives to regain the lost School position while moving forward. One can recognize success by the fact that the lightest contact can cause flexion in the jaws, just as it can induce the correct flexion in the haunches.

As soon as possible after the correct gait has been achieved in the School position, the rider should no longer hesitate to perform the School halt. This will depend on the ability that the horse has now acquired.

To conclude a School gait or School jump, the School halt should be done on ground that is not too soft. One should hear more clearly when the hind feet are set down than in the halt in balance. Also, the hind feet in the halt in balance do not press into the ground as deeply and are farther apart from each other than in the School halt. The more the hind feet step forward to the line of the horse's center of gravity, the closer they come to one another and the more they are burdened.

If it is possible to perform the School halt as consistently as stated, then the rider can combine a more difficult exercise with it in the third session. Because of the greater flexion in the haunches, the rider can sustain this submission consistently in walk and trot. This is done by switching the bent-straight position of the horse to the straight position and then returning to the bent-straight position.

Because one of the haunches is less flexed than the other in this lateral bend, the horse will seek to evade with the less burdened hind leg by moving it incorrectly. If the rider is able to feel this evasion as it occurs, then he should immediately give the horse a half-halt and demand a change of the bent-straight position, so that he regains control of the haunch that the horse is trying to free. The School half-halts are the preferred means of correction. Mainly through them, one gains the full submission of the trained horse and maintains the correct movement, but not via bodily pain, which is caused by the spurs. If, on the other hand, it is necessary to use the spurs with severity, then one should not refrain from performing the full and School half-halts, but also the exercises of the School itself, and correct the horse in campaign gaits.

The following lessons one begins right away, first with School position and School trot. However, it is preferable to practice the School trot in the first session, but not with sustained lateral flexion or turns that are too tight. If practiced too early, they will usually disrupt the regularity of the School trot. This trot can be regarded as the soul of the entire School work and can be considered to be the yardstick by which one can judge the progress of the training. If the tempo is still irregular, that is to say mixed with counter-tempos, which results from the fact that a haunch becomes too free, or if the horse begins to rush because of spur pressure, which is actually meant to prevent this, then one may not yet go on to the following movement that involves greater flexion in the individual haunch on two tracks. Instead, one corrects the horse with a half-halt, that is, with alternating greater flexion in one haunch then the other. This also occurs in reinback.

Plié

Even if the horse is well on the hand due to the previous exercises in the first session, the jaw flexion in School walk and trot cannot be perfected until it has been prepared by the School shoulder-in, i. e. by the greater flexion in the inside haunch. In a few riding books, this movement is also known as plié. This name is considered quite appropriate, in that it is the most descriptive for the effect of this movement. It will, therefore, be used here because it is shorter.

The term, "plié," however, is not understood to mean bending on the spot, but rather only when the horse is moving forward on two tracks. Just as the School began with the School position, so too does this begin with flexion on the entire inner side of the horse. In the School position and the School gaits with the horse positioned straight, the haunches are loaded to an equal extent in an alternating fashion. In the shoulder-in or plié-position, the inside haunch is loaded more and for a longer time than the outside one. It must bend more as a result. This can be caused by the greater effect of the reins on the same side, but only if the inside hind foot is positioned in front of the line of the haunches, which can be explained by the effect of the curb. (See the Double Bridle.) The horse's forehand then follows the pressure on the reins by changing its straight position to a bend to the inside and around the inside hind foot, in that it brings the inside feet closer together and compresses the ribs on the inside more than the outside, which are more open.

Although the bend in the jaws can be achieved in this plié-position at a standstill, it only serves to indicate to the horse the position it is to take in the subsequent movement.

Therefore, it can only be perfected in the School halt after it has been achieved via plié-position.

Shoulder-in in forward motion has already been explained in the first part, but only with respect to balanced gaits. One will be able to apply those explanations, since the legs are moved in the same way in shoulder-in and in plié. This movement does little to bend the haunches when practiced on circles, because the outside hind foot steps sideways too much and can stiffen more easily and escape the burden. It suits the purpose of this plié-exercise better to ride around the whole arena, and later on to transition to smaller rectangles. At any rate, now the rider's outside leg aids are used more often than those of the inside leg. This is so that the haunches cannot evade the burden. It is more difficult to prevent this, but more important than keeping the horse going on two tracks.

The second session with these positions and movements of the horse that were just mentioned should be done with greater bending in the inside haunch. First ride them in walk, and be satisfied with a few good steps, especially in School trot, and then execute a proper halt. The halt is correct if the inside haunch is flexed more than the outside haunch and the horse remains in the plié-position after this plié-halt. After an incorrect halt, whereby the inside haunch stiffens, it can be very effective to correct the horse with plié-reinback.

The third session must either be a repetition of the first, or an exercise in short collected trot in balance. This is especially true if the horse has adopted somewhat restricted or uneven steps. None of the following movements determine how the horse steps forward into the reins and with correct bending in the jaw and good contact on the hand in plié, so the rider should know how to maintain this plié in all of the remaining lessons. Depending on the contact and flexion, one must determine the duration and necessity of this exercise. Do not continue too long with horses that like to go forward and allow themselves to be bent easily. Instead, connect it to renvers and travers, i. e. the exercises for bending the outside haunch, so that it is not necessary to change the horse's head position as one changes which individual haunch is flexed more.

Renvers

In renvers, the horse moves its four legs in almost the same way as in the School shoulder-in. The only differences is that it is slightly more on two tracks or sideways. In addition, both movements differ less with respect to how the legs are moved and loaded than in the lateral flexion of the entire horse, depending on whether these exercises are in right or left position. In right shoulder-in on two tracks, the right side of the horse is the inside, the right hind leg is the one that carries more, the horse steps left and is bent to the right. If the horse is bent to the left with the same leg movement, then the right side becomes the outside, the right hind leg remains the one that carries more, the horse steps left as before, and the movement is called renvers-left. Naturally, the turns are to the right.

The direction of the forward motion in renvers is in accordance with the position of the horse's body; the horse looks in the direction it is going. In shoulder-in, in contrast, its position is opposite to its forward motion.

Renvers is prepared via the School plié and, in the campaign training, via the exercise of counter-canter position. The horse thereby gains practice carrying its body more on the outside hind leg in turns whilst going on one track.

As long as the horse is not yet on the hand, only practice renvers when changing from one direction to the other. Use the longest lines of the arena — the diagonals — to do this as follows:

It is assumed that the horse has thus far been confirmed in School walk and School trot, with and without lateral flexion, in turns across the half arena, on circles and in large and small voltes and squares, and that the first session has been completed and can be ended with a School halt.

One then begins the second session with plié. Ride it in School walk around the entire arena right and left to the spot where one of the diagonal lines begins for a change of hand across the whole arena. Give the horse a half-halt here, and immediately assume the School position for renvers, that is, bring the outside hind foot more under and to the center of the horse than the inside one so as to more heavily load that haunch by using the hand. The horse is now positioned diagonally in the direction it should step. Imagine two diagonal lines running parallel through the arena. One starts from the front legs; the other from the hind legs. Have the horse go on these diagonal lines in a collected manner using the aids that have already been stated. The rider now focuses all of his attention on the hind legs to make sure that they stay close to each other and to prevent the outside foot from stepping next to or too far over the inside foot. If the latter occurs, the horse can no longer go in correct School collection. The hind legs will either becomes sluggish or the croup will evade behind. To prevent this, the horse is halted after a few successful steps, which is repeated two horse lengths before the end of the diagonal line. From this spot, one can ride on from the halt in two different ways: If it becomes easy for the horse to change the movement of the legs, then one maintains the renvers to turn in front of the corner and ride along the wall. If, however, it does not have the necessary carriage, then after completing the diagonal, change the horse's bend, but keep the legs the same, i. e. transition to plié-left.

In order for the horse to stay collected with good contact, it is essential to transition from plié to renvers by changing the sideways-stepping of the legs, and not by changing the horse's position or flexion. In contrast, transition from renvers to plié by changing the position and bend. This is because it is easier to keep the horse collected if it is already bent than if one tries to collect and bend at the same time. This can first occur in the following travers exercise.

In renvers, both haunches are loaded to almost the same degree in an alternating fashion, but the outside haunch a little longer than the inside one. Therefore, the reins must be held more against both hind legs, but against the outside one a little longer. One may only make an exception if one of the hind feet tries to evade. In the renvers-turn, the outside haunch must be loaded more. Thus, the hand is held against it. The outside rein plays the main role in this, in that it is used before and after the inside rein. Along the wall, one keeps the horse so collected by means of the inside leg and spur that the horse's inside buttock may touch the wall — but not the tip of the hock. Alternatively, one keeps the hindquarters a foot away from the wall. To conclude this session with a halt, position the horse straight at the end of the wall on two tracks, ride it at an accelerated pace in the half-pass to the next wall, and halt it on the spur opposite the wall.

The third session must be a repetition of the first. If the horse has acquired such carriage in these School gaits due to the continued exercises such that the gaits are pure without counter-tempos, then it is time to prepare it for tighter turns and the School canter via greater collection. This can be done in lessons in which one works the horse with its forehand placed along the wall.

The first of these lessons, as preparation for the second, namely the travers, is "riding into the corners" and "Doubliren."

The corners of the arena where two walls meet form right angles. In order to ride into a corner, the horse's forehand first goes through and then the hindquarters follow in the same way. It is necessary for the horse to willingly bend both haunches at the same time. It has been well prepared for this by the previous halts.

The first session of the following lesson begins immediately with the plié. Instead of rounding off the corners on two tracks as in the past, one guides the horse's outer side using the inside leg and a steady rein until it is a horse length in front of the corner along the wall, then positions it straight and collects it with a half-halt. In this way, one attains the necessary School position to correctly ride into the corners.

If the halt is successful, then the horse will go straight into the corner. If it is not successful, then one must not force it into it, but rather must continue working in plié. Then, when the horse least expects it, choose another corner. After successfully collecting the horse, halt in the corner in such a way that its forehead almost touches the wall. The opposing wall will make it easy for the rider to succeed in setting the horse back on its haunches even more by using the collecting aids.

By holding against the inside haunch with the hand and using the inside leg more, the horse will be positioned more on the inside hind leg. Then holding the forehand in a similar but increased manner will guide it through the corner. The rider's outside leg is responsible for preventing the croup from falling out.

As the horse moves out of the corner, it is necessary to bend its body in a half-circular shape, which prepares it for the School canter position.

After successfully riding through one of the corners before the long wall, one guides the horse by means of the renvers-line to renvers and to plié in the other direction. Repeat the previous procedure for riding into the corner, and halt in one of the corners to end the session.

The second session, ridden mostly in School trot, is even better for the turns on the inside haunch.

One works the horse in the meantime away from the wall in the canter position, quickly alternating right and left, on a circle, on squares, and full and half voltes.

If one rides towards a wall and turns in front of it, then the turn must be rounded, but coming away from the wall, it is a doublé. In this turn, the flexed haunches form an axis around which the forehand turns. It is in the School what "right and left about face" is in campaign-riding, and could be called a normal pirouette because of its precision.

If a horse is to perform these pirouettes equally well to the right and left, then the rider must know how to position the horse as required for the doublé via preparatory half-halts before every pirouette. This is done first by using both legs, then holding the hand against the outside haunch shortly before the pirouette. In this moment, the outside hind foot is the main support for the weight, and therefore, must not evade. This is the only way to adequately fix it to the ground. If the horse has been given the doublé-position, this pirouette will easily succeed if the rider holds against the inside haunch and almost simultaneously increases the use of his outside leg or spur, especially if he goes in the direction of the horse's weight with his weight.

If the necessary rein contact has been lost as a result of these difficult pirouettes, then one rides around the whole arena with rounded corners in lively School trot to complete the second session, i. e. in an octagon rather than in a rectangle. One then executes a pirouette without the horse suspecting it by means of a doublé in the middle of the arena, and concludes the session with a full halt. Alternatively, correct the horse with reinback and flexions, if it goes hard against the hand in this doublé.

The third session of this lesson is a repetition of the first.

If the horse has now been prepared to transition to the following difficult movements via these lessons, then travers can be ridden on the travers line. This line has a different name depending on its length and direction, just as the renvers line does.

The first two sessions of the lesson that was just described now must form the first session of this lesson in School trot, if possible. After the plié, one shortens the renvers line by first riding across the half arena in renvers, or after riding out of a corner, immediately turn around in renvers and ride back on the same line in renvers that one just rode on in plié. This pirouette is called the passade without change.

The aids for this are the same as the ones indicated earlier, but they are used more quickly depending on how tight the turns become and how quickly the changes follow each other.

One also practices this lesson with the horse on full and half voltes and on the circle. One should also ride figure eights, the dimensions of which must depend on the horse's carriage.

The halt that concludes one of the sessions should never be done in a pirouette. This is because it is, as already stated, a rule that the horse always halts on one track either in straight or bent-straight position, and it should only be able to step forward about a foot to the halt. Because of the following transition to travers, the most suitable position would be a horse length before the corners.

Travers

The term, "travers," actually applies only to the movement on two tracks that is ridden in School gaits. This is because this is a movement that requires greater bending in the haunches than is needed for balance. Because weak horses cannot sustain this, it is better to not perform travers with them. If it must nevertheless be done, then only in campaign-walk. One can teach such horses at most the leg yield or the half-pass with fewer disadvantages than in trot. These movements are also only done in walk.

The horse goes more sideways in travers than in plié, with the forehand on the outside line of the arena and the hindquarters on the inside line, thus with the forehand along the wall and with the croup directed toward the inside of the arena. This position causes its hindquarters to bend more, because the part of the horse that goes on the narrower path is naturally used more. However, the shoulders must precede the haunches by at least half a foot.

The leg sequence that has already been described remains the same in the three gaits when doing travers, except that the legs on one side are not placed in front of the ones on the other side. Instead, the outside legs cross over the inside legs.

In order to accomplish this movement, the horse must carry its weight on its inside haunch longer than in the previous turns at the moment when the outside feet cross over the inside ones. It also moves its outside shoulder with more freedom. This shoulder must be lifted higher in travers, and the humerus will be bent more with the elbow moving forward visibly. The horse was prepared for travers by the plié and renvers exercises, especially by the latter, in which, however, it was not allowed to cross over with its outside hind foot, but only set it down in front of the inside one. The hind legs move on a larger track here, especially while turning. Therefore, they were used less than in travers.

The horse will have little trouble beginning travers in this second session if the final halt of the first session were successfully executed in front of a corner. In dressage generally, the good beginning of an exercise depends upon the good completion of the previous exercise.

One collects the horse for travers in the appropriate School position a head's length in front of one of the corners. One then proceeds as was stated earlier for riding the horse into the corner. The rider's inside leg induces the horse's inside hind foot to step forward, while the hand holds against the inside haunch to load it. The outside leg prevents the croup from falling out. Lively action with the inside leg while holding with the outside leg, combined with restraining with the inside hand to cause flexion in the jaws, causes the horse's inside shoulder to come closer to the inside hip, which has already moved forward. In other words, the horse bends in the ribs. Thus, the previously mentioned School position for canter is also achieved via this preparation for travers. The rules for the aids to begin travers are derived from the rules that govern the bending of the legs in this movement.

First, lifting the hand to the inside and then sideways will cause the inside foreleg to begin the movement. Thereupon, the outside hind leg must immediately leave the ground and step sideways, crossing over the inside leg. The rider supports this by holding the reins even more against the inside haunch, setting his own position against it and increasing the outside leg aids at the same time. Hereupon, the outside foreleg is lifted, crosses over the inside hind leg, and almost at the same time, the inside hind leg is placed sideways. The rider supports the outside shoulder as it lifts by holding the hand more firmly and putting his weight on the outside. This frees the inside hind leg to move sideways. The same aids that created the first step of travers are repeated to produce the second and third steps, and to maintain the steps that follow for which lesser degrees of these aids are enough. The direction in which the inside legs should go sideways depends on the direction in which the horse should go in travers. If one steps sideways a lot and only a little bit forward, then the horse must accelerate its tempo and turn around. Therefore, in order to travers along the wall, the rider must prevent too much sideways movement by using his inside leg and rein. The horse's outside legs will then be able to properly cross over, and the horse will not lose its tempo and rush.

The rider will succeed in doing all of this only if he uses his outside leg more strongly when the horse's outside hind leg is stepping forward, but more gently when the inside is stepping sideways. The degree to which he should use his inside leg to counteract will depend on the relationship of how these legs are moving. In general, the rider must pay the most attention to the necessary inside leg aids in travers. This is because this leg has two tasks, both to cause the lateral flexion of the horse's inner side, as well as to maintain its forward motion. Therefore, it must always be close to the horse, in order to be able to drive partly by using its weight, partly by using pressure. The degree of its use will depend on the circumstances. This also has the benefit that the rider can fully determine the direction in which the horse is to go and be able to follow the horse's motion. He will not find it difficult to put his weight on the inside hip at the correct moment and avoid the common mistake, called "hanging behind the leg," which prevents him from following the horse's motion.

Horses usually resist going with their heads to the wall in the beginning, suspecting what is coming. Therefore, one should first ride travers one or two head-lengths away from the wall and be content with a few good steps at first.

As with every turn, the horse must accelerate its tempo to travers through the next corner. In general, the tempo of the forelegs will be more energetic in the travers-pirouettes, the more the rider is able to load and bend the inside haunch. The inside hind foot serves as the pivot point for the horse's weight.

This energetic movement cannot be demanded immediately. One must be content in the beginning if the horse keeps its hind feet almost on the spot until the forehand has completed the half-circle pirouette in still slow, albeit accelerating, steps. If the horse creeps behind the bit, which happens very often, return to one track and position it again by riding into the next corner, resuming travers as it leaves the corner.

To change directions, initially ride travers across the whole arena on the diagonal lines, which are now called travers-lines. At the beginning and in the middle of these diagonal lines, the horse must be collected with half-halts and, at the end, with increased collection with a full halt. The aids for this, as mentioned, are given when reaching the wall at the end of the renvers. The change of the travers-position after it has returned to the wall after completing the travers-lines begins with a half-halt to straighten the horse. A repeat of the process is then carried out, as already stated above in the School-position for travers.

In the third session, one should practice the previous exercises. Choose the ones that were most difficult for the horse, and then determine the gait accordingly.

To finish the lesson, ride the horse in School trot with canter position, ride into a corner, so that this will induce a few short canter strides out of which the horse is halted. The same thing is repeated in the other direction.

If the horse has been sufficiently prepared via repeated exercises of the last lesson, which can be easily ascertained by the regularity of the tempo, it must be kept in School canter and prepared by the tighter travers-pirouettes.

The first session cannot begin immediately with the School canter, but rather must be initiated by repeating the previous lessons. Therefore, start with renvers. The skill the horse has acquired up to this point will determine whether this will be in School walk or School trot.

Renvers will always be easier for the horse than travers. This is because the haunches are used more in travers. One transitions from renvers to plié only to ride into a corner. After a travers-line across half of the arena, collect the horse along the other wall with a halt, and then proceed with the same exercise in the other direction.

The second session is ridden only in travers, which, depending on how one changes direction in the arena, has a different name. These can be full and half travers-voltes, half pirouettes, passades and full pirouettes.

The travers-voltes in the middle of the arena, executed on a square, will be easier for the horse than in front of the wall or corner, if they are not ridden too small. Therefore, practice them in the middle of the arena first.

The half travers-voltes have the shape of a semi-circle or rather a triangle. One rides them to change direction by transitioning from travers-right to renvers-right, for example. One can also use them to change the horse's direction, position, and gait at the same time as changing direction by riding travers-right and turning to the right by means of a half travers-volte, that is, by a half-circle pirouette to the right, and then bringing the horse back to the line it just left and changing direction.

The travers-eight consists of two circles, the circumferences of which meet at one point, thus forming the figure eight. In this exercise, the horse must always change its position and gait after a circle is completed.

The half pirouettes and the passades are most successful in the beginning if one combines them with travers in one of the corners. They consist of turning the horse around, whereby the hind feet step on one spot while the forehand describes a half circle, and the horse's position and gait are changed.

The full pirouettes can only be ridden away from the wall. They are the hardest turns for horse and rider, especially when changes are involved. The forehand must describe full circles, while the hind legs serve as the pivotal point for the greater part of the horse's weight.

All of these pirouette's and changes can be made away from the wall at any point in the arena one chooses.

The rider's procedure for executing the pirouettes was sufficiently explained partly here, partly in the riding lesson. In these complicated pirouettes, a lot depends on the quick use of the prescribed aids.

Before beginning any pirouette, one must have complete control over the outside haunch if one wants to turn on the inside foot as tightly as possible. This rule generally applies and depends on the degree of the pirouette and the horse's skill.

The rider must halt the horse after a successful pirouette at the beginning and let it rest for a few seconds as a reward. If it were deficient, he must halt to regain the position that the horse lost, unless he prefers to correct it by repeating the exercise, which would be easier for the horse. Likewise, in order to change the horse's position and gait in the beginning, one must first straighten the horse out of travers, then attain the travers-position in the other direction by first halting and collecting before riding on.

At the end of this and at the completion of the third session, one walks around the whole arena in School position for canter. One tries to get a few collected canter strides both right and left while riding out of one of the corners, without, however, demanding the regularity of the School canter described below.

Only via these pirouettes and changes does the horse gain the necessary degree of skill to be able to put its and its rider's weight more on one haunch or the other, or on both equally at any one moment.

The haunches can no longer resist the quick and energetic transitions between loading and unloading. They are completely flexed. The horse, submitting to the rider, finds immense relief in carrying the weight via the springy interplay of the hind legs. Afterwards, it feels free of any constraints, and goes forward with zest and a new, previously unknown power and energy.

The last School lessons must be continued until one notices this swinging motion, especially in School trot. Now, it is time to perfect the horse's collection, for which the School canter is especially suited.

Chapter II

On the preparatory flexing in the haunches on one and two tracks in the School canter

One must gradually give the horse a School position with an even greater flexion in the haunches. From this, the gallopade, the canter with short strides that is almost on the spot, is developed.

No horse, neither in a state of freedom nor under saddle, can transition from a standstill to canter without first collecting itself with a few steps in walk. It will, therefore, have to be collected by first stepping in place. The hind legs almost always step back into their hoof prints in short steps. The rider's hand will determine the degree of weight to put on the haunches that is required to develop the canter by how much it restrains. This degree can be easily recognized by the fact that the hind legs make springy movements. In short strides, the horse will be able to bound right and left as in canter, depending on how much the rein hand loads one haunch or the other.

The gallopade, which is almost on the spot, is developed in this way on both leads as a necessary preparation for the School canter. The rider's legs have only to prevent the haunches from evading. If the horse in its zest and zeal begins the gallopade by itself upon the use of the rein hand later on, then the legs have almost nothing to do. One then attains the most beautiful posture on horseback by stretching both legs down vertically.

One's control of the horse can be perfected by these exercises, such that imperceptible movements of the hand become the sole impulse for the horse's forward movement. This can be regarded as perfection in the School riding. It also makes it clearer what power the curb bit exercises over the levers of the horse by virtue of its own lever-like properties. The obvious truth of this is contained in the following principle:

"The surest and most beautiful successes in dressage can only be obtained if the horse's skeleton is primarily affected."

Only the School offers the means by which to act predominantly on the skeleton. If that is the situation in which the rider finds himself, whatever it may be, then the skillful use of such methods will always be of the greatest value to him.

When the horse collects itself for the gallopade on the spot in a walk or in trot-like steps, the rider's legs, which are stretched down long and are sometimes softer on the horse's sides and sometimes firmer, maintain the motion without the rider doing anything. They are also in harmony with the horse, because their movements originate from it. It is the horse's motion that causes our legs to move. They maintain the motion and, combined with the reins, become collecting aids for the horse. At first, one may have to use the spurs alternately by using brief periods of pressure, but without changing the leg position when transitioning into the gallopade. If one feels the walk steps become more animated, then this is the moment to collect the horse for the gallopade.

The leg aids, which cause the horse to move in springy steps, are different from those that cause trot-like movements. In the gallopade and in School canter, the horse lifts its forehand higher off of the ground and moves forward less. The hind feet follow in shorter, quicker strides than in the ordinary canter. One must use the appropriate aids to ask the horse to do this and to maintain it.

After the horse is collected according to the rules, one must lighten the forehand. To achieve this, give gradually increasing half-halts on the reins on both haunches in quick succession, along with alternating leg and spur just behind the girth. In so doing, the thighs and knees are slightly raised, and are, therefore, not as tightly closed.

At first, these aids follow the tempo of the shortened canter, but then are gradually given in quicker succession. After several repetitions, this will cause the horse to make a few short bounds, with which one must at first be content.

The gallopade can easily be developed from these short, jump-like movements in which the horse may not be bent at first. The hand directs the half-halts at the outside haunch, while the outside leg, placed at the flank, holds the outside hind foot. The inside leg, close to the girth, determines how the inside hind foot steps forward and down. The true ribs on the inner side come together, whereby the correct lateral bend is achieved under the inside shoulder. This furthers the lifting of the forehand, if the hand induces it. The same methods in conjunction with the squeezing and opening of both of the rider's legs and knees, along with simultaneous gentle spur use when the forehand is down, will cause sufficient flexion in the haunches to lift the forehand. This is done to put the horse in the School canter and maintain it via intermittent restraining against the outside haunch. The light contact and correct bend in the jaw will make it easy for the rider to guess the correct degree of flexion in the haunches. Another indication of this is the opening and widening of the horse's chest and ribs, which will allow the rider to sit farther back in the saddle and closer to the horse's center of gravity. If, on the other hand, the rider is thrown forward in the saddle, then he can conclude that the haunches are still pushing too much, whereby the horse loses volume between his knees.

Collected to such a degree, one canters the horse only from one corner to another. Ride into the corners to use them to collect again.

The rider should prevent any crooked position of the horse, if the School canter is not to become an ordinary canter. On a hard surface, one can differentiate between these two types of canter very clearly by how the feet are set down. In the totally collected School canter, one can hear the steps of each individual foot. This is because it has four beats, as is known, whereas the ordinary canter only has three beats. As soon as it is collected on a single track, guide the horse away from the wall and ride it on all of the various lines crossing the arena. The first changes are made, as already explained, by means of the diagonal lines. After reaching the end of a line, evening out the reins, and positioning the horse straight, do not refrain from using the spur to bring it to the wall, and encourage it to perform a more successful halt. This is especially true if it becomes careless in its tempo when it is near the wall, which usually occurs because it anticipates a halt. The entire side of the horse, i. e. forehand and hindquarters, must be brought alongside the wall at the same time. With the horse positioned straight, the last strides before the halt are sideways on two tracks. This resolute connection to the wall will now be a very important method for the rider either to change the gait or to transition to greater flexion in the haunches of the higher movements that follow. This is because the horse's hindquarters cannot easily escape the stronger effect of the rein hand. The straight position of the horse, however, is very important to keep in mind. If the horse is crooked, the rider can lose the free use of his outside leg.

The change will be successful after the halt if the rider switches the aids he used for either right or left lead School canter.

It will be easy to deduce the process for changing over the half arena, on both circles of the figure eight, and in half voltes from what was said in the first chapter. If the horse is completely confirmed in this, then one can practice it in the School canter on two tracks. This is so that, if one haunch still stiffens, it will submit completely.

One practices the shoulder-in in School canter with the horse on all of the various lines of the arena, if it still stiffens the inside haunch and shows the tendency to creep behind the bit. This makes it easy to recognize the horse's inclination to go crooked.

This lesson is much harder in School canter than plié on two tracks in the School trot, especially for the rider. This is because both haunches are loaded almost equally at the same time. It is very easy for the horse to make a flying change to the wrong lead when the rider increases the use of his inside leg.

The aids for the plié-canter, as well as how the horse's legs are supposed to move, are the same as those stated for the plié in School trot in the first section of this lesson.

Similarly, one connects plié-canter to riding into the corners, renvers-lines and renvers-turns until the horse has regained the proper contact on the hand and the bent-straight position in School canter, whereby the rider's procedure in the penultimate lesson must also be mentioned.

As soon as the horse dares step onto the hand in the cadenced School canter, do not hesitate any longer to perform travers in this gait. One begins this after riding through a corner either along the wall, or if this is too difficult for the horse, on the traversal line across the whole or half arena. The renvers exercises served to prepare for this.

Depending on the increased flexion in the haunches, these exercises are continued on ever-tighter turns, as already outlined in riding travers in the School trot. The School canter that is ridden on voltes and on small circles is called redopp. A horse can only perform good pirouettes if it has been confirmed in redopp. These canter pirouettes are the tightest and fastest turns a horse can make. It carries itself almost exclusively on the inside hind foot, which, pivoting almost on the spot, only steps next to or even into its foot print, while the forehand canters in a circle around the hindquarters. In order to collect the horse for a pirouette, first ride redopp on the circle, making it tighter and tighter. Use a half-halt to momentarily fix both hind legs to one spot. Then with a subsequent half-halt, set the inside hind leg upon which the rider puts his weight while the hand gives intermittent half-halts on it. The inside rein must be at least two inches shorter, partly because of the bend, but mainly so that the rider can use this rein more easily each time the forehand lifts up while turning. The inside rein must cause the inside haunch to flex without which the horse cannot pirouette. Only then can the outside rein determine how the forehand turns by putting pressure on the neck.

The outside spur, positioned on the flank and pressing at the moment when the inside rein is used, is only used to prevent the croup from evading and to cause the outside foot to cross. The rider's inside leg encourages the forehand to lift, and its pressure makes it easier to follow the movement each time the horse lifts up while turning.

This use of hand and leg, as well as the rider's weight distribution, which has already been described, may last only for as long as the forehand is turning in the air. They must be repeated each time the horse lifts up.

To halt out of the pirouette, the inside leg aids must support the hand. If one wants to change direction, then first ride circle-redopp again onto the other hand.

If the horse has finally reached the point at which it consistently remains sufficiently loaded, fixed, and bent by the use of the inside curb rein without any counter-action on the outside rein such that it can pirouette on the inside haunch with the outside rein determining how the forehand turns, then the exercises in the lower School have achieved their goal of making the horse agile.

For anyone who has correctly ridden redopp and pirouette a few times on School horses, it will be easy to establish this procedure in the turns, even with less well-positioned horses. Whoever undertakes to train a horse to this perfection, but does not proceed as correctly as is described here, will soon feel the disadvantages which are the inevitable result of an overly hasty, not methodical or orderly dressage training. The horse will allow itself to be thrown around on the spot in canter, but loses its balance in the campaign gaits. Thus, the purpose of the School fails.

HIGH SCHOOL

Chapter III

On the perfect flexion in the haunches
(Piaffé, Passage, Pesade)

The purpose, especially of the higher School, is to bring the long-recognized value of riding as an art form new validity. The creations of other artists differ from those of the rider. Those (eg. plastic and paintings) exist for centuries, while ours vanish due to the short lifespan of the horse. One would be deceiving oneself if one were to regard the lower School riding as an art form. It may well be considered to be a step to the higher School, but only the High School proves the true value of the art and, therefore, can never be dispensed with. The exercises contained within it will convince the thinking rider even more than the previous studies.

First: The functions of the horse's muscles, tendons, and ligaments depend on the position of the immobile parts in the dressage training.

Second: The good position of these immobile parts is due to the proper position and movement of the rear extremities. Only these should be targeted in order to subjugate all resistance from the soft parts without causing detriment to the horse.

The usefulness of the correct position of the hindquarters, which is the source of good gaits, will first be realized in its entirety in the movements of the High School. This is assuming that we can determine the flexion in the hip joints and mainly the stifle joints to the exact same degree as the hocks.

The different angles that are formed by the various positions and connections of the bones in the haunches, namely the pelvis, the pelvic bones, and the femurs, act in the opposite direction when their spring-force is activated. Thus, the hip and hock joints will push, and the stifle joint will carry.

This can be proven by pushing an elastic rod against the ground. After releasing the pressure, it will spring up in an opposite direction to how it was bent.

The forward pushing or lifting force is, therefore, located in two places in each hind leg, whereas the backward or carrying power only in one. Therefore, the horse's dressage training always regulated the pushing force before the power of the stifle joint was unlocked via perfect flexion in the haunches. This is what differentiates the higher School from the lower School.

For the same reasons that one chose walk or trot in the previous dressage training depending on the conditions and inclinations of the horses, i. e. depending on the carrying or pushing forces of the hindquarters, it is up to the thinking rider to choose one of the following movements — piaffé or passage — to use to perfect the other. Horses that have a tendency to suck back, i. e. over-flex in the stifle joints, which neutralizes the pushing force of the hip and hock joints, must be improved via frequent passage or School walk as early as possible. However, do not practice the passage too early with horses that use the pushing power of the hindquarters too much. Instead, perfect the piaffé by practicing the piaffé itself and by reining back. Everything depends entirely upon a proper relationship between the carrying and pushing forces.

Piaffé

Trot-like movements on the spot are used to perfect the School canter all the way up to the courbette and to develop all of the springing forces that can be seen in the School jumps. In these movements, which are called "piaffé" in their perfect state, the horse raises its legs such that the forearm is horizontal and the hind hoof is about one foot off of the ground.

When collecting the horse for gallopade, the rider's aids are meant to induce a trot-like movement on the spot. These aids are also used in piaffé, only with more precision.

The effects of these aids will be clear to everyone after the following explanation.

If the horse is straight and brought into the proper School position, then the initial rein aids work to compress all of the angular connections of the hind leg bones that point backwards. This will induce a tendency in the horse to go forward at first. If the rein pressure increases, then the horse will lower its croup. This is because the stifles are now compressed and their angles become sharper. If the reins and the rider's weight increase this compression even more, then the horse will show a tendency to step backwards. If the rider prevents this from happening as it arises, then the hind feet will step back into their footprints, and the horse will begin to piaffé. The forelegs, whose action is determined by the hind legs, are lifted higher off of the ground than the hind legs. They are held for a brief moment at their peak height.

One allows the pitter-patter movement of the legs in the first exercises, in which the horse is still moving more in balance than on the haunches, until the horse shows no more tendency to evade with the haunches to the back and to the side.

It requires a lot of skill on the part of the rider to counter the horse's natural agility in these unfavorable movements. Due to the spiral movement of the hip joint, the legs can move sideways, which is quite opposed to bending in the haunches. This can cause the horse to suck back, spin around, rear, and even fall down.

The horse's initial introduction to piaffé occurs far more expediently under the rider, especially through proper rein back in prolonged sessions than by the almost universally recommended exercises between the pillars without a rider.

It has been proven that the rider's hand, legs and weight can cause the horse's stifles to bend and carry — upon which everything depends — better and more quickly than the pillar halter and whip can. The pillars are actually only supposed to be used out of convenience to teach the student the first lessons in the higher School on already trained horses. (See the Pillars in the first section).

As with all exercises recommended thus far, it is of the utmost importance to be satisfied with just a few steps in the beginning. One should not demand regularity in the steps right from the start. Before the horse decides to begin stepping when the rider gives the driving aids, it is usually very resistant. Courageous and strong horses become extremely angry. However, if one knows how to deftly counteract this untoward behavior, then the desired beautiful piaffé steps usually follow immediately afterwards. Be satisfied with a few steps, and then transition to the collected School trot, which must always end these exercises in the piaffé.

Those who do not wish to increase the resistance in the angry horse refrain from undertaking this movement in the manner indicated. They avail themselves of the pillars as an emergency measure.

Determined and skilled riders, however, should not believe that the pillars are necessary to introduce a horse to the piaffé. They should not refrain from practicing this movement because they have no access to pillars. If they do not do it, then they will not gain the great advantages that this movement can grant to them and their horses.

Advantages for the rider are gleaned from the piaffé with respect to his seat, insofar as it convinces him that any stiff posture of his upper body and hips is counterproductive to a firm knee contact. It is also counterproductive to the perfect collection of the horse (the main goal of this movement), as well as for achieving a fine rider feel.

With respect to contact, practicing this movement allows for a correct assessment of how receptive the horse's mouth is to the bit. In other words, one learns to distinguish a light contact on the reins from a firm one, and depending on the circumstances, learns how to more correctly connect both with leg aids and balance.

The special methods to counteract all cases of resistance that horses try before they know the rider's will and submit to it should be reviewed in the section, "On Resistances," at the end of the first part. The rider must already have a good seat and know how to control the horse depending on the circumstances, and have a completely developed "rider feel" (see above), in order to adequately meet the horses' extreme actions.

The correct School seat requires the rider to sit deep in the saddle. One's seat has as many points of contact on the saddle as possible. Six parts of the seat are in contact with the saddle, namely the two seat bones, the crotch in the front, the two buttock cheeks in the back, and the tailbone or coccyx in between.

It is the contact of these parts of the seat, not the legs and knees, the pressure of which is now to be regarded only as an aid, that provide the necessary support that allows the School rider to assume a beautiful posture.

It is only possible for the rider to sit in the prescribed way if the horse's spine is in the correct School position. Since the position of the backbone is determined by the correct use of the hind legs, the rider's seat can only be perfect if the horse piaffes correctly. Therefore, how pleasant the seat is will become the standard by which to judge whether the piaffé is correct or not.

The rein hand, which initially holds both reins to the same degree in the School position for piaffé, will restrain right and left during piaffé and will use the right or the left rein more depending on which hind leg is being set down. In so doing, however, the hand does not move from the wrist, but rather it is more of a matter of it moving with the upper body as it follows the alternating flexion of the hind legs.

For example, at the moment when the horse supports itself on its right haunch in the piaffé, the right side of the croup lowers. The weight of the rider's upper body, correctly distributed on well-placed hips, follows the movement of the croup, leaning slightly back and to the right. These movements of the upper body and shoulders cause the rider's more elevated hand to be carried almost imperceptibly to the right. If this hand aid is insufficient, only then may the flexion in the right haunch be increased by bending the hand to the right from the wrist.

It is easy to determine the flexion in the left haunch in the piaffé by using these aids. At the moment described above, with respect to the necessary leg aids, the right leg or spur is used before the right hind foot has left the ground, whereupon the rider shifts his weight, hand, and leg aids from right to left at the same time.

To execute the School halt, which should conclude the piaffé session after a few good steps, the rider gives both leg aids at the same time. He also puts the weight of his upper body, which is placed on both hips and remains flexible, on both haunches evenly. At the same time, the rein hand, which is raised to the middle of his belt, but never as high as the navel, restrains with a rounded wrist.

Once the horse has performed the last piaffé steps perfectly, the flexion in the haunches must be perfected by a step that is springier than it has been up to now. A halt will prepare for the transition to the movements with a more elevated forehand.

At the moment when the horse has set down all four feet in the halt, keep holding the forehand for a few more moments and then reduce the rein pressure as much as possible without giving up the rein contact. In order to evoke the previously mentioned springy step, restrain on the reins again until the collecting effect of both legs or spurs causes the horse to make a short hop under itself with its hind feet. This will cause the forelegs to lift a little, or at least, become unburdened.

The School horse must also learn to piaffé in bent-straight positions. It may not lose its tempo when the rider is alternating between hand and leg. This is the proof that this movement has reached the desired level of perfection. In piaffé, one rides the horse forwards, backwards, and sideways, and in all of the turns, even in pirouettes, using the same aids that have already been described in the lower School.

Passage

Horses with power and energy develop another trot-like movement as a result of previous exercises, namely the "passage." It can be regarded as the apex of the trot-like School movements. It is distinguished from the School trot by the floating motion of the legs and by the slower tempo.

All well-built and well-trained horses can learn to piaffé, but only those with a lot of energy can passage. That is why one must work the horses according to their own abilities and never force the passage. This is because the purpose will not be fully achieved, and it is usually detrimental to the correct tempo of the School trot. This trot is too valuable and should be preferred to the passage, which is seldom done properly, anyway.

In the correct passage, the horse moves forward about a hoof's length with every stride.

If the hind feet step too close together and too short, or step too far forward, then the beautiful bend in the knees is lacking and the forelegs are lifted up too high. The correct rein contact is also lacking. One must then not be deceived by the high shoulder movements that are made when the front leg is stretched out in front. The horse is either behind the bit or is leaning too much on the reins and is going incorrectly. If the horse covers too much ground with each stride, then the action is more eye-catching. Because it is of a floating or swimming nature, it is also called "the swim step." However, this movement only occurs if the haunches are stiff and the horse supports itself on the rider's hand. Therefore, it is not passage and may not be counted as a real movement.

The horse must not forget the good School trot during the passage exercises. If this happens, then one must return to the School trot.

The rider must be very skilled to train the horse's trot in in such a way that he can ride passage, School trot, or the trot in balance at will. A rider who is able to do so is more valuable than one who neglects to train his horses in these gaits and exercises them more in canter movements, which can never be successful without first being prepared by proper trot exercises.

The advantage of the passage is not limited to only the fact that the student is taught in the forward movement in the arena, but also to correctly determine the flexion in each individual haunch. The student's posture also acquires the necessary suppleness that can never be achieved on hard-trotting horses. This posture is necessary for the following movements, especially for the School jumps.

The same movements that were recommended for the School trot should also be practiced in the passage. It requires the greatest attention on the part of the rider, especially in the turns, to measure the aids so that no disruption in the tempo takes place. As a result, the rider must focus all of his attention on the horse. As soon as the haunches have achieved this perfect flexion, the rein contact alternates almost exclusively between the soft contact and the light contact. In the highest state of perfection, it can often consist of the weight of the reins alone. Riders who have never schooled horses to the point of developing a light rein contact out of a firm contact or a soft contact do not know the difference, or they misinterpret it. Accustomed to only the firm contact and the soft contact, or even to riding with no contact, they consider the light contact of a perfectly trained School horse to be "behind the bit," or they understand it to be the so-called "riding without reins."

The rein contact is determined by the action of the hind legs in the forward movement, which may now be directed forward, sideways, backwards, or upwards. The more the pushing power of the hind legs is engaged, the firmer the previously light contact becomes. If the former light contact is completely lost, then the forward movement is not correct. It is correct if the pushing and carrying power of the horse's hindquarters have entered into a relationship corresponding to the desired gait, and the previously firm contact on the reins becomes light. To feel this, the rider must possess the finest sensitivity that can only be given to him by horses that go with the greatest perfection in the movements that have been mentioned.

Therefore, the highest precision in controlling the horse is maintaining the light contact in the following movements. This is similar to how the soft contact had to be the rider's highest aspiration during the exercises of the lower School and the campaign School.

Assessing the value of a rider is based less and less on his posture when mounted, and more on the skill with which he manages to control the horse. The greatest compliment will always be if he is told that he has a "good hand."

The light contact is the result of perfect flexion in the haunches. However, this can never be maintained if the horse is still able to assume the crooked position that is so natural for it. Since this is mainly prevented by the rider's inside leg, its use deserves our undivided attention from now on.

In the passage, the horse is less inclined to push against the outside leg, i. e. to fall out with the croup, than to push against the inside leg so that it can go crooked, as this makes it easier for it to regain its usual way of going. Accordingly, it is mainly the rider's inside leg that will maintain the passage. This use predominates not only in passage on one track, but also on two tracks. Even more precision is required in travers. This is because the horse is more inclined to assume a crooked position than in any other movement.

The importance of this leg was already considered in travers, among other things. It was used to obtain the correct lateral flexion of the entire horse, starting from the haunches, and to maintain the proper School tempo. In the travers-passage, the use of the inside leg is of a finer type, in that stepping on the inside stirrup is often sufficient. It is also indispensable for keeping the tempo, because as soon as the regularity of the rhythm ceases, so does the light rein contact.

Using the outside leg at the correct moment is made a lot easier for the rider by the fact that the inside leg is allowed to hang more freely due to stepping on the inside stirrup, whereby it gains significantly in its elastic counteraction. The differing degree of this effect induces the horse to move forward of its own accord for the most part, which is better than due to the rider's will. Since the rider's attention in the travers-passage is mainly on the inside rein and leg, this movement may correctly be called "travers on the inside leg" to distinguish it from the normal travers and half-pass. In order to explain this effect even more clearly, it should be remembered that bending in the ribs, as well as in the jaws, can be achieved by holding against this side with a steady hand and applying pressure with the rider's inside knee. These special aids direct the horse's forehand onto the inside haunch.

Since the inside haunch carries more than the outside haunch, it develops greater springiness. This is expressed in the direction in which it is moving, and is transferred to the forehand. The travers is developed in this way.

The horse's outside hind leg serves as a support only for as long as the inside hind leg is swinging the mass sideways and until it is set down. If the latter can overtake the outside hind leg, the horse will stop passaging. This is always the result if the rider uses too much outside leg in combination with his weight. Even the travers will suffer, if not degenerate into an ordinary half-pass.

The remaining special aids for riding passage will come partly from the lessons to be practiced in the School trot, and partly from the rules for the piaffé exercises.

The benefit of piaffé and passage for the dressage training of a naturally gifted horse that has been prepared for them depends on the correct use of one or the other of these movements, which in turn depends on the horse's personality. Only the alternating practice of both movements causes the perfect flexion in both haunches, maintains and perfects the horse in the movements it has learned thus far, and prepares it for those to follow.

On the other hand, if the exercises in piaffé and passage damage the horse's campaign and School gaits, then their use was either premature or not conducted properly. It is a preconceived notion to believe that properly executed movements are worthless, and that they should be regarded as "tricks." Only one who is totally ignorant of School dressage and the horse's anatomy could believe such unfavorable allegations about the riding arts.

Should a horse who is familiar with these movements be kept in good condition for ordinary official service, then the rider must be able to distinguish how the pushing and carrying power of the haunches stand in relation to each other. He does this not only via the sensitivity of his legs, which has previously been discussed, but also by the momentary rein contact.

If the horse leans firmly on the rein hand in any gait, then it is to be expected that the strength of the extensor muscles in the neck will soon be combined with the strength of the extensor muscles in the hindquarters or with their pushing force. This will result in extended strides. In this case, the exercise of the piaffé will be the appropriate means to restore the forces that have gained too much freedom with respect to their proper condition.

On the other hand, if the horse adopts the familiar habit of sucking back by refusing to take rein contact, then the flexor muscles of the haunches get out of proportion with those of the neck. This leads to strides that are too short. Passage is the correct choice to restore order. From this, it can be concluded that a horse is harmed by piaffé exercises and all of the related gaits (the ones that require an unusual flexion in the stifle joints), if it does not step onto the hand enough. By contrast, passage, as well as all exercises in extended strides (whereby the pushing forces of the hips and hocks have more freedom than in the piaffé and in the shortened gaits) are of no use as long as the horse still leans on the hand.

Furthermore, one concludes from this that exercises in piaffé perfect the horse in the shortened movements, while the passage perfects the lengthened ones. This is true not only for those of the School, but also for those of the campaign rider. If these exercises are used properly and are combined with the pesade (still to follow), then they will successfully prepare a strong horse for the School jumps.

Pesade

The next preparation for the School jumps is the pesade. It forms the second beat of each School jump. It is just as necessary a preparation as the aforementioned brief lifting of the forehand or the gallopade to prepare for the School canter on the spot.

The perfect pesade requires the most continuous flexion in the haunches that a horse is able to maintain. This is so that it can evenly balance its and the rider's weight on both hind feet for a few moments. The horse's body then forms an approximately 45 degree angle to the ground. Above that, perfect flexion in the haunches does not take place. Instead, the pesade degenerates into a rear, which must not be confused with that movement.

The forehand is only gradually lifted to the specified degree. This depends on the natural elasticity and strength of the haunches to carry, which was developed in the preceding lessons in the rein back, the full halt, and mainly, the piaffé.

Before the rider prompts the horse to lift its forehand, he has to make sure that it piaffes perfectly straight, and that there is an even contact on both reins, which is not disturbed by an incorrect bend in the neck. From this position, the forelegs are pulled up and held in a bent position such that the knees form sharp angles and the hooves come close to the elbows. This is the characteristic mark of the perfect pesade. Deviations from this are called "levades." In these, the forehand is raised to a low elevation above the ground. As already mentioned, if it is too high, it is just a "rear."

The rider's hand and leg aids are almost the same as those that have already been recommended at length for the full halts and to collect the horse for the gallopade on the spot.

However, they are given with more energy. One executes a full School halt out of the piaffé or out of the passage, and later out of the School canter. One must maintain the strongest upper body position and sit deep in the saddle. Keep the horse in that position by restraining with the hand, then move both shins and spurs closer to the horse's chest just behind the girth. Give either pressing or poking aids in quick succession and with increasing strength until the forehand lifts up off of the ground. In the first of these attempts, the horse usually piaffes in a hurried fashion instead of raising the forehand off of the ground. This is because it had previously been punished when it lifted up when the hand continued to restrain after a School halt. In this case, do not disturb the piaffé any further. Instead, restore order with just a few quite energetic steps, in order to be able to finish the session with a second School halt. This is similar to how the halt ends the piaffé, which has already been explained. This should occur before the horse's strength fades along with its good will and mind.

This exercise, repeated several times with the proper combination of the aids, will soon cause the horse to lift its forehand a little. After being praised for it, it will perhaps lift up too soon and too willingly the next time in order to please the rider. Because the horse can carry itself on both haunches at the same time, and the use of one haunch does not counter the other, as is the case in the forward movement, the horse soon learns to love lifting up. This makes preparing for it between the pillars, as well as the whip aids, unnecessary.

To develop the pesade, it is necessary to keep the forehand in the air, which has already been explained. This is probably one of the most difficult tasks for the rider, but it will gradually become easier the more the pesade is correctly developed, i. e. the more accurately the rider can bring the horse's center of gravity to the middle of its support point (between both of the hind legs). With this, his seat and the horse's position become more stable.

One should not yield on the reins for the duration of the pesade. Instead, the rein contact switches between soft and light, which is sufficient to transfer the necessary weight onto the haunches.

Reducing the tension on the reins is used to lower the forehand in a controlled manner. The slightest increase on the reins raises the forehand if the rider's legs continue giving the indicated aids, albeit less forcefully while working together at the appropriate moment.

The position of the rider's hand and weight control the alternating burdening and unburdening of the haunches in the pesade. The steady but almost hovering position of the hand, with the upper arm close to the body, contributes to this. It hardly needs mentioning that one should not lose the steady position of the upper body over the hips, or the suppleness of the spine.

The lowering of the forehand should in no circumstances be onto the shoulders. If this happens, it is impossible for the horse to set the forefeet back into the same footprints it just left and to immediately transition into piaffé. This should be done after every pesade, because it proves that the horse remained sufficiently collected.

As the forehand is lowered but before the forefeet touch the ground, the rein hand must keep restraining to prevent the haunches from being unburdened too suddenly.

So that the horse learns to distinguish between the aids for the pesade and the reinback, which are very similar, one should practice the reinback after the pesade in the beginning. If the horse shows no inclination to lift up, then it is confirmed in the pesade. The rider must not induce the horse to lift up in the reinback via incorrect, ill-timed leg aids. Keep in mind that to pesade, both legs must work simultaneously and more on the forehand. To reinback, in contrast, the legs are used alternately, and more on the hindquarters.

If the horse lifts up regardless of proper aids, or if it rears, either proceed as stated in the chapter, "On the Resistances," or refrain from practicing the pesade as it is still too soon.

The exercise in pesade on a School horse confirmed in it perfects the rider's correct posture in the saddle, without which the leg grip (eg. with obstinate horses that rear) does him no good.

One will no longer make the usual mistake of most equestrians to lean forward. Instead, one will seek to counter the horse's movements with one's own body, i. e. by directing the upper body and legs backward at the moment the horse first lifts up.

In many cases, one leads oneself into the same danger that one sought to avoid by leaning forward. This relieves the part of the horse's body that must be regarded as the junction point of the forces of the forehand and hind end, namely the haunches.

As far as the pesade's usefulness with regard to the horse's dressage training is concerned, it requires a more detailed explanation here. This is true both for the systematic ordering as well as because it has not yet been sufficiently highlighted.

Horses with a light forehand try at times to evade collection by rearing. In other words, they resist the required greater flexion in the stifle joints, which as has been sufficiently demonstrated, is where the carrying power is located that is indispensable for collection.

When a horse rears, it over-flexes the hock joints (which are almost the only joints that are bent). Because they are overloaded, they can no longer push. The shape of the forehand of a horse that is rearing is quite different from that of a horse that is performing pesade. It stretches its head and neck out instead of going into the bridle. It also stretches its forelegs out, rather than bending them.

The pesade is thus to be regarded as the pinnacle of the carrying capacity that can be developed, and consequently, of the collection via the flexion in the horse's stifle joints.

Only after this force has been acted upon does the pushing power develop. Its energetic action becomes all the more indispensable, if the rider intends for the horse to jump forwards and up and no longer just remain horizontal, i. e. that it perform a School jump.

From the first moment the horse's training began, it was prepared for the pesade via School position at a state of rest. This was done by the rider relieving both forelegs of a part of the load at the same time and shifting the burden to the hindquarters simultaneously and equally. Thus, it is to be regarded as the most perfect School position. Just as it — in its perfection — prepares the School horse to develop the greatest possible springing power via School jumps, it also brings about jumps in balance by using it to a lesser degree with less-trained horses.

The closer the forehand is to the ground in the pesade, the less springing power can be developed for School movements, but more for balanced movements. Every horse must bend in the stifles as it starts to raise the forehand, even if only for a moment, before it can stretch up to rear. If one uses this moment to increase the flexion, then it will induce a correct jump, whereby horses that do not like to go forward and stand still so that they can rear will be corrected the most thoroughly and with the most lasting effect, as has already been mentioned.

The rider who does not know how to feel the moment and the degree of bending in the horse's stifles with his seat must deduce this from the previously stated differences in the rein contact and by the horse's head and neck position so that he can gauge the degree of aids to use accordingly.

Chapter IV

On the perfect flexion in the haunches via the School jumps Courbette and croupade, ballotade und capriole

The forward motion of the horse in which all four feet leave the ground is called a jump. It is called a School jump if the hind feet are set down before the front feet.

Just as halts, reinback, bending, etc., belong to all School lessons and serve as a means for dressage training, so does jumping. The rider who trains horses should be so well acquainted with both the School jumps and the balanced jumps, both of which are good and proper for dressage, that he can avail himself of them during the course of the dressage training.

The School jump is just as suited to a well-built horse as are the three gaits — walk, trot and canter. Its degree of perfection will depend on the strength of the individual. The rider is, therefore, directed by nature, as it were, to use the School jumps as a training method. If he uses these drastic measures rarely and selectively, taking into account the conformation and the energy of the individual horse, then he will achieve the main goal of dressage more perfectly than if avoids these jumps out of fear.

In the School dressage, the jumps are less indispensable than in the training of campaign horses. This is especially true because they will perfect the horse's movements in a shorter period of time. If riders who practice dressage with their horses not only read about but also practically test the theories on the jumps that have been stated here and those that are still to follow, then they will be convinced of this truth, if they are in doubt, by the better movements that a horse of power and energy is ready to make after a correct jump. It is not only necessary for the prospective trainer to ride horses that have been trained in the School jumps in order to learn how to train School horses and jumpers in particular, but it is also of a very significant value for the rider who trains horses for the campaign riding service. This is because School jumps will familiarize one with the movements that are made by disobedient horses that are young or badly ridden. Hence, the riding instructor can count on greater success with his teaching, if he puts the budding rider on School jumpers, and if he makes them fully acquainted with the aids in a systematic manner, which one uses for the different degrees of collection, in order to counteract resistance in the horse.

However, one can only expect the riders who, by practicing the previous movements, have been convinced of the benefits of the perfect flexion in the haunches to recognize the manifold value of the School jumps. They will also admit that riders can only receive a complete training via School jumps.

The more one considers the use of the School jumps to be inessential in the instruction and that they are unnecessary in the horse's dressage training, the less the value of the riding schools will be recognized, and with it the art of riding and that of its followers.

The demands that were made on the trainer's skills in the past extended to the training of a horse in the School jumps. The mastery they give the rider over the strongest horse was correctly recognized. Now known almost only by name, they are usually no longer considered to be essential. There are even trainers and riding instructors who reject the higher movements entirely, especially the School jumps.

One can, therefore, not fail to notice that the educated and enthusiastic men who are lacking this foundation now turn their backs on the riding schools, and prefer to seek their riding education via empiricism.

Both the teachings on the lever that were explained in the General Section and the mechanism of the jump that were imparted at the end of the first part provide the proof that, in essence, the lesser amount of aptitude a horse has for School jumps is less a result of deficient musculature, but rather is a result of the imperfect placement of the bones that form the haunches and the horse's low energy. A horse with extensive musculature in the hindquarters does not always possess sufficient take-off power for the School jumps if the bones in the haunches are not in harmony with each other. Similarly, one often sees old and physically weak but well-built horses, or those that, because of their slender build are thought incapable but that possess a lot of energy, correctly execute the most difficult jumps.

Depending on the talent and the skill the horse has acquired, the rider should first make a correct assessment of its ability before he subjects it to practicing the School jumps. Never try it with weak horses of fierce temperament. It would only aggravate them more.

Only ask strong horses to jump after the excessive stiffness and hardness in the back have been removed by extended movements. Otherwise, such horses will resist too long before they correctly flex in the haunches. By then, they have usually harmed their extremities by making too many incorrect jumps (*Lanzaden*, etc.). For the same reasons, one must not demand that horses that are visibly built downhill bend their haunches to the great degree that is required for the School jumps.

Fast trotters are rarely good School jumpers, but it is easier to train skilled jumpers in the correct trot-like movements. This is what experience teaches. The discussion on the mechanism of the movement, which has already been explained here in part, and which is about to be discussed, will prove conclusively that, since the trot is already naturally separate from the canter, and seldom are both gaits found to have the same degree of perfection in one individual, even the art form should not stubbornly demand that the trot and the canter or the passage and the School jump be of the same quality.

Courbette and Croupade

Collecting the horse for the pesade out of the piaffé, the passage and the School canter prepares it for the most perfect jumps. All of the previous exercises have prepared for the canter with four beats, which is regarded as the most correct jump-like School movement. It has reached its perfection when the rider is able to perform a School halt out of it so well that the horse is made light to the degree of the pesade, which is a requirement of the most perfect School jumps.

Depending on the degree of this elevation, the School jump can be initiated by performing a half or even a whole courbette. It consists of three distinct beats. The first is the School halt, which, depending on the horse's temperament, strength and skill, prepares for the following beat. The more energetically the hind feet jump forward and under, the higher and more easily the horse can lift its forehand. Although the School canter is the most suitable gait from which to perform a School halt, it still has to be prepared by piaffé, in order to develop the courbette out of it, just as all movements that were previously unknown to the horses were introduced by trot-like movements.

The second beat is indicated by a pesade-position, whereby the elevation of the forehand is due to the degree of the previous collection. However, it must not exceed the median height of the perfect pesade.

In the third beat, the hind feet hop together and at the same time circa 1-2 feet forward, as soon as the front feet touch the ground again.

These three beats, executed in this order, actually form a two-beat canter with the difference that, due to the increased elevation of the forehand and increased flexion in the haunches, it jumps only a small distance, as just stated. The jumps also follow each other more slowly.

The courbette is the transition between the balanced jump and the School jump. It has probably been counted among the latter because it has a greater relationship with them, and usually precedes the execution of a more advanced School jump.

The rider's aids to collect to a halt and then lift the forehand into pesade, and also to maintain it until the front feet are back on the ground, have already been explained in detail. The success of the third beat depends entirely upon maintaining this position, in order to keep the horse bent in the stifles when the legs or spurs induce the hind legs to hop forward and under. This beat appears to be combined with the first beat of the second courbette jump, but the rider can distinguish between the two by feel. It is clear enough that the pushing force, even if it lasts only for a moment, ends the first jump, while the carrying power of the hindquarters begins the second one. Since the latter outweighs the former, this change will not easily escape the rider with a trained sense of feel. It is necessary to correctly feel this change between the forces of the hindquarters, in order to be able to exactly assess and use the moment the hind feet step down. This is when the aids for the halt should initiate the second jump. They will be unsuccessful if they are given too early or too late.

At first, one must be satisfied with one or a few half courbettes. Continuous courbettes are extremely strenuous for the haunches, because it uses the carrying force almost exclusively, which, as is well known, is much less naturally abundant in horses than is the pushing force. However, if one seeks to ride the horse in these jumps soon in bent-straight position, to change direction often, and to turn it, then one haunch is always used more than the other, and both gain in endurance.

The croupade is to be regarded as the first actual School jump. It uses much more of the springing force of the hindquarters than the courbette. The haunches and the hocks are also flexed more than in the courbette.

This allows the horse to push up off of the ground with the hind legs while the forehand is elevated.

The chief characteristic of this jump is the bending in the hind legs that takes place again immediately after the take-off. The higher the horse hops, the closer it pulls its hind legs to its body. It keeps the hind legs tucked in while it is in the air. The jump ends when the hind feet touch the ground before the front feet. As a result, the horse covers less ground than in the courbette. Referring back to the previous section with the better explanation, collecting the horse via piaffé to the School halt forms the first beat; raising the forehand to the median height of the perfect pesade forms the second beat.

Since the necessary aids have already been given above, no further explanation is needed here. However, those aids that are used in the third beat of the croupade and are intended to get the horse to act in a quite unfamiliar way are explained. They demand that the rider possess a lot of correct feel, but when precisely used, they ensure the best results. The third beat requires that, when the rider balances the horse in the second beat, i. e. in the pesade, the rider restrains on the reins energetically with the hand, as though he wanted to pull the horse to himself. This causes the haunches to noticeably bend more. At the moment when this can be felt, the legs must be pressed against the horse, and both spurs must be used on the flanks at the same time and with equal force. The reins are not in effect until the horse pushes itself up off of the ground, and thereby jumps back onto the hand. The first actions of restraining on the reins are repeated, in order to prevent the forehand from lowering until the horse's hind feet touch the ground first, and thus has correctly completed the jump.

Riding forward in any School movement or performing a second jump can only succeed if the rider's hand and leg can collect the horse again after the front feet have touched the ground. In this way, the halt can be performed correctly, and the horse will be able to elevate its forehand in the second beat.

While in the third beat, the hind feet are still in the air and are beginning to be lowered to the ground. If the horse has lowered the forehand too soon, then hand and leg aids must be given vigorously at the same time. In the best case scenario, the horse will be in balance, i. e. it will complete the jump with all four legs touching the ground at the same time. The rider must be content with this for the moment, and not punish the horse. The jump in balance is not incorrect, and is usually the result of the collecting aids being given too late. Afterward, however, he must use these aids to try to get a few piaffé steps, in order to restore the flexion in the haunches.

After a well-executed School jump, the horse piaffes almost without being asked.

Only in the second beat, i. e. during the pesade, the rider is able to determine whether the courbette or croupade is to be executed; in other words, whether he can cause the horse to use the pushing power of the hindquarters to lift up the hind end with the support of the front legs (as in the courbette) or without using them (as in the croupade) in the third beat. Only in the third beat does the take-off power develop when jumping forward and down with the hind legs. Depending on the flexion in the horse's stifles, this propels it forward to a greater or lesser extent.

Thus, the development of the jump in balance and the actual School jump depends on the elevation of the forehand. The courbette, regarded to be neither a School jump nor a jump in balance, is perfectly suited to prepare the former and to perfect the latter. Horses that are trained in the School jumps must have previously been confirmed in the courbette. This is so that they perform the School jumps only upon request, and do not think that they are being asked to do so every time the forehand is lifted, or when there is even less collection than that. If the rider allows the horse to do this, then the exercises in the School jumps usually result in detriment to both.

Under a skilled rider, the School horse, which has been properly prepared by previous schooling, soon learns to distinguish the irregular aids that one has to use in the third beat of this jump. This will happen if courbette and croupade are not both practiced at the same time in the beginning. The most important difference between the courbette and the croupade is that, in the courbette, the carrying capacity is developed to a lesser extent than in the latter. Thus, the aids must be explained. In general, hand and rein play the main role in the courbette. In the croupade, however, the legs do. While holding the pesade position, one must teach the horse to refrain from jumping for as long as the rider's legs press softly and repeatedly, using the spurs gently close to the girth, thus still working on the chest. However, the horse should commence with the croupade jump as soon as the rider is able to change the light contact on the reins, or the alternating transition between light to soft contact, into a resolute pressure on the reins with his legs firmly back and spurs on the flanks.

One must first have familiarized the horse with the courbette for the reasons given above and with the aids that induce the hind legs to jump up. It will accomplish this more willingly, if the rider leans forward a little with his upper body as soon as the forefeet are on the ground. This will make it easier for the horse to move its hind feet.

If the horse is confirmed in the courbette, then it is possible to combine it with the croupade, the perfection of which is subject to the same conditions with respect to the flexed haunches. After it has propelled itself up off of the ground, the horse should draw its hind feet to its body, and bring them forward in such a way that the hind hooves reach the line of the center of gravity with greater flexion in the haunches. Only in this way can the hindquarters touch the ground before the forehand.

Anyone who has acquired the necessary skill to carry out such School jumps will know how to develop more endurance in campaign horses, which will tire easily under other riders because they cannot keep them sufficiently collected. This is especially true if the horses are worn out by being ridden fast over terrain with many obstacles where frequent high jumps make greater collection particularly necessary.

The usefulness of the jumps described above with respect to the training of the campaign horses does not yet seem to have been sufficiently proven in theory. However, the fact that these are of practical use is proven by the skilled rider who trains such horses.

In general, perfection in the School jumps should not be demanded, especially in regard to the perfect pesade during the second beat, as is shown as the norm in illustrations in most riding books. This is only necessary for the training of a School horse that is intended for teaching in the arena. Some riders, who attempt School jumps with not yet sufficiently prepared horses, are probably totally scared away from the School by the failure of these attempts, partly due to the difficulty that they encounter, but also because the riding books contain too few depictions to sufficiently highlight and illustrate the general benefits of the School jumps.

In order to train horses as they used to be in the old days such that they performed several School jumps in quick succession almost on the spot, they have to be positioned almost perpendicularly via pesades. This almost entirely sacrificed the horse's extended movements.

To meet the demands that are now made on a perfectly trained dressage horse, the training should regulate the horse's natural impulsion, but the horse should not be robbed of it. Experience shows that this goal is achieved in most young horses by positioning them in balance. However, this is often not enough with older and very strong horses. Such horses can only meet the requirements via the School.

The School jumps, especially courbette and croupade, must be considered to be crucial for the collection in the higher training of the campaign horse. In any case, the rider must adapt their use to the horse's personality. This is understood to mean that the jump, whether perfect or imperfect, or even a single step of one of the jumps indicated above, must be done according to the ability and strength or the inclinations and resistances of the horse.

With regard to the individual steps of the School jumps, it is not necessary to repeat the explanation for the School halt for the time being, since it has already been frequently discussed and sufficiently explained.

If both legs gradually collect the hindquarters, as has been explained to execute the third beat of the courbette, it will be easier for the horse if it pushes off of the ground with its forefeet. This will not be detrimental to a horse with well-set hind legs that are free of defects, as the elevation of the forehand is initially low and not prolonged. When combined with the timely use of the legs and spur pressure afterwards, a wide rather than too narrow croupade jump will be the result. As a consequence, the horse, in connection with the previously explained exercises, is successfully made submissive to the rider's will in a shorter amount of time.

A detailed examination of the movements with perfect flexion in the haunches, as is required of School horses that are trained for years in dressage, is provided here mainly to give the campaign rider a yardstick by which to measure the success he has achieved and to gauge further demands that are made.

Balotade and Capriole

The goal of the previous dressage training with respect to collection was reached with the perfect croupade. The agility that the horse has acquired is now to be regarded as a permanent feature of the horse, as it were.

The weight of the forehand has now been used to regulate the pushing power of the hindquarters via the flexion in the haunches such that the extensor muscles in the haunches (which represent the pushing power) now only resist to the extent necessary for the horse to balance on its hind legs. The carrying and pushing forces, which mutually support each other, meet in the hock joints. If one of these forces is more dominant, then the desired springiness will be created depending on how much this occurs.

The part of the horse that contains the most vital organs necessary for life, the forehand, is most weakly supported by nature and is usually most burdened by the rider's weight. Now that it is relieved of all constraints, it can move with more freedom and endurance. The functions of these vital organs (the lungs and the heart) proceed unhindered, and support the ancillary organs located in the hind end more. This is why a School horse reaches a greater age than many others.

Even if the School horse is particularly well suited to all movements that require agility above all, but despite this and its stamina, it may not meet all of the various demands that the rider must make on the horse. Where there is a need to change location quickly (for ex. in war), the horse's speed becomes the main requirement. The question then arises whether the School also offers the means to reach this goal?

It is assumed that the previous dressage training did no damage to either the solid or the soft parts of the horse's body, and that the rider got control over the pushing power of the hind legs, but that this power was neither put to sleep nor destroyed. To avoid this, the School halt had to be developed, not only from the piaffé and from the School canter for the pesade, but also from the passage. Therefore, those movements should always be practiced in conjunction with these jumps. The regularity of the tempo arises because the extensors and the flexors of the hind legs act alternately with the same force in the passage. In the School, therefore, the passage is used to revitalize the extensor muscles. In the campaign-training, the canter, the carrière, and the jumps in balance are combined to achieve the same purpose. In the higher School, croupade is used to achieve perfect regularity in the horse's collected movements. However, the capriole, the most perfect extension of the hind legs while the horse is in the air, is used to reestablish the horse's extended movements, but in a more controlled manner.

The capriole differs from the croupade only by the strike. The extensor muscles of the hindquarters are used to kick out. The hind hooves often come as high as the stifle. It takes place in the third beat. The first two beats are identical to those of the croupade and, like the aids, do not need to be described again. The balotade, which is more akin to the capriole, lies between these two jumps, as it were, because it hints at striking out with the hind legs. It is actually the predecessor of the capriole. Before the horses decide to do the capriole, or if they do not possess the strength necessary to execute this powerful jump, they usually perform the balotade first.

In order to teach the horse, which already fully understands the croupade, to strike out, it is necessary to use a rather long whip on the buttocks while the horse is in the air. This is indispensable.

After the rider's legs and spurs cause the horse to push off from the ground in the third beat, they must not induce the horse to strike out. This is because the rider must close his legs firmly and stretch them down into the stirrups during the strike. This gives his hips support so that he can maintain his position when the horse kicks out behind and jostles his seat.

The reins must not be taut at this moment. Instead, there should be a light contact, or they could even be completely dropped. They will be taken up again after the strike to collect the horse.

It is essential that the rider's spine remain supple at this moment. Because the vertebrae are pushed back instead of being lifted up toward the chest, if the rider's back is stiff, then the force of the strike is not absorbed by the curved spine, but rather acts on the entire upper body. This will cause him to lose his strong position. It would then be impossible for the rein hand to keep the horse's forehand in the air after the strike. This must be done with arms held firmly to the body if the jump is to end correctly, i. e. with the hind feet touching the ground before the front feet. The horse should only leap over the ground indicated for the croupade.

A rule especially applicable to the capriole is not to execute it on a turn or right after one. In the first case, it is because of the turn itself. In the latter, it is because the rider's hand and leg are supposed to be used less after turns. Depending on the degree of the collection at the moment, select one of the School jumps that have thus far been practiced to perform with a horse that is already familiar with them. At first, the rider must allow the horse to choose to do the capriole and not immediately force it. If this rule is not adhered to, then incorrect and resistant jumps usually result. The intelligent horse almost does not require the use of the spurs anymore, especially if they can be replaced with gentler methods. This includes, in particular, the whip aids, which, however, must be applied differently in each of the three beats. For the halt, the whip must touch just behind the girth. To ask the forehand to lift up, tap the chest. To leap up and strike out behind, touch the buttocks.

The latter is easiest to teach the horse in-hand without a rider in the beginning. This is done by repeatedly tapping the buttocks with the whip. If one praises the horse for lifting its haunches even slightly, then it will learn it just as quickly or even more quickly than raising its forehand.

In the courbette and croupade exercises, the springiness of the hock joints was partially developed by the energetic, rapidly successive use of the flexors and extensors. Now the balotade and capriole induce the horse to allow the extensor muscles of the hindquarters to work more strongly and with more freedom than before. The even greater degree of springiness this creates causes the horse to leap higher than in the croupade. In the capriole especially, the hindquarters kick up more strongly, so that the horse is no longer hovering diagonally, as in the other jumps, but rather horizontally over the ground. This horizontal position of the horse's body in the air, however, depends on how fiercely the horse kicks out behind.

The purpose of striking out with the hind legs is to restore balance between pushing and carrying after perfect flexion in the haunches has been achieved. The correct capriole, therefore, represents the highest possible perfection of the School dressage. It is the transition to the campaign gaits. By allowing the horse to gradually leap farther and farther in the capriole, it will touch the ground with all four feet at the same time, i. e. in a balanced jump. Even though the extensor muscles of the hind legs were sufficiently active to develop, in conjunction with the flexors, the necessary strength for all of the previous movements during the horse's dressage training, the hind legs will still not be able to strike out right from the start with the strength and energy that are required for the perfect capriole.

Maintaining the pushing power of the hind legs during the exercises that lead to perfect bending in the haunches is considered to be the most difficult task in dressage. That this is so is proven by how rare it is to find a horse that is good at capriole, among other things.

The pushing power of the hind legs can only be suppressed by misuse, namely by incorrect jumps or by incorrect jump-like gaits. This is clearly indicated by a dragging movement of the hind legs in extended gaits. If it has not been possible to properly maintain this force during the School dressage, then the horse will neither be able to execute the movements correctly, nor be used with certainty for the campaign service. If this occurs, then the purpose of the School dressage has failed.

One should not deceive oneself in this respect and believe that a School horse can no longer go in campaign gaits if a horse properly trained in courbette and croupade no longer shows its former élan in extended gaits, for ex., in lengthened trot. For this purpose, the springiness of the hock joints is not yet adequately regulated by the practice of the croupade, which is only regained once the horse's gaits have been gradually lengthened out again.

It is just as big of a mistake to suddenly ride a horse still in the School dressage in extended gaits, as it is to collect a green horse too soon. Just as the horse's flexor muscles have more tension put on them gradually, so must one allow the extensors of the horse performing croupade to gradually be used more in the extended gaits, which are unfamiliar to it. Developing such gaits again does not pose any great difficulty. It requires only cautious transitions at first. Although more difficult, but most perfect and least damaging for the horse's limbs, the balotade and capriole are used to achieve this goal. It is certainly not insignificant, but rather of great importance, whether the horse, by the effect of the extensor muscles of its hindquarters, has to push its body mass forward, as is the case in the airs on the ground, or if it engages the pushing property of these muscles by kicking out with the hind legs (as in the balotade and capriole), whereby their action is not disturbed in the slightest by being burdened.

For the same reason that not all horses have the same natural freedom of movement in the forelegs (considering the position and the structure of their shoulders), the ability of the hind legs to kick out depends on the construction and the position of the pelvis. If it is difficult for the horse to kick out high due to unfavorable conditions or lack of energy, then one should seek to only train the horse up to the balotade.

As soon as the extensors of the hindquarters use their full strength, the capriole will not only be the highest of the School jumps, but will also be the most suitable one to most fully develop the springiness in the hock joint. This has been explained on page 21 and 22*** of the General Section and as follows.

Since the joints in the haunches have no flexor muscles in and of themselves, they are only bent by the hind legs and by the load. The hock joints, on the other hand, have both flexors and extensors. They develop strength by being used in an alternating fashion. These joints are to be considered to be the sole source of the springiness and impulsion.

The higher a School jump is executed, the more the springs are compressed by the weight of the body landing on them upon its completion. As they uncoil again, they will develop an even greater springiness. This is released in the same direction from which the load first acted upon them. After this, it will be easy to understand why strong horses can perform several caprioles in a row (and almost on the spot), and immediately afterwards step into any gait at will. This is to be regarded as the highest perfection of all School dressage.

The impulse to move forward, combined with the horse's complete submission to the rider's will, is brought about by the weight landing on the hind legs that are the only support at the moment the School jump ends, but not by the transfer of this burden at the beginning of the jump. This flexion in the haunches is the only method to elicit the highest degree of the springing force. Without it, the springing power does not develop completely. The degree to which this develops depends on the flexion in the haunches, which is determined by how much the forehand is elevated.

Because the movements and the School jumps are indispensable for the highest training of the horse, riding and even more so, training fully trained School horses, is of manifold value for the rider. This was also acknowledged by all of the old riding experts. No movement, however, is better suited to training the rider's sensitivity and to further the perfection of his seat and overall control more than the School jumps, and especially the third beat. With this, the time has come when he changes the contact on the reins, and when he must allow the stronger or weaker leg grip with which he can most clearly feel the forcefulness of the horse's movement.

A horse fully trained in the School dressage will meet all reasonable demands of the rider. It will be possible to use it in fast gaits to the same degree that it demonstrates skill and endurance in collected School movements.

THIRD PART

On riding in the natural position of the horse

Riding in the natural position of the horse is to be understood as primarily meaning that the hindquarters either push too little or too much.

In this style of riding, the hind feet step either too far forward or not far enough. In other words, they do not reach the footprints of the forefeet due to too little bending in the joints in the haunches, or they track over them. The former is the case in too constricted gaits, the latter, on the other hand, in too lengthened gaits. In both cases, the greater burden of the horse's body and the weight of the rider are supported more on the forefeet when going forward. The center of gravity of both bodies falls between the front legs.

This riding style on the one hand and the School or primarily using the carrying capacity of the hindquarters on the other constitute the extremes in equitation, as it were. Between them lies riding in balance. This is the norm in riding, in which the forces of pushing and carrying are equal. This is better for determining the horse's all-around utility.

It is useful for the rider to be familiar with the riding in this section in multiple respects. This is for the following reasons:

First: To be able to better distinguish the gait in balance from one in the natural position of the horse, and the one in which the forehand is overburdened, and to form a more correct assessment regarding the firm rein contact in particular.

Second: To use horses with weak hindquarters (i. e. with too little ability to carry or with defective hind legs), which could entirely lose their already low value for riding service by being ridden in balance.

Third: To accustom young horses with unsteady carriage to taking a firm contact on the bit, which is usually still lacking, in a short amount of time, and to go forward more willingly as the rider desires.

Fourth: To further the training of colts more expediently, and to use those young horses, whose still undeveloped power in the haunches does not yet allow dressage with flexion in the haunches, such that the strengthening of the hindquarters, which increases with age, is not hindered by this style of riding.

Fifth: To test horses that are intended for breeding.

Sixth: To be able to develop the highest possible degree of speed in the horse for changing location.

When riding in a natural position, one only acquires the steady connection that is required between horse and rider via the rein contact in lengthened gaits. If, on the other hand, the horse in this position goes in restricted gaits, then it is behind the bit. The firm rein contact prepares for the light and soft contact. This is why the rider must first obtain a firm contact. This is created by primarily using the pushing power of the hindquarters, and especially the fetlock joints.

All well-built horses, even if they are still green, have a natural tendency to take a firm contact. Therefore, they are suited at once to dressage training with flexion in the haunches. Most green horses, however, usually take either a hard contact rather than firm due to their abnormal conformation, in that they push too much (especially with the fetlock joints), or they seek to avoid it (i. e. they go behind the bit) by developing too little pushing power.

The former, namely the well-built horses, are most suitable for training by the method described in the first part. The latter, the ones that have abnormal conformations, on the other hand, can be ridden in natural position. This is the best way to prepare them for riding service because it suits their meager strength.

One begins with lunging here again. However, this differs from that of the first part by the use of the two auxiliary reins described in the first section of the eighth chapter. Here, the side reins are used hardly at all. The draw reins are used depending on how much the horse is to be prepared for shortened or extended gaits. In the first part, the intent was to lighten the forehand and to engage the hindquarters. Here, the hindquarters of the young horse should not be burdened by the forehand. The horse is to retain the natural position of the spine in all three gaits. Therefore, it is neither in balance nor on the haunches under the rider. Consequently, the forward motion is most appropriately described by the expression, "Riding in the natural position of the horse."

The choice of which of the two types of lunging depends on the horse's inclination to take either a hard contact or no contact. In the first case, if the horse pulls hard on the reins out of eagerness and a desire to go forward, the lunging of the first part is to be used. Otherwise, choose the lunging of this section whether the horse is weak or strong.

When riding, the same relationship occurs with regard to the loading and unloading of the hindquarters. If the pushing force is too powerful in strong hindquarters, then the rules that were given in the first part apply. In the opposite case, the following rules of riding in the natural position of the horse will be the most suitable.

Depending on the horse's current tendency to push too much or too little or to carry too much or too little, the most appropriate means to counter it must be applied immediately (without, however, going from one extreme to the other). Thus, it is often necessary to change between the riding styles of all three sections for a few moments with the same horse, depending on which one is required at the time.

In all cases, however, the horse's front legs suffer from being ridden incorrectly and for too long without lightening the forehand. The later utility and longer endurance of the horse will be nipped in the bud the more one fails to proceed according to certain rules.

In an attempt to systematize this riding style in accordance with rules, only riding methods that are the least detrimental to the horse can be suggested. It is not to be feared that the excessive use of this riding could cause the School to fall into oblivion. This is because the advantages that the School offers are so important and convincing that nothing can challenge its rightful position.

In the first and second parts, the rules are given on how a strong horse can gradually be brought into balance by loading the hindquarters more. In this section, on the other hand, it is shown how to train a horse with a measured burdening of the forehand. This is done partly by how the schooling of such horses meant for riding service, whose weak or afflicted hindquarters do not allow positioning in balance, must be conducted, and partly how the rider has to proceed in order to develop the highest degree of speed and endurance in the horse.

Although this method ruins the front legs more quickly if used in excess to achieve the highest degree of speed, the disadvantages it causes can be mitigated somewhat with horses that have powerful hindquarters. This is because their ability to carry has not been destroyed. In the previous sections, it has been proven that the free movement of the front legs can be restored to a certain degree by using this characteristic, but not if the springiness of the hindquarters has already been impaired. Thus, the riders for whom it is either too difficult to ride their horses in balance or whose horses are not suitable for it, are advised to choose riding in the natural position of the horse because it is easier.

Furthermore, as this riding style seldom angers the horse, it is recommended for the schooling of ladies' horses.

The position of the horse's head and neck determines the restricting and awakening of the pushing property of the hind legs when lunging and riding in natural position of the horse. By setting the head with a very rounded neck, one soon causes the horse to restrict its pushing power, i. e. to shorten its steps. By contrast, stretching forward with the head and neck releases more pushing power, and the horse takes longer strides.

In both cases, the horse's spine remains in its natural position. It has been proven that the weight of the horse and rider is carried more on the forefeet. As a result, the carrying capacity, which results from the bending of the joints in the haunches and was called "collection" in the previous sections, cannot be developed. On the contrary, the carrying capacity of the hock joints is used almost exclusively, which are no longer supported by the haunches but rather by the fetlocks. That this is the case is proven by the almost unavoidable over-exertion of these parts, which manifests itself through weakness and diseases, but above all through the loss of the spring in the hock joints.

The positioning of the head and neck, as described above, is to be done, to a certain extent, both when lunging and riding the colts, as well as when riding fully grown horses with weak hindquarters. If it is allowed to go on the forehand and take support on the bridle, then its hindquarters do not have to bend. If the haunches have to bend, then it causes pain, and, as a consequence, makes the horse resistant to going forward.

Accordingly, the method to be chosen must also be oriented toward making such horses reasonably useful for the riding service by going in shortened strides (whereby it is allowed that the hind feet do not reach the hoof prints of the forefeet). The complete dressage training, as described in the preceding sections, may not be undertaken with them. The schooling of such horses for riding service is more of a "breaking" than a "training." It works much more on the soft tissues of the horse's body, whereby the fixed parts change their natural position very little, if at all. It goes without saying that the lever theory, which is presented in the General Section, only applies in the previous sections and not in this section. Because the soft structures are more subject to diseases, the schooling sessions may not consist of three sessions in every lesson, but rather only one.

The rider's posture in this riding style must not be the strong one that was previously described. Instead, it must fully correspond to the horse's position. In addition to the seat bones, the third point of support is no longer the coccyx, but rather the crotch. In order to make this posture easier, choose a saddle with a high cantle, eg. the Hungarian saddle. It is better for the stirrups to be long rather than too short. Because it is necessary for the rider to do without the most advantageous point of support for the upper body, he has to try to replace it by rotating the legs and gripping firmly with the knees and calves.

This also helps maintain the natural position of the horse. Due to the low neck and the vertical position of the head, combined with the so-called fork seat of the rider, the hindquarters are almost completely unburdened by the forehand. Instead, the head and neck serve to support their pushing power by pulling the body forward.

In order to obtain a shortened stride on such horses in the three gaits of walk, trot, and canter in a short time, despite their weak hindquarters, and to teach them to let themselves be thrown right and left, allow them to go crooked. Encourage this by bending the neck. It has already been mentioned that weak horses seldom become angry when ridden in their natural position. Since their shoulders are usually strong in comparison to their hind legs, and because the weak hindquarters may not be overburdened, these horses can be gently used for a rather long period of time before they are fully worn-out due to this style of riding.

Horses with strong haunches, however, ruin their front legs faster when ridden in the natural position. This is not because of any weakness in the haunches, but rather because their strong hindquarters overburden their forehand more forcibly. Therefore, such horses require a regular dressage training.

The rider, who, in order to ride a horse in shortened strides, attempts in vain to collect the horse out of the natural position but does not understand how to balance the horse, should be satisfied with the suggested schooling of the cavalry horses. This is especially true if the hindquarters are weak. Only very experienced and skilled riders will succeed in balancing weak horses (provided, however, that their hind legs are free of defects). This is because it requires the necessary experience to gauge how much to use the strength available in the haunches to sufficiently collect such horses so that the weak horses suffer no harm.

Less experience is required to learn the following style of riding, in which the horse, though also in a natural position, does not go in shortened strides, but rather in lengthened ones.

———————

Since the races modeled on the English races were introduced on the continent, the principle of assessing the value and choice of horses for breeding due to their exterior has been put in doubt. The principles of horse breeding in England have been recognized as the more correct ones, and breeding has been almost universally conducted accordingly.

If the performance in the natural position of the horse under the rider in lengthened gaits is the goal, then it is best to check the quality of the vital organs (especially the lungs), the animal's energy, and the elasticity of the tissues, and judge the choice of the breeding horses accordingly. Now that the descendants of horses bred and tested in such a manner largely satisfy the current demand for speed, it is to be expected that these newer principles of breeding are here to stay, and with them the style of riding known as "English Riding."

This is also understood to mean riding in the natural position of the horse. However, this is no longer done in shorter and more restricted gaits, but in such an extended forward movement that the hind feet track over the hoof prints of the front feet.

All horses that willingly move forward under the rider are suitable for riding in lengthened gaits. However, if this willingness does not exist, it must be created by the preceding appropriate lunging.

The most suitable is this

Lunging

to awaken the impulse to move forward in lengthened gaits. The horse's head and neck are positioned in such a way that the auxiliary reins do not hinder the pushing power of the hind legs, yet make it more difficult to misbehave (by jumping around, etc.).

Usually, only the colts destined for the racetrack are mounted and ridden in their second or third year after they have been prepared for it by lunging.

This English Method, which is already widespread on the continent, is for use with horses at the youngest adolescent age. This is partly to train them, and partly to adequately prepare them for any kind of future use. It deserves a more general application, i. e. not just as preparation for the colts intended for the racetrack, but to train all fine and valuable horses. It will, therefore, be useful to say something about the beginning of this training in order to highlight its utility.

The eighteen-month-old stabled colts and fillies must immediately have their hooves trimmed. However, if they are still too mistrustful for this, then it can be done after some of the following exercises on the lunge line, which are suitable to adequately familiarize the young horses with people.

This type of lunging requires only one strong man, but one with a pleasant personality and a lot of love for horses.

The necessary equipment is as follows: A wide lunging surcingle with a hook and two buckles on either side. A suitably heavily padded cavesson with a ring to attach the lunge line. A snaffle with a thick bit and a chinstrap that has a ring on it.

In order to give the head and neck the necessary position, one uses the draw reins that were described in the eighth chapter of the first part in addition to the snaffle reins, which, as previously stated, are used to set the head and neck in such a way that they can only bend sideways when the cavesson is used.

Although setting the head and neck in this way brings every horse under the trainer's control very quickly, it must not be attempted with colts or fillies before they willingly move away from the trainer and follow the lunge line. Also, avoid the use of any scary methods with the colts, especially the rough use of the lunge line, which may cause them to go backwards or even fall down. In any case, only one man should to be used to lunge the young horse so that it soon loses its distrust. This is because the presence of more people will add to the suspicion and fear felt by the young horse that is not yet used to dealing with people.

However, it is absolutely necessary, should one man be enough, to handle the colt well, to praise it a lot, to feed it, and not immediately demand that it go in a circle around the trainer. Rather, he should walk it in straight lines, stand still often, and praise and pet it on the forehand while talking to it.

The draw reins are shortened depending on how willingly the colt follows the lunge line. One should not spoil its desire to go forward with them, but rather just prevent it from leaping forward, something that young horses are inclined to do.

It is usually the leaps the colts make that cause the diseases and defects in the extremities that appear later. Colts raised in the traditional way, i. e. their misbehavior is not only not prevented, but rather encouraged because some consider it to be beneficial for the horses to run and jump about wildly, have a tendency to develop wind puffs, curb and even spavin, etc., usually in their fourth year of being stabled. These problems then crop up during the dressage training, which robs the horse of its value, the breeder of his asset, and the trainer of the fruits of his labor.

If the young horse tolerates the tauter tension on the auxiliary reins without being restricted in its forward movement, then the head and neck must gradually be put in such a position that the conditions that are required for the lengthened gaits are fulfilled, namely that the hind feet track over the footprints of the forefeet. The result of this head and neck position is the intended steady contact, whereby the young horse will be properly prepared for riding. A whip that is not too long is limited to just preventing the colt from coming into the circle in these exercises. Special driving aids with the whip (as with lunging in the first part) are unnecessary. This is because the young horse, being less restricted by the attachment of the reins, will go forward enough on its own.

Although it is preferable to exercise the young horse in walk and trot on the lunge line, cantering may never be forcibly impeded, but must rather be permitted. Also, one should conduct these exercises outdoors and only on rather large circles. Do not hesitate to put a saddle on the colt as soon as possible. An over-girth will be attached over it, which will cause the saddle to lie more securely. It is useful to place straps, cloths, etc. on colts that are very sensitive and scared when touched. This may make them more fearful and even almost wild in the beginning, but they will soon learn to tolerate their touch.

It is not necessary to fasten the head to one side by means of a cavesson or snaffle reins in this type of lunging. This is because it is not the carrying capacity of the hind legs via greater burdening that is promoted, but rather the pushing power that should be developed much more.

If the rider's weight is in the correct proportion to the animal's strength, which is still weak, then there is no disadvantage associated with mounting early. Instead, it contributes significantly to the colts' training, especially if they are prepared for the faster gaits by prolonged walking under the rider and if nutritious food is not spared.

When the colt is stabled, it receives a 12-14 year old boy as a caretaker. The horse soon becomes so happy with him that it learns to tolerate first being saddled and then mounted by him in a few days without great difficulties. It will soon tolerate the weight of its young caretaker on its back just as willingly. It will go forward when the trainer rides a horse of quiet temperament alongside, and the colt is led by a lead line attached to the cavesson or the snaffle.

After a few rides, let the colt go behind the lead horse, but make sure that it follows exactly in its footsteps. If it breaks away, then the trainer takes it in hand on the lead line again, quiets it down by longer walking sessions, and makes it obedient again.

If the colt has no tendency to buck, then the side reins can be removed during the ride. However, the draw reins are still to be used by the rider initially, as they are a very suitable means to prevent other disobediant jumps.

The first purpose of the early riding of the colt is attained when the rider can give it the proper movement in lengthened trot or canter, which is necessary for it to flourish. The more willingly it offers its power in these gaits, the more the quantity of nutritious feed should be increased. Thus, the feeding of the young horse can best be determined by its regulated movement. This must always be continued until a low level of fatigue sets in, if the state of the colt's health allows it.

It is not the intention here to describe the training of the colts, but rather to only make recommendations about their initial schooling, which are connected, as the most expedient. If this is combined with more care and expense in terms of supervision and better feeding, then if the breeder uses, for example, one knowledgable man to train 20 colts, then the greater effort and expense will be sufficiently offset by the quicker development and strengthening of the colts.

Each of the boys may well be given three or even more colts to groom and ride.

The foals may move around freely in the foal stalls or so-called "Kaffstalle" as before. They will — bearing in mind how little exercise they get — behave more quietly, especially if the lads watch over them.

After the foals have been stabled, if stable-feeding is not preferred, their grazing should be restricted to the most fertile months of the year. This is so that the benefits gained from the exercises described above are not lost, and the foals do not become wild again and hurt themselves by resistant or disobedient actions in the next exercises in lunging or riding.

Before discussing the riding style known as "English Riding" more fully, it is necessary to mention the bridling that is peculiar to it.

The Bridling

The bridling of a non-artistically positioned horse must be as simple as possible, especially when speed is intended.

At first, choose a simple snaffle and attach the martingale to it, but not the draw reins. The martingale proves to be very useful with horses that carry their heads too high and stretch their necks out. It also allows for the effect of the reins to suddenly increase significantly, as well as be done away with entirely. This cannot be done so quickly with draw reins.

If one uses two sets of reins, which is highly recommended, only one set of reins will be drawn through the rings of the martingale. One strong snaffle bit is more expedient than two fine bits, because their unsteady position makes the horses less inclined to take a firm contact upon which everything depends.

The best bridle for a horse prepared for the lengthened gaits with snaffle and martingale is the Pelham. It is more severe than the snaffle by virtue of the curb chain, which is prevented from riding up by the chinstrap, and due to its other construction features, but not as sharp as the curb bit. With horses that pull hard on the reins, it is better to use the English hunting curb bit, which must, however, be placed very high in the mouth so that its significant port corresponds to the width of the mandibular canal.

The lever-like effect of the hunting curb is limited to the horse's head and neck. It cannot reach the haunches in these lengthened gaits, because the balance is missing, i. e. the hind feet track over the front footprints.

Different shaped curbs should be used depending on the horse's sensitivity and temperament. With horses that are inclined to take a hard rather than firm contact and go powerfully with their noses stuck out, it is advisable to use a bit with long shanks and a thin mouthpiece, which, if it has rollers, produces a stronger effect. If, on the other hand, the horses do not take a firm enough contact, this severe bridling only confuses them. In that case, one should use a more appropriate bit with shorter shanks and a thicker mouthpiece without rollers. The upper cheek bars of this curb must be longer than usual and bent slightly outwards. This is so that they will not injure the cheekbones if they are pulled on strongly. However, since the sensitivity and the temperament of the horses differ so much, the length of the shanks, the thickness of the mouthpiece, etc. cannot be given for individual cases in general terms. Instead, the choice of bit among the innumerable types of curb bits is left to the rider's discretion.

Since the rider's main endeavor, for example, a rider who intends to ride horses in their natural position over any terrain, is to achieve firm rein contact, he should choose the Pelham for a horse with an unsteady neck and sensitive mouth. Because of its gentle and negligible lever-action, it does not suppress the horse's drive to go forward right from the beginning. In cases that the rider cannot avoid taking a hold on the horse's mouth for a moment, as can happen while jumping, this bridling will prove to be very useful.

The Pelham is also simple to use when guiding the horse. If the two reins, which are attached to the lower rings on the shanks, are divided between the pinky or fourth finger, and the other two, which are attached to the bit, are divided by the fourth or third finger, and if these latter reins are held constantly with full contact, then the slightest taking back on the two aforementioned reins will refresh the mouth's receptivity to the effect of the reins.

If, however, one uses the reins on the lower rings right from the beginning, then one cannot prevent the Pelham from rising up when restraining or tugging strongly on them. It then hurts the horse's cheeks, which usually causes the horse to over-bend in the neck.

In order to tug strongly on the Pelham, use either both hands or alternate between one and the other. Increase the tension if necessary by alternating between the two reins on each side and by lowering both hands and then raising them again from time to time, or use them together by rounding the wrists.

The martingale can be very useful when combined with the Pelham, but one has to use it with reins that have been attached to the bit rings. Any German curb without a port or without a jointed bit can easily be used on a hunting bridle, if one shortens the cheek pieces, makes the noseband completely ineffective or even removes it, and uses a long curb chain. This achieves the intended purposed of making the curb ineffective.

On riding in the natural position of the horse in lengthened walk, trot, and canter

Due to hunting with horses, which has become more and more popular in recent times, steeplechases, and above all, the hunting races, which also have become prevalent on the continent, riding in the natural position of the horse in lengthened gaits has quickly become widespread.

It is also undeniable that this riding style offers multiple and not insignificant advantages, even if it is hardly taken into account that it leads to the horse wearing out faster, and perhaps the total sacrifice of the horse for the purpose to be achieved at the moment. A horse that is ridden in a natural strung-out position, for example, for hunting, is able to follow the hounds more quickly than the artistically positioned horse, since it covers more ground in every stride than the other. This is because its hind feet track over the footprints of the forefeet. On long excursions where speed is the main requirement, this riding, properly performed, will make things significantly easier for both horse and rider. Even in inspecting young horses to determine their value or worthlessness for breeding at an early stage, riding the horse in the natural position with lengthened gaits is not only adequate, but rather necessary, as already pointed out in this section and steeped in reasoning.

As for this type of riding itself, it is understandable that the seat and aids of the rider who allows his horse to go in a natural position must be different from those used by the rider who intends to perform artistic movements. The main purpose of the lengthened riding is, as mentioned above, usually to develop the greatest speed when going from one place to another. Therefore, the rider is to avoid wasting time in everything he does from the moment he mounts to the moment he dismounts.

With this style of riding, the rider should not neglect to examine the bridle, the saddle, and especially the stirrup leathers before mounting. The first, whether it allows for a strong pull on it. The second, whether it can slip back or hurt the withers or not. With respect to the stirrup leathers, whether they can offer the rider's body a solid support. As far as the shape of the stirrup is concerned, it should be borne in mind that it is about four and a half inches high from the tread to the leather. This shape of stirrup or stirrup bars that have springs on them prevents the rider from getting his foot caught in the stirrup in the event of a fall.

The stirrups, which are appropriately very short, make it almost impossible for the rider of a small stature to mount the horse according to the rules laid out in the first part. It is even difficult for the taller rider. Mounting can be made much easier if the rider lifts his foot and puts it in the stirrup on the left side of the horse, such that his right side stands behind the saddle-flaps. At the same time, he holds the rein ends with the right hand, takes a firm hold with the right hand at the back on the saddle panels on the right side. The left hand holds the riding whip and grabs either the mane at the withers or the saddle pommel. This is the first step in mounting. In the second step, one swings into the saddle without stopping, immediately takes the reins with the left hand, grasps the riding whip with the right, and takes the stirrup with the right foot. With this style of mounting, however, the steps should not appear to be too spread out. This grants various advantages. Firstly, it is easier to reach the short stirrup with the left foot. Secondly, impatient horses that do not wait to be mounted can be more easily followed by hopping forward instead of backward, and thirdly, one is in the saddle more quickly. This is because one mounts in two steps.

To dismount, the right hand grasps the reins again, and the left takes the riding whip and the mane. The right hand, supported on the saddle pommel, serves as a support for the upper body as the rider swings himself out of the saddle. Back on the ground, he must be in the same position as described in the first step of mounting, i. e. standing next to the horse.

However, in this kind of mounting and dismounting, the horse must not have the bad habit of kicking at the rider whose right leg, both at the time of taking and leaving the left stirrup, is in danger of being kicked. In this case, one can only protect oneself via the School-correct mounting.

If the rider intends to ride on in walk, then he must keep the steps even and lengthened, but not too hurried.

Horses that walk in lengthened strides without swaying their hindquarters back and forth give the rider the required firm contact as fast as possible. By this means, it will be possible for him to gradually give the horse the appropriate head and neck position, which allows it to survey the terrain in front of it. This position must be maintained in all gaits. However, the rider should mainly pay attention that the lowered position of the head and neck does not overburden the forehand too much. If this is the case, then the more lengthened gaits are not without danger, especially when jumping.

The rider who is attentive to his horse will recognize that the forehand is overburdened by the transition from the firm contact to the hard contact; the horse takes too firm a support on the rider's hands. By taking and yielding on the reins in a timely manner, but without disturbing the gait, the rider will be able to prevent the incorrect contact and control the movement. With a more casual and somewhat more forward-leaning upper body position, going with the horse's motion, he combines a firm but elastic contact with his legs, whose driving aids are determined in part by the horse's gait.

The trot in the natural position of the horse is very uncomfortable for the rider if the hind legs push strongly and the fetlock joints of the forelegs are short and upright. The horse, too, by having to suffer a jolt by the rider's weight on its back with each trot stride, will tire sooner. The forward reaching movement of the forefeet, on which the jolts are mainly acting, will be hindered rather than furthered. The halt on the forehand and this bumpy trot give the most palpable proof of how little spring is inherent in the front legs, assuming that the position and construction of their bones is not proof enough. Therefore, as the forehand pushes off from the ground, the burden placed on it is affected less the more the horse extends in the fetlocks, whereby the cannon bone and the pastern form a greater angle.

There are only two ways to avoid the discomfort of hard trotting when riding in natural position of the horse. These are to either grip strongly with the legs to get the seat in the closest possible connection with the saddle, or if strength is lacking, proceed in the English style when trotting.

The rider can continue this so-called English trot on important excursions without tiring, if he goes with the movement of the horse. In this case, the ordinary trot is probably preferable when riding in the natural position of the horse.

The rider's hand must remain quiet and steady in the same place, while the body rises higher than in the normal trot. The seat bones should not fall back hard on the saddle. This can be done by leaning forward with the upper body, by rotating the legs so that they are very flat, and by finding firm yet elastic support on the stirrups.

The pushing movement of one hind foot is predominant in the English trot. It comes about almost by itself from the rhythmical rising of the rider's body in the saddle. This foot is called the lead foot, which the horse changes from time to time, especially when the rider does not follow its movement.

It is not to be assumed that the horse's front legs always suffer a lot in a correct English trot, that is, with proper harmony between the hand aids and the distribution of the rider's weight. In a controlled process, the front legs reach forward more. This is partly because they cannot move high above the ground, and partly because the more definite and more effective aids of both calves cause the hind feet to step forward farther. Thus, this trotting is highly recommended for horses with too high shoulder action and that use their hind legs too little. It is only correct if the contact on the reins is steady, but is not a support for the rider upon which he lifts his body out of the saddle.

This rising trot must by no means betray any effort on the rider's part. It must only result from the movement of the horse's one forefoot, which, burdened by its diagonal hind leg, has just been set down. The noticeable flapping with both arms, as though a pair of wings, do not make it easier to rise from the saddle. They also interfere with good rein contact. Giving checks on the reins and aids with the leg can be easily connected to the movements of the upper body; one checks on the reins when rising up and gives the leg aids when lowering back down.

Of all of the movements, the canter is the most strenuous for the horse in the natural position. This is especially true for its front legs, and even more so if the horse's natural speed and endurance is to be tested in this gait. None of the other gaits is as suitable for this testing as the canter. Although early damage is caused by an excessive strain on the horse's legs, the knowledge that is gained about its value for breeding it undoubtedly of great benefit. Horses that distinguish themselves from others by their achievements in the lengthened canter in a natural position certainly deserve special consideration in improving their breed.

The more freely and unimpeded the long extensor muscles of the back and the haunches can act, the more freely the hind legs can move. The rider's weight burdening them limits the action of these muscles. This is especially true if the rider's bouncing around causes them to react against it. Therefore, if the rider directs the position of his upper body according to the horse's center of gravity while galloping fast, i. e. he leans forward, then he will be able to follow the horse's motion with ease. Firm knee and leg contact and the stirrups replace the support of the back part of the seat that the rider has given up by leaning forward with the upper body.

The horse will start to canter on its own, if the leg aids speed up the trot and the hand restrains with repeated half-halts. Whether the horse canters on the right or left lead does not matter here. Steady contact on the hands at the withers will support the upper body position in the fast gallop. It will also serve to prevent the upper body from swaying and make it easier for the horses to keep the pace. For riders who are accustomed to riding their horses only in an artistic position, it is more challenging to not use the aids than to use them. These aids are almost only limited to the rider's hands. In particular, intermittent and timely half-halting on the reins prevents the horse from escaping the control of the hand, bolting, or falling down. If the horse is prevented from going forward in a spirited fashion by frequent checks on the reins and from taking the necessary contact on the hands, then it will lose speed just as much as though one were to let the horse go with loose reins. In racing, for example, the horse's weariness is often exacerbated just before the finish line. This is because the rider relinquishes the rein contact in order to use the whip. However, if the horse is out of breath, this will have as little effect as the rider's most vehement jabs with the spur.

If the rider has to encourage his horse with the whip and spurs (a method which he should only use in the most exceptional case), then arms and legs must work together as energetically as possible.

The turns the horses make in lengthened gaits are actually just throwing the forehand around, whereby the head position is disregarded. Exceptionally fast horses, whose most extended gallop stride has only two beats, show themselves to be the most agile.

When riding in a natural position of the horse, the rider mainly uses the outside rein in the turns. During the right turn, for ex., the right rein is held steady, while the left one throws the forehand to the right by putting more pressure on the neck. At the same time, the rider must transfer almost all of his weight to the right side, support himself more firmly on the right stirrup, and use both legs equally.

It must not be the rider's intention to make the horse very agile by means of shortened gaits if it is to remain fast. The turns in the natural position of the horse are almost only executed at obtuse angles, and therefore, require no special agility on the part of the horse. The first preliminary exercises in turning the young horse are done on the lunge line on a circle. How long this is continued depends on the horse's personality and the use for which it is intended.

If the turn is not to be made at too obtuse of an angle, then the horse must reduce its speed before the turn and take a less firm contact than is allowed at a full gallop. The same rule applies to the halt out of the lengthened gaits.

Jumping in the natural position of the horse is different from the jumps in balance and those of the School, in that the horse can jump higher and wider. At the end of the jump, the forelegs touch the ground before the hind legs. A jump executed in this way is called a deer jump.

The rider's actions over these jumps are usually limited to preventing the horse from stopping or running out in front of the obstacle in a timely fashion, and to follow the movement without hanging on the reins.

To compute a precise calculation and to apply the combined aids — as with the jumps described in the previous sections — would only confuse the horse when jumping in natural position, because it is unfamiliar with many of the finer aids. This may cause it to jump too short or too low, which could result in many accidents for the rider.

All that matters here is that the rider has some courage and acts as passively as possible when jumping. After having chosen the most appropriate spot for jumping over the obstacle, let the horse do the thinking.

If one rides in walk and trot, then one should not let the horse jump over every small obstacle. This will tire it unnecessarily and use up the strength it needs for more significant jumps that may still be coming. Therefore, do not allow it to jump over a wide, dry and shallow ditch, over a small embankment and the like, as it can partly go through these obstacles, and sometimes step over them. One encourages this by totally yielding on the reins, burdening the horse's forehand by leaning forward with the upper body to make it more difficult to lift for jumping, and touching the hindquarters with the riding whip.

A horse ridden in natural position may not wait for the rider's aids as would one that is trained in the artistic position, but rather collects itself in front of a jump, whether on the spot or in any gait.

Before this happens, however, the rider will be made aware of the horse's willingness to jump by its determined and spirited approach to the obstacle. If the horse pulls hard on the rider's hand and gets very strong on the approach, then the rider has to be more active. To regain the correct contact, he must quickly and repeatedly half-halt on the reins. This not only furthers the horse's collection for the jump, but also prevents it from suddenly running out in front of the obstacle.

One should not force a weak horse that does not trust its own strength to jump right away without taking into account beforehand whether the jump is commensurate with its strength. Instead, only choose obstacles that it is capable of clearing. A strong, well-built horse will, if properly ridden, almost never refuse an obstacle. However, if this happens, then one must force it to jump. To do this, speed up the approach, raise the horse's head with lively half-halts, and do not allow it to see the obstacle until it is close to it. Then the rider gives complete freedom on the reins and uses the spurs as strongly as possible at the same time.

If one rides over terrain that has many obstacles, then one tries to spot upcoming obstacles early enough so that one can implement the appropriate measures in a timely manner. Just before arriving at the obstacle, allow horses that like to jump to choose the spot for take-off on their own.

The jumping pens, which have arisen in England in which young horses are exercised, are very practical and therefore, generally recommended. They consist of a high fenced area with a diameter of 80-100 feet. There is a second circle inside with a diameter that is 20-30 feet smaller. Between the two fences, there are several obstacles and ditches that are placed at various distances for the horse to jump. If the young horses go between this enclosure and the fence, either with or without a rider, one can stand on the inside of the smaller circle or follow them on the jumping circle, and easily use a whip to make them jump. It goes without saying that the surrounding fence should be high enough that it is impossible to jump over.

The horse gains the best jumping practice, however, by following the hounds in the hunt. It should not be separated from the experienced hunting horses, even if the obstacles are difficult. It is, therefore, not always the rider's extraordinary skill and fearlessness that makes it possible for him to chase the wild animal to the kill. Instead, it is mainly the excellence of his horse and the inclination it has to follow the hounds.

In general, it is still considered to be more advantageous to hold the reins just with the left hand and the whip with the right one before the jump. If the horse falls, this hand has to use the horse's crest for support as the rider's feet hit the ground. If, at the moment of landing, the rider's upper body is thrown back violently, then he will not only prevent himself from falling if he is supported by hand and leg as just noted, he also makes it easier for the horse to pick its forehand up again, because he is not burdening it. He also avoids falling off to the side. The horse will get up quickly if the rider acts in this way and can be ridden again immediately, provided that it did not suffer injury.

If it is not possible for the rider to maintain the position just described when the horse falls, then he must at least try to roll off of the horse's neck when falling. This is so that, if it falls to the side, he will not be under it. However, it is very important that the rider not let go of the reins so as to prevent the horse from running away. If he does not succeed in keeping the reins in his hand, however, he must be able to get up before the horse. While the horse is still standing there stunned and indecisive after falling, the rider should quickly grab the reins again.

———————

In this section, two types of riding in a natural position of the horse were discussed. The first is used to give very weak horses enough carriage via shortened gaits so that they can be used for ordinary cavalry service. The other is suitable for use with weak as well as strong horses in extended gaits for various purposes.

Both types of this riding style cause premature damage to the horse's forelegs. They do not correspond to the main purpose of dressage, which is "to balance the horse so that it can move the most easily, the most safely, and with the greatest strength and endurance."

Unfortunately, the first type of this riding style will often be used as an emergency measure due to the large number of weak and afflicted horses, but it fulfills its purpose only very imperfectly. The other, in contrast, corresponds perfectly to several essential purposes of the rider. The early exercise of the colts, which can also be considered as a very suitable preparation for the future dressage training, is one of these purposes. Another is to recognize and select the most suitable horses for breeding by testing them on the race track.

Although English riding has spread quickly and widely on the continent, one can generally consider it to be just a fad — with the exception of hunt riding. Although the hunt riding ruins the horses prematurely, it should nevertheless be more widespread and more widely supported because it creates courageous and determined riders.

If it were more generally permitted in Germany to ride across fields and if one could encounter more significant obstacles, then the native horses could be given more opportunity to develop their jumping ability, which they possess if finely bred to a sufficient degree.

English riding in the frequent hunts through the forest is always detrimental to the horse's forelegs to a greater or lesser extent. If the rider is able to keep the horse in balance over such terrain, then he will not only be able to follow the hunt the most quickly and safely, but he will also be able to protect the horse from harm.

If the rider knows how to ride a strong and well-positioned horse according to the principles set out in this work, as well as in the position of balance and in English-style, it will be very expedient to switch between these two styles of riding, depending on the hunting terrain. Horses that fully meet these two demands of the rider will prove to be the most useful over any hunting terrain.

The longer utility of a horse, which one uses only in natural position in the most extended gaits, is conditioned in many cases upon the skillful procedure of the rider, who must combine his aids just as the School and campaign rider must. Its value is often underestimated by those riders, since they do not take into account the difficulties in controlling the horse in its most lengthened gallop, usually due to a lack of experience. The rider, however, who knows how to ride in its natural position in the most extended gaits, or trains them to do so, certainly deserves greater and more general respect from the art connoisseurs than he usually gets in large part. His experiences give him an infallible measure by which to correctly assess the horses and their gaits, as opposed to those who have never practiced this riding have been able to acquire in practical terms.

It is regrettable that the riders who successfully ride horses exclusively in the most extended gaits usually lack the necessary education to help other determined and well-informed riders who wish to acquire the skill for themselves via a well-ordered theory.

Although the lack of such theories is partly replaced by the valuable information in the "Hippological Journal," which has appeared in Germany since the introduction of racing, it is nevertheless to be wished that a work on the most recently discussed riding style would appear that is as systematic as possible.

Appendix

Selecting a horse suitable for any riding service

Since the value of a horse suitable for any riding service depends on developing its natural strength, which is dependent upon its main attributes, speed and agility — the proper interaction of which results in endurance, then the first inspection when selecting such a horse must be on how the parts of its body are put together if it is to be made based on its exterior. This is because this will determine how the horse moves. However, much experience and ability are required to assess how the horse will move while it is standing still. Usually only horse connoisseurs, who pay special attention to the exterior of horses that have distinguished themselves by extraordinary achievements in lengthened gaits, have this ability.

If the riding horse's value could just be determined by its achievements in the extended gaits and by its noble parentage, then horse experts would only need to look at the collected biographies of noble horses, eg. race reports, etc. The more difficult task of assessing the horse by its exterior would then no longer be necessary.

It is vital for someone to know these two types of assessing a horse, however, if he wants to recognize for himself a horse that is fast, as agile as possible, and has stamina.

He who only desires speed and innate stamina in a horse should choose according to the race reports. However, if one also wants agility, and because endurance only arises from the regular exercise of this characteristic, it is necessary to base one's decision mainly on the collected gaits. Achievement and parentage, however, should not be overlooked as often as they are, because one can make a horse more agile than fast with training, and those without it always remain incomplete.

The first question is: How does one assess the forward movement or gait by looking at the horse's exterior while it is standing still?

It has already been explained that distributing the horse's weight from one hind leg to the other in an alternating fashion is what causes the body to move forward. (See General Section). The muscles that transfer the weight of the forehand to the hindquarters, which causes the movement, are not in the legs. Instead, they run along the entire spine and are attached to the spinous processes. Because the forward movement or the horse's gait is determined by the energy of this muscular activity, the spine from the croup on deserves special consideration in the initial assessment of a horse. This is because it is the connecting beam between the forehand and hindquarters, and not the four legs.

Therefore, when choosing a horse for the riding service, one should not first turn one's attention to the legs, either to look for strong bones or to discover one fault or the other, and if one finds one, regard the horse as not worthy of further consideration. Only those less experienced in the natural sciences think they can determine the animal's strength by its legs, or even in the larger volume of its bones. Without properly developed muscles and tendons, the greatest power of which emanates from the haunches, the larger bone mass is useless in the riding horse. Although the flaws in the limbs need not be overlooked, their conformation, the way they are connected to the rump by more or less substantial muscles, and the presumptive shape of the bones to which they are attached deserve more attention than minor leg defects that do not cause lameness. The strength of these muscles determines the action of the hind legs and the position of the backbone.

When assessing a horse, it is necessary that it be standing without a blanket on level ground with its four legs vertically under it and positioned straight.

The inspection of the horse begins with the careful examination of the position of the pelvis, the croup, the loins, the spine, the shoulders and the chest, along with the surrounding muscles. The width, length, and substance of these muscles suggest the dimensions of important underlying structures. The larger bone volume proves to be just as useful here as in the extremities.

The position of the fixed parts can be seen to some extent, and with some experience in inspecting, can be assumed with reasonable certainty.

After all this, the expert will know how to deduce whether the horse has good gaits or bad ones. If the horse's conformation does not correspond to his wishes, then he will avoid wasting time and effort by continuing the examination.

Step behind the horse to examine the hips. They should be far apart from each other, and must appear prominent rather than short and rounded. The position of the hip bones should be between horizontal and vertical. Between the hips lies the croup, extending from the last lumbar vertebra to the dock of the tail. If it is of significant length, then its horizontal position is not a sign of weakness. A short croup must be more rounded rather than sloping or slanted, if it is not in a straight line. The shape and position of the hips and the croup will determine the strong position of the muscles surrounding them. They cannot be too wide or long. If this is the case, then all of these parts that make up the haunches have a nice shape in addition to possessing strength.

The long and visibly divided muscles on the outside of both buttocks and upper legs cannot be too broad. In addition, there must be enough muscle mass on the inside of these parts so that the hind legs are not visibly separated from one another.

The haunches shaped in this way always indicate great strength. This is also revealed when the examining expert, standing behind the horse, sees that the strongly protruding muscles of the croup and, if he steps a little to the right and left, those of the buttocks and upper legs almost lie on the same plane with the hips.

After inspecting the croup, it is necessary to stand at the horse's side and examine the kidney or lumbar region. This is the next most important part of the examination. It is perfect if it is not too long, has significant breadth, and much muscle mass. One can judge this part best from above.

Rarely is a long and narrow kidney region associated with a strong croup, as previously mentioned. However, if this is the case, the horse's hindquarters usually make a swaying motion when it goes forward. Such horses are never fast and have endurance at the same time. They also present great difficulties in dressage and tire easily under heavy weight. If the horses also have weak haunches, then they can almost never be used for the riding service.

The next part of the assessment is the back. It begins with the withers — the higher the better. This speaks to the high position of the first vertebra, and consequently, to the propensity to go in balance (see General Section). If they are flat, this points to the chest cavity not being very deep. One can conclude that it has little stamina. In addition, the shoulders have less room to move freely if the withers are not only low, but also wide.

These drawbacks of badly shaped withers are combined with the bad position of the saddle, which rides up on the shoulders. This makes it almost impossible for the rider to distribute his weight equally on the forehand and hindquarters. The withers of donkeys and mules are low and their shoulders are flat. This makes them uncomfortable to ride. No saddle stays on them well without a crupper.

The somewhat low and even hollow back, which is called "swayback," is comfortable for the rider. As long as the horses are ridden in shortened and collected gaits, this is not disadvantageous. Regardless of its length and propensity for greater speed, the hunting horse needs strength in the back and lumbar muscles, which is more greatly developed in the higher position of the spine to carry the burden of the rider over obstacles. Its back must be almost straight, of average length, and well connected to the shoulders and loins. Roach backs that are too high have opposite disadvantages for the rider.

A long back is associated with greater speed, but also causes fatigue more quickly. If the horse has a short back, its movements are more restricted. If connected with a short croup, the hind feet usually grab the front shoes and often pull them loose. This also makes an unpleasant noise that the rider can hear when he lets the horse trot out in the extended gait. However, a horse with a short back is usually very strong and suited to strenuous work.

The next part of the horse to be assessed is the chest. It is seldom properly examined even though it contains the most vital organs.

The shape of the chest can best be judged by standing to the side of the horse rather than in front of it. This is because the good characteristics of the chest depend on the length and curvature of the ribs, and not on the width between the two points of the shoulder.

The rider encircling the horse's chest with his legs is the best judge of the correct breadth of the horse. It is well-formed if he sees a lot of volume in front of his knees and feels a lot between them. Horses with a narrow chest stand with the front legs close together, and are, therefore, of little value.

The depth of the chest is indicated by the vertical line from the fourth vertebra to the sternum. Since this vertebra has the longest process, one can correctly assume a deep chest if it has high withers.

A broad chest allows so much space for the respiratory organs that their performance can be brought to the utmost perfection by proper exercise. In the case of the horse's swift movements, speed and endurance mainly depend upon this. Horses with a narrow chest do not become fatigued because they lack the muscle strength, but rather because they run out of breath due to low lung function. If the chest, viewed from the front, is very wide, this also impedes the horse's speed. This is partly because of greater air resistance, and partly because of the larger circumference over which the effect of the muscles must spread.

Along with the three main parts of the rump that have been discussed, the croup, the back, and the chest are also to be regarded as the horse's real foundation (its power). If these parts are shaped as described here, then they will adequately make up for any deficiencies in the horse's conformation. However, if they correspond too little to the conformation that is indicated here, then even if all of the other parts of the horse are perfect, one will never be able to expect the same achievements that one may expect from a horse with a good foundation.

Along with the examination of the horse's individual body parts, one should also conduct an assessment of the state of the horse's health. In fact, examine each side of the chest just behind the elbow to see if there are any noticeable signs of inunction or *Haarseil*.[4] These can be assumed to be evidence that the horse has already suffered from pulmonary diseases. The respiration must later be tested by a lively gallop, as it can be assumed that, as is often the case, lung maladies persist after illnesses. Also, the skin on the chest between the two front legs should be thoroughly examined for the same reasons.

If the hair is sparse, bristly and going in different directions, then this betrays a recently performed inunction. Small, bare, nodular spots are signs that *Haarseils* or *Fontanelles* have been applied.[5] One should not assume that one of these markings indicate that a horse is unhealthy. They are merely evidence that the horse has been treated for a disease that often results in lasting maladies.

Standing behind the horse, compare the two hips to each other to see if they protrude the same amount. It is often the case that a piece of the hip bone has broken off in some accident. If it is small in size and if the horse is not lame, it should only be considered to be a cosmetic defect.

The scrotum will sometimes contain a soft, swollen mass, which can be compressed. It varies from the size of an egg to that of a child's head. It is formed by the presence of the

---

[4] Translator's note: *Haarseil* was a surgical method in which a string of horse hair was threaded into the skin to cause pus to form.

[5] Translator's note: *Fontanelle* was the insertion of a pea into a cut to cause pus to form.

intestines. It is usually only found in one testicle of stallions. ("Scrotal hernia.")

Because this disease is so rare, the scrotum is less frequently examined. However, it should be carefully examined when buying a young horse, especially one intended to be a breeding stallion. This should be done whether both testicles are present or removed, or in other words, if the horse is a stallion, gelding, or cryptorchid. It is not advisable to buy the latter. Recognizing this presupposes the ability to judge correctly.

The examination now turns to the four legs, and for now, how they are connected to the body, then their position to the body and to each other.

How the hind legs and front legs connect to the horse's rump can differ as much as their purposes. In other words, the hind legs carry the body and propel it or push it forward, while the forefeet are only suited to carrying.

Via the femoral head fitting into the socket of the pelvis, which it half encloses, the hind legs receive a steady point of attachment to the body, which becomes even more fixed by the fact that the upper part of the femoral head attaches to a strong, short sinewy membrane at the bottom of the pelvis without, however, hindering the free articulation of the joint. This allows a spiral movement as do the points of the shoulder in the front.

The connection of the front legs to the chest is less internal and not created by two bone ends meeting in a joint, but rather they are attached to the shoulders by means of muscles and tissue. This way of connecting the shoulder to the rump is also necessary because of the freer mobility and the greater length of the shoulders.

It is of no benefit, however, if there is too much mobility in the joints connecting the hind legs to the body in regard to the rider's use of the horse. On the contrary, he must get control over them and use them to free the forelegs.

Even the greatest burdening of the hind legs by means of the halt will never cause the femoral head to pop out of the pelvis as can sometimes occur. The cause of this dislocation is always either due to the horse falling down when it slips, or a local injury that was very forceful.

The different places where the body connects to the front and hind legs that have been mentioned are never the cause of stiff hip joints or lameness, or at least rarely, as is usually believed. However, rheumatic ailments easily arise where the front legs connect to the body. Moreover, the shoulder point is exposed to more external influences, as it is closer to the horse's skin than is the hip joint.

On a horse with good conformation, the distance between the two shoulder points is exactly the same as between the two hip joints. This equality determines the correct position of the four feet to each other.

If one stands in front of one of the front legs, and if one notices that the middle of the coronary band of the hoof lies vertically below the point of the shoulder, then the leg is well-set. If it covers the hind leg at the same time, then the same is true for the hind leg. The middle of the hind coronary band will then be almost vertically below the patella.

The horse's feet, correctly connected to the rump, should neither be positioned too far out nor too far in. Of these two cases, however, the former is less detrimental.

The position of the front leg, viewed from the side, is more correct the closer the vertical line comes from it to the tip of the withers.

On the hind leg, the stifle should be on the line of the haunches and almost in a straight line under the hips. It is better for the distance of this joint from the hock joint to be long rather than short. This is because the tendency to go forward arises mainly from the greater length, although the horse's endurance depends on this less.

The angle that the femur makes with the cannon bone must be too obtuse rather than too acute. A line from the posterior part of the buttocks, drawn vertically, should also hit at least the tip of the calcaneus if the horse is standing correctly on its four feet.

The initial assessment of the horse with respect to its exterior is hereby concluded. The examination of the horse's other characteristics now begins, as usual, with its forehand.

No definite measure can be determined for the most suitable height for a horse. This is because it must be in proportion to the size of the rider. Horses of average height with wide rumps and short legs are more suitable for any rider and are preferable to the overly tall horses, which are usually narrow and leggy, and not very comfortable. In general, when choosing a good riding horse, its width, which has already been described, should be taken into account more than the fact that it is too tall.

The horse's height is determined by a vertical line from the tip of the withers to the sole of the hoof. It is obtained in three ways, either by the hand measure, by the angle measure, or by comparing it to the body size of the examining person, which is preferable because it is the simplest way. One can also acquire great skill in it with some practice.

The average height of a horse is 5'2" to 3". If it is of this size as described above and has good movements, then it will be suitable for any use as a riding horse. When worn out, it can still be used for pulling better than an overly tall horse. The medium-sized horse also has the advantage that it is more sure-footed over terrain with obstacles, easier to collect, and therefore, easier to maneuver in turns. Even if the overly large, leggy, and therefore, long-strided horse is faster in a test of speed over a short distance, the medium-sized horse will win over longer distances in most cases.

The horse's age is an important subject of the inspection that follows. Usually, checking the front teeth of the lower jaw is sufficient.

Although few horses will be on the market before the age of three, many riders may wish to know how the foals' teeth erupt and change as the horses age.

The horse is subject to the secondary dentition just as humans and all four-legged animals are. The first teeth that come in, the "milk teeth," remain only for a certain period.

The six to eight-month-old foals usually have all 12 milk teeth. Soon after they turn two years old, these fall out two at a time. This makes room for the permanent or "horse teeth." These teeth, also twelve in number, are fully visible when the horse turns five years old. At this point, it is called "adult," and it now has 12 molars, two canine teeth, and six incisors in each jaw.

Each of the permanent incisors has an oval hollow area on the surface when it first erupts in the jaw, which narrows towards the bottom of the tooth. This is called the "valley." If the teeth are worn down by friction, then gradually the width and depth of these valleys disappear until they finally become completely invisible. As this occurs in certain periods, the general decrease in the valley gives the surest indication of the horse's age. It is a mistake to say that "the valleys are filled in." This is not the case, as they are rubbed by the upper teeth.

The following explanations concern only the formation of and the change in the lower incisor teeth.

About eight or ten days after birth, two incisors, called the "nippers," appear in the middle of the jaw. Between the second and fourth month, two others emerge to the side of each nipper. These are called "central incisors." Between the sixth and eighth months, a third pair, called "cuspids," appears next to them. From that time on until the permanent teeth appear, one can tell the age by the valley of each tooth.

In the twelfth month, the valleys of the two nippers are completely obliterated. They are also diminished in the central incisors. At eighteen months, these four teeth no longer have any valleys. The surface of the nippers becomes almost triangular, in that, depending on how they are worn down, the tooth takes on the shape of the root.

At two years of age, the valleys of all six teeth are obliterated, and the nippers appear significantly narrower than the other teeth. They become loose after 2 1/2 years, fall out and make room for the first permanent teeth, which quickly reach a height equal to the remaining four milk teeth. They are wider and darker than the milk teeth. On their surface, called the "crown," they have a deep groove that is quite different from the hollow of the milk teeth.

From this period onwards, the colt is often the subject of deceptive trade practices. It can be made big and fat by means of soft and nourishing food. It can be made to appear to be four years old, partly to sell it for more money, and partly to save a few months of food and maintenance.

For this purpose, the lower milk teeth are pulled. This is so that the permanent central incisors can grow in faster. As a result, the horse can be sold as a four year old for more money. However, it is really only a few months over three years old.

This fraud can be easily detected by examining the teeth in the upper jaw, if the animal's juvenile appearance is not sufficient proof that it is not yet mature enough for work.

The permanent central incisors usually appear at three and a half years of age. Even before the colt is four years old, they stick out as far as the baby corner incisors, which now turn yellow at the top and lose in circumference where they connect to the jaw.

At four and a half years old, the permanent corner incisors erupt. When the horse is five years old, they stand at the same height as the others. Shortly before that, the canine teeth appear, but the majority of the mares do not have canines. From now on, the colts are called "horses."

At six years old, one no longer notices the valleys in the nippers. At the age of seven, the valleys of the central incisors, and at eight, those of the corner incisors have disappeared. The valleys of the upper teeth, which are later obliterated, are not a reliable indicator of age. This is because the teeth wear down extremely irregularly. One will hardly find four horses whose upper teeth look the same, even if they are the same age.

These merit as little consideration as the canine teeth in this regard. Even though there may be some truth in accepting them as markers with respect to the change, their height, sharpness, and the degree of obliteration of their valleys are so irregular and subject to the action of the natural dentition to such a degree that, in most cases, it is futile to use them to form an opinion. Rarely can one find two cuspids that are alike, even in the same jaw.

After the eighth year, it is difficult to determine the horse's age using the incisors in the lower jaw. Nevertheless, one may be required to use them if a definite opinion is needed. Their shape, although by no means as certain a marker as their valley, is characteristic enough to enable us to approximately estimate the age of an older horse, although it may be a year or two off. Nobody will be able to claim that they can determine the age after this time. This is because it is practically impossible to draw an infallible conclusion for the reasons that have been cited.

At ten years old, the nippers are narrower on their surface rather than being almost oval, as they were at the age of seven. They are also narrower from one side to the other and wider from front to back. At the age of eleven, the surface of the central incisors, and at the age of twelve, that of the corner incisors takes this shape, which gradually begins to resemble a triangle.

The further determination is difficult and without great benefit. This is because, if a horse is over twelve years old but still under twenty and is still fresh and strong, it is almost irrelevant whether it is several years older or younger. If it had been handled well in its early years, it will be just as useful in its fourteenth or sixteenth year as many a horse of ten years that were worked too soon and too hard.

Besides the teeth, it is possible to recognize the horse's age by its appearance. If it is very old or worn-out (words that can now be considered to be synonymous), then it is excessively lazy, seemingly blind to the surrounding objects, heedless to whip and to the trainer's voice, and seemingly insensitive to pain. The gray hair on the eyebrows and the forehead, the sunken eye pits, and the droopy lower lip give such horses a particularly pitiful look.

Although the teeth are continuously worn down, they seem to grow longer with age. The reason for this is that the gums that surround the teeth recede over time.

Horses that graze in sandy pastures lose their valleys sooner than those fed in their stalls because their teeth are worn down more quickly by the harder, sandy fodder.

A fraud that is used to make valleys must be mentioned. The surface of the valleys of the teeth are hollowed out with a chisel designed specifically for this purpose. They are then burned out with a hot iron or with calcium fluoride acid. This usually only happens with the corner incisors of eight to ten-year-old horses, which are then presented as seven-year-olds. This is done to the central incisors and the other teeth to make the horses appear to be five or six years old. However, one can recognize that a horse is twelve years old or even several years older by the shape and length of the teeth.

These frauds can be identified partly by the roughness of the sides where the teeth were hollowed out, and partly from the unnatural darkness of the valley, but mainly from the lack of the enamel ring that surrounds every natural valley. This, along with the length of the entire tooth and the shape of the tooth's surface, can reveal the deception. Such "rejuvenated" horses usually are reluctant to have their teeth inspected. This is because they are afraid of experiencing a repeat of the pain they suffered during the operation.

Along with the examination of the age, one looks at the four front incisors for signs of "cribbing," also called "crib biting," "wind sucking," etc. If the older horse has this bad habit, these teeth will appear ground down on the outer edges. The impression left behind by the straps of the cribbing collar, which is used to prevent cribbing, is often still evident near the place where the head and neck connect. In young horses, cribbing can only be discovered by giving them the opportunity to do it. They grasp the manger with the teeth, press the head back against the chest and swallow air, emitting a grunting sound.

The disadvantages caused by "cribbing" are not as great as one might expect. They are often limited to fodder being strewn about, because the animal starts to crib while eating and drops the food that is in its mouth onto the ground. Often, even this does not happen. If the horse is otherwise good and corresponds to the requirements made, one should not be afraid to purchase it. This is especially true because, in most cases, this bad habit will lead to a reduction in the purchase price.

With regard to the "eye examination" of the horse, it is particularly important to know the diseases of the eye.

Describing these diseases individually with their outcomes would digress too much. Therefore, only the main maladies, which are often the consequences of earlier illnesses, will be addressed.

To examine the eyes, do not look at them in bright light at first. The pupil dilates in dim light, which allows one to look inside the eye. Afterward, quickly put the horse in the light and watch the sudden contraction of the pupil.

A not uncommon but usually minor eye defect consists of a darkening of a part of the transparent cornea. Such a darkening, called "wall eye," is easy to recognize.

Such corneal spots interfere with the vision to a greater or lesser degree, depending on their size and location. They are the reason why horses that are afflicted with it tend to shy. If the spots reach a significant size, namely in the lower half of the eye, then the horse should be considered blind. It is incorrect to view the corneal spots as untreatable. They are generally difficult to eliminate, especially if they have been present in old animals for a long time, but no such spot should be pronounced as incurable in advance.

Apart from the corneal spots, the most common is the "cataract." It consists of the crystalline lens being impossible to see through, and is not always easy to recognize. In its emergence, the cataract is a small white dot at the back of the eye. This gradually increases in size without changing very noticeably until it causes complete blindness. However, before this occurs, the disease is visible to everyone, even from a distance, on the contracted triangular shape of the upper edge of the eyelid. In the first stage, the cataract is best recognized when the horse is led out of the bright light and into the shade. Then, as mentioned, the dilated pupil allows viewing into the inside of the eye. When there is cataract, one notices a small milky-white point in the interior of the eye. It is brighter and whiter at its center, and more transparent at its periphery. Make sure it is not just a reflection of a bright or shiny part of the garment worn by the person examining it. Therefore, in order to not be deceived, hold the brim of one's hat (if it is black) opposite the eye, and observe if the white point vanishes, which it will do if it were just caused by a reflection. Less common is "glaucoma." This is a degeneration of the so-called vitreous body that lies in the posterior chamber of the eye. The eye does not appear to be diseased at first blush, but upon closer examination, one will notice a greenish substance within the eye. This, along with impaired vision, characterizes glaucoma.

Another important eye disease is periodic eye inflammation, otherwise known as "moon blindness."

In the case of this disease, the eye appears slightly greenish, but the pupil remains constricted despite the change of light. It remains only as wide as the back of a knife. Bald patches on the cheeks, which are caused by draining tears, can also serve as a sign of eye maladies. However, this does not mean that if these are found, moon blindness is also present. This is because it is very common for the tears associated with moon blindness to not be very frequent or stinging.

Since only experts can recognize periodic eye inflammation on one hand, and they disappear at certain times, but return later and ultimately cause complete blindness on the other, Prussian law has established a period of 28 days from the date of sale within which time this disease may not appear. If it does, then the purchase can be rescinded, if necessary.

The most significant eye disease of this kind is "amaurosis." It consists of a paralysis of the optic nerve or the retina (the skin on the inside of the eye), without having any further effect on the eyeball. It is associated with vision loss. Since its recognition presupposes specific expertise and the disease only appears long after its initial cause, a legal warranty period of 28 days has also been established for it.

Other diseases of the eye are of lesser importance than those just given, for the most part. To mention them all here and to present their symptoms would be to digress too much, nor does it belong here. If one should discover an eye disease in a horse and cannot give an account of it oneself, then it is advisable to consult with an expert and to make any purchase contingent upon his opinion.

When observing the horse's head and neck, it is advantageous for the horse's movement if they are not too heavy. A heavy head hinders the School gaits the least, the campaign gaits more, and the gaits of the horse that goes in its natural position under the rider the most. It usually leans hard on the hand, is more prone to stumbling, and becomes insensitive in front sooner than it would under more favorable conditions.

The weight of the head usually determines the strength of the neck. Just as a short, thick neck is suited to a heavy head, a thinner, less arched and shorter rather than longer neck is suitable for a lighter head.

This is probably sufficient for what shape the horse's head and neck should be, as it relates to all riding uses.

The head should be small and slender. The moderately long neck should be wide rather than narrow. This width must be formed by the muscles that run along both sides of its upper part. From the withers to the head, it may arch moderately in the middle, but certainly not form a high neck or a "fat neck." Even the so-called "ewe-neck" would be preferable to a neck that is too heavily laden on top.

The windpipe must be broad and freely connected to the neck, so that the air has an unobstructed passageway going to and from the lungs.

Although less important for the horse's soundness as it relates to the conformation, but rather just pertaining to its elegance, the ears should be small and pointed, the eyes gleaming and large, and the forehead wide and flat.

If this is combined with a dish-like formation in the face from the lower part of the forehead to the nostrils, then the head acquires a beautiful shape. From this point downwards, the nose itself must be convex. The nostrils must appear wide, so that when the horse goes fast, the respiration is increased. The surrounding red mucous membrane can be easily seen when the horse is breathing hard.

The various movements of the ears and the nostrils betray the will at the moment, and thus the horse's disposition. It is not so much for the rider to study the latter as for horse handlers. It is of special interest to those who paint horses and draw pictures of them.

When both ears are laid back against the back of the head together or one after the other, this shows duplicity, and along with widely flared nostrils, which take on an almost rectangular shape, the greatest anger in the horse. Good-naturedness, on the other hand, is indicated by relaxed tips of the ears and by nostrils that retain their natural oval shape.

A small labial commissure and thin, tight lips make the head beautiful. It can move the most freely where it connects to the neck, if the lower jaws taper at the back from where the ear begins to their center, and if there is a wide space between the lower jawbones (the throat).

Concerning the diseases and defects in the parts mentioned above, one can conclude that there is a "malady of the mucous membrane" or "strangles" if there is a discharge of a thick mucus from the nostrils. Although it is rare for horses with glandular diseases to be put up for sale, there are plenty of cases in which inexperienced people have been sold horses with glanders. This is done by concealing the symptoms of the disease. Even though the law has established a guarantee of fourteen days for such cases, the damage caused by a horse with glanders is often irreparable.

The young horses usually receive the best care in the merchant's stable, but little exercise, on a daily basis. Therefore, subjecting them to strenuous riding tests before the sale are too much effort for them. As a result, they usually develop strangles after sale in the buyer's stable. This is especially true if they receive worse care than before. Foreseeing this, the buyer should be on his guard. It may well come to pass that the horse, as a result of the effort just mentioned, catches cold, gets pneumonia, and dies.

A thin, liquid discharge from the nose is the first indication of a cold. Even slight pressure on the larynx causes the horse pain. Although many a horse suffering from colds are purchased with no adverse consequences, the buyer should never put such a horse to work immediately as he would a healthy one. A few days of rest, a well-ventilated stall, and feeding it warm bran mash a few times are sufficient to eliminate the malady in many cases.

If the horse that one has just purchased only "coughs" from time to time and is free of discomfort, then it does not warrant any further consideration. Such a cough often soon goes away again. However, if the cough is raspy, dry, and if it occurs after feeding and drinking, or after the horse gets into the open air, it can be concluded that it is chronic. Although it is not very detrimental to the horse's health, it always remains unpleasant, if only to the ear. In such cases, the buyer would probably do best to first seek the advice of an expert.

If the horse has swollen throat glands, then one must examine the nasal mucosa membrane more closely. If there is a viscous, yellowish, sticky discharge, then this is very alarming. This is true even if there are no ulcers on the mucous membranes yet, which characterize glanders.

If there is no nasal discharge, then hardened glands that have been present for a long time are the result of earlier colds and are harmless.

The next part of the horse to be considered is the abdominal cavity or the belly.

It should have the shape of a cylinder from the girth to the flanks. If this is the case, then there will be enough room for the digestive organs.

The abdomen of a horse with a good shape keeps the balance between fat and thin. Horses with a fat belly and fat, overly full flanks cannot be fast. They must be distinguished from those with a slender body and rounded ribs. This always indicates strength, agility at a run, and the ability to "go under heavy weight." It is less common for horses with shallow flanks to have the good qualities mentioned above.

Regarding the desirable front leg position for the rider and how they are connected to the horse's body, it has already been established that feet that turn out are preferable to ones that turn in. This is because there is less danger that one foot will hit or strike another in this case than in the latter.

The shoulders should not slope at too great of an angle toward the front of the chest. The surrounding musculature must protrude, but not be too fleshy. There should be no fat that obscures the position or the path of each individual muscle.

The neck and shoulders should be connected in such a way that the neck seems to be sunk into the shoulders. The point of the shoulder should not stick out sharply, but rather be flat.

The forearm should be broad and long. Mainly at the top part, both on the inside and outside, it should have muscles so voluminous that there is only a moderate space between the forelegs directly under the chest. The definition of these muscles should be clearly visible. The elbow is at the top back part of the forearm; it runs parallel with the rump when the foot is well set.

The front knee or carpal joint must appear to be large and perfectly straight when viewed from the side, but appear wide and flat from the front.

If it is bent forward, it is said that the horse is "buck-kneed." Such horses are usually under a lot of strain already. Therefore, one must not reckon on the safety of their movements. The knee that is bent toward the back is called "calf-kneed." This ugly defect, which is detrimental to the horse's durability, is due to weakness in the knee's flexor muscles. It should not be considered to be minor.

If deviations from the straight, strong position of the front knee are allowed, then a slight bend forward is not as great a disadvantage as the calf-knee.

The cannon bone, which runs from knee to fetlock, must be fine, flat, and not too long when viewed from the front and back. However, when seen from the side, especially at the top just below the knee, it cannot appear to be too wide due to the broad and clearly defined flexor tendons that run along the length of the entire leg. These must lie free, as it were, and separate from it.

Just like the knee joint, the fetlock joint must also be large and wide. Although the short and almost upright pastern reveals much strength and endurance, and is therefore, very expedient for gaits that are not too extended, they do not further the speed of the horse or the comfort of the rider. Long and sloping pasterns bend more with each step, whereby the elasticity of the pastern lessens the impact caused by a fast gallop. The best pasterns are those that are a balance between the former and the latter.

If the pastern is too long, the leg is very susceptible to sprains. If the horse is driven to exceed its natural speed, then it is prone to collapsing. If the pasterns are too upright, then the horse goes as though on stilts, and is, therefore, very uncomfortable. As a result of the more severe shock to the bones under the knee, it easily suffers from "ringbone" or the so-called "knuckling over."

The hooves should be as round as possible. The keratin walls should be smooth and show no sign of porosity or of "brittle hoof," in which the keratin pieces break off around the nail holes. The heels must be open. The frogs should look dry and healthy and emit no nasty odor. The sole should be only moderately concave. If it is flat, then, especially in the case of horses with high and very plodding action, it is to be feared that they will become convex over time. This is because these conditions often lead to hoof inflammation, which then results in the so-called "dropped sole."

The front knee requires a special examination because "bald spots" on the front are almost always a sign that the horse is already lame in front. Even if the spot with no skin originated due to an accident, the general opinion speaks against it. As a result, the horse's value suffers.

Just below the knee joint on the inside, bald spots can occasionally be found, and the lowest of the seven knee-joint bones is raised. This is due to the other foot striking it. This is found only in horses with too high action in the extended trot. This fault, which can be called "interference," deserves consideration when choosing a horse for extended movements.

A bone distention is often located between the knee and the fetlock joint on the inside. This is called a "bone spur." It sometimes causes lameness as it forms, but once it has developed, the lameness disappears again. Only if the bone spur grows in size or is sharp under the tendons such that it interferes with their activity does it cause lasting impairment.

If, on the other hand, the tendons do not lie freely along the cannon bone, then an inflammation of the tendons, "Tendinitis," is usually the cause. Horses with long pasterns are often prone to this malady if the fetlock overextends. If the swelling is significant, then it always remains doubtful whether it will completely heal.

It is difficult for some to detect tendinitis as it first emerges, if one does not compare both legs to each other.

Rarely is this disease found in both legs at the same time, but if it is, then usually to a differing degree.

Older cases of tendinitis have often contracted so much that they are invisible to the eye. If one runs the thumb and the first two fingers down along the tendons, however, one will easily be convinced that this malady is present.

Bristly hair is a sign of previous inunctions. This does not necessitate special examinations in the first instance.

"Wind puffs" (enlargements of the tendon sheaths and joint capsules filled with fluid) are often found on the fetlock joint. Therefore, it must be examined thoroughly, both with the eye as well as by feel. These are evidence that the horse has already had to endure strain.

The inside of the fetlock joint, like the knee joint, should also be examined with regard to "interference" and be compared to the other leg.

A bone spur called "ringbone" is often located on the cannon bone. It is easy to recognize by its elevation. Although horses that have it can go for years without lameness, it always remains questionable whether to buy a horse afflicted with it.

The "hoof crack" is a separation of the hoof wall. It is usually on the inside of the hoof with a length of 1/2 inch, but it can run the entire length of the hoof. If this crack has wax or some resinous substance stuck onto it, then it often escapes the buyer's notice. Although the horse is not always noticeably lame with a hoof crack, it usually shows up if the horse is subjected to prolonged and strenuous work on hard ground. The "sand crack," which splits the hoof cross-wise, has the same disadvantages as the hoof crack.

With "contracted heels," the hoof is narrower across than it is long and the heels are more or less contracted. Often, however, this hoof conformation is not detrimental.

When one hoof is contracted more than the other, this is usually a consequence of earlier lameness, which may well have its root cause either in the leg or in the hoof.

If "thrush" is discovered while examining the bottom surface of the hoof, then it must by no means be regarded as insignificant and overlooked. One identifies it by the discharge of a smelly liquid when squeezing the heels of the hoof, or by the fact that the frog is narrow, soft, and shriveled up. The horse with thrush has a lower value than it would otherwise, as lameness often develops, which may become significant when worked on hard ground. However, if the horse is otherwise good, and the thrush is only just emerging, i. e. not yet associated with significant discharge, then it is not difficult to cure this ailment.

"Stone bruises" cannot be detected without first removing the horseshoes. One should be suspicious if there is a higher temperature in the hoof heels and one cannot find any other cause for the lameness. They are found on the heels between the wall and the frog. At first, there is some blood under the sole. This makes the keratin appear red in color. The stone bruises are at first not a significant problem. However, if they are festering, then one always does well to retain the advice of an expert before purchasing the horse.

The "dropped sole" has already been mentioned; the "flat hoof" can be considered as a lesser degree of this malady. In both, the position of the hoof wall is very sloping. Rings form on their outer surface, hence the term "ring hoof."

One should always examine the horseshoe, especially to see if the horse interferes. This can usually be prevented by making the inner branch of the horseshoe considerably thicker.

The nails are usually only hammered around the toe on the outside. This branch of the horseshoe is thus positioned so low and under that the hoof protrudes over it a bit.

If the toe of the front horseshoe, if not somewhat new, is very worn, then one can conclude that the horse interferes. As a result, it does not move safely.

If the horse's free movement is affected by "laminitis," then this can be recognized partly by the altered shape of the hoof, and partly by the modified stepping of the feet. Instead of bringing the sole of the hoof into contact with the ground on all of its points at the same time, the horse first steps onto the heel. This is best seen if one has the horse trot straight toward him. However, a previous case of laminitis is best characterized by the shaky movement of the front feet. This ailment not only hinders the free movement of the horse, but it also returns after exposure to minor causes, such as a bit of prolonged use on hard ground. In this case, it usually makes the horse lame forever.

Now the hind legs will be considered. The conformation of the hock joint can really only be tested when the horse is moving because it determines the springiness of the hindquarters. All too often are the value and choice of a horse determined almost exclusively by the external conformation of its hock joints while the horse is standing still. The position of the body parts, which comprise the foundation, receive too little consideration as they relate to the hocks — the source of the horse's power.

If the hock joint is free of defects, if the whole leg is well-set on a strong croup, and if the femur is long rather than short, then there will always be enough springiness, assuming that the rider knows how to develop it. This strength can be developed to an almost unbelievable extent, if the hock joint appears very wide when viewed from the side, due to a significantly long calcaneus. This forms the real lever of the hock joint. At a certain length, the muscles work to stretch the leg out more, especially the Achilles tendon. As the pushing property of the hind legs is conditioned on this extension, the width of the hock joint, which is attributed to the length of the calcaneus, is of great importance to horses used in fast and extended gaits, such as racehorses, for example. On the other hand, the flexor tendon, which runs down along the front surface of the hock joint, also deserves closer attention if the horse is to be as willing to collect as to extend under the rider.

In addition to strong haunches, the position of the legs will have to be a main consideration. If, for example, the points of the hocks are too close together, then they are "cow-hocked." Horses built in this way are usually good trotters, but they are difficult to keep collected in jump-like movements. This is because the sudden burden on the hind legs causes them pain. Regardless, the cow-hocked position is to be preferred by far to one in which the hock joints point outwards.

The hock joint is correctly positioned and has the correct shape for the purpose just stated, namely to further the horse's speed, agility and endurance, when it is in the middle between the two faulty positions just mentioned. If it appears to be free of defects and not "swollen," its quality will be confirmed by the horse's movement.

The rear cannon bone or radial bone should not be too long, just as in the front. Similarly, it should be wide, flat, and straight. Horses with very long cannon bones move more easily and are more agile in School movements, but are not as fast.

The cannon bone and the femur should form only an insignificant angle with the hock joint. The toe of the hoof must be placed with a moderately sloping position of the pastern almost vertically under the stifle joint. The conformation of the tendons and the fetlock joint can be the same as described earlier with the forelegs. However, the shape of the hoof should be more of an oval.

The hooves of the forelegs and the hocks of the hind legs are, in general, the parts that are subject to diseases more than any other part of the horse. Hence, they deserve special attention.

Growths are sometimes found on the calcaneus under the skin on the Achilles tendon or in their sheaths. These "nodules" are usually only considered to be a cosmetic defect, and are normally a consequence of previous bruises or injuries.

A growth located on the posterior side of the lower end of the hock joint, which originates in the tendon sheaths, is known as "curb."

The "curb" is best seen if the buyer takes a few steps to the side of the hock joint. If it is of a limited size, then it is less disadvantageous for horses that are to be used for extended movements than for those that are to undergo a regular dressage training. In this case, even the smallest curb makes it inadvisable to buy the horse.

The "thoroughpins" are of the same nature as the wind puffs on the fetlock joints. These are usually of lesser significance than the "curb," unless they are very large or chronic. They are located both on the inside and outside of the hock joint.

The "bone spavin" is a diseased condition of the small bones where they connect to the lower inside part of the hock joint. The spavin often extends from between the joint surfaces all the way to the upper edge of the cannon bone. This common condition usually causes lameness.

Recognizing spavin is often not very easy to do. To the contrary, a horse can be noticeably lame without being able to say with certainty whether this was due to spavin or some other malady. It is a mistake to assume that there is no spavin if one cannot see it. This is because its emergence is imperceptible and it grows slowly. Inflammation and pain are associated with it from the very beginning. These precede the exudation of tissue fluid. The horse may already be lame from spavin before a noticeable bony distention indicates the presence of the disease. The lameness associated with spavin is peculiar in its appearance. It can be identified by the inflexibility of the hock joint or a pulling motion of the leg, which is lifted up higher off of the ground. The lameness in horses suffering from spavin usually lasts from its emergence to its formation, and then transitions to stiffness in the hock joint. However, this stage of the disease in its lesser degrees is often not recognized as spavin. If one picks up the leg, which is suspected of being afflicted with spavin, and squeezes the hock joint for a few moments, then the lameness is more obvious if one has the horse trot away immediately after releasing the foot.

The horse afflicted with spavin is always less lame after it has been going for a while. Thus, it would not be advisable to buy a horse that one can see has been ridden before the examination without being particularly cautious.

There is occasionally a distention of a blood vessel, the hock joint vein, on the hock joint. This "blood spavin" is of no consequence, as it is not associated with any significant disadvantages.

The parts under the hock joints are worthy of just as intense an examination as previously prescribed in the observation of the front extremities. Possible defects can be assessed by standing in front of the horse.

After the most exacting examination of the individual parts of the horse at a stand still, it is necessary to also closely observe how it moves. This is because significant faults that cause lameness may have been overlooked, which only become apparent when the horse is moving.

In order to discover such flaws most easily, have the horse be led on stone pavement, and do not allow its head to be held high. This is because lameness is easily recognized by the bobbing of the head. Thus, some try to conceal lameness by holding the head high, which makes it impossible for the horses to move their heads. Let the horse be led with long reins first in the walk and then in the trot. Pay attention to both the movement of the head and neck, as well as the legs. If both forefeet or both hind feet are lame, then it is more difficult to recognize by the bobbing of the horse's head than if only one of the feet is lame.

The malady known as "goose-stepping," whereby the horse lifts one or both hind legs unusually high, convulsively as it were, is not a consequence of spavin. However, it is detrimental to the horse's stamina and prestige.

To further examine the horse's forward movement, have it be ridden after it has been led around, and lastly, ride it oneself, if possible, but in the open and without accompaniment. This is because horses are often very willing and hard-working in company, but when ridden alone, are obstinate, lazy, spooky, or difficult to handle.

If a test ride is not granted, then one has to draw a conclusion from the visible observations of the horse about its character and temperament. For this purpose, note the manner in which it carries its head, how it observes the surrounding objects, how it moves its legs, ears, nostrils, eyes, etc, etc.

If one is obliged to deal with someone whose strict integrity cannot be established, then one does well not to let the horse to be examined out of one's sight even for a moment.

If the purchaser is permitted to carry out his own examination of the horse he has chosen, then in addition to the character and the temperament, also examine the horse's respiratory organs via a fast and not too short ride, especially at a canter. If the breathing remains robust throughout, the flanks betray no overexertion by a dicrotic or too accelerated movement shortly afterwards, and if the larynx does not produce a nagging, scratchy cough when it is compressed, then the lungs can be assumed to be healthy.

Another not uncommon disease, "roaring," will sometimes betray itself during such a ride. This malady is caused by a narrowing of the glottis and usually results from an earlier inflammation of the throat (quinsy). The constriction will determine how loud the sound is that is produced by the accelerated breathing. Roaring is not usually heard at a state of rest.

All of the above-mentioned diseases are among the most prevalent. One's ability to recognize them is conditioned less on expertise, but rather more on a correct eye. More uncommon maladies that could hinder the horse's use entirely can only be diagnosed by an expert. Since not everyone can be one, the law forbids deliberate fraud. It has set a period of time for certain diseases during which none of them may emerge. Otherwise, it is assumed that the disease had been present prior to the sale. In that case, the sale will be rescinded. These diseases are: *)[6]

Staggers with a warranty period of 28 days;

---

[6] *) According to Prussian law.

Heaves with a warranty period of 28 days;
Obstinacy with a warranty period of 8 days;
Glanders with a warranty period of 14 days;
Moon blindness with a warranty period of 28 days;
Amaurosis with a warranty period of 28 days.

This concludes this attempt to enable those who do not wish to consult an expert to choose a riding horse. With some practice, the necessary examination will require little time. This is vital, for ex., in a market where one usually has to choose among a large number of horses. If, in such a case, one does not know how to assess the value of horses at a state of rest in the manner indicated, but rather must spend a long time watching each one being walked around and being ridden, then one must expect that the desirable horses will already be snatched up by experienced buyers. The less than perfect conformation of a single part of the horse will seldom deter them from purchasing the horse. This is because, as has been proven, the presence of a well-formed part supports the weaker surrounding parts, and perhaps even more distant parts, to a certain extent. For example, a well-formed shoulder rarely exists without good withers, deep chest, and well-set front legs. Anyone who knows how to correctly assess such features immediately, even without a special examination of the dependent parts, will be able to correctly evaluate a horse within a short period of time.

It will be difficult to find a horse that is perfect for every riding use. This is because speed and strength are rarely found in one horse in equal measures. Rarely is a good racehorse suitable for campaign service, and vice versa, a good campaign horse for the racetrack.

This is not the place to more thoroughly discuss the good qualities of the other parts, which have not been specifically discussed, that make one horse faster and the other stronger. This is the subject of anatomical and physiological studies.

One who intends to select a riding horse ought to keep in mind that the differences in the horses' performance depend mostly on the relationship and the position of the bones to each other (see General Section). The muscles, as the initiators of the movement, make the horse strong depending on their development. However, since the bones are the levers upon which the muscles can first develop their strength, the horse's movement will be either good or bad depending on how closely the bones to which they connect come to the prescribed relationships.

However, this does not only concern the bones in and of themselves, but also their position to each other and the nature of the joints connecting them. It is generally said of the latter that the larger and broader they are, and the longer and coarser they appear, the more surely the attached muscles and tendons can work with significant strength, unless they stick out due to defects. The position of the individual bones also has, as already mentioned, much influence on how the entire limb works, especially on its extension. The longer the shoulder blade is, for ex., and the more it slopes down from the withers, the more extended and powerful the forelegs can move. On the other hand, if the shoulder blade is close to being vertical, then the movement of the entire leg is limited. This results in a weaker expression of muscular activity.

Moreover, the bones not only support and form the horse's structure, they also contribute much to its weight. Therefore, a large bone mass is disadvantageous for horses that are intended for speed. Conversely, it has little effect on shortened gaits.

However, the normal body conformation is not the only subject of importance when choosing a horse that is suitable for every riding service. Experience shows that the buyer's expectations are disappointed many times by a horse that appears to be faultless, while another, appearing to be of little promise, astonishes even experts with its unexpected and extraordinary achievements. A lack of energy can reduce some of the value of even a well-built horse, whereas a less well constructed but very energetic and lively horse often surpasses the former. If energy is combined with a good conformation, then such a horse will prove to be invaluable for all types of riding.

Naming the parts of the skeleton

1. The upper jaw
2. The lower jaw
3. The seven cervical vertebrae
4. The eighteen vertebrae with their dorsal processes and ribs, the first eight the true ribs, the last ten the false ribs
5. The six lumbar vertebrae
6. The five sacral vertebrae and the caudal vertebra
7. The scapula
8. The humerus
9. The radius
10. The ulna
11. The carpal joint or anterior knee, consisting of seven bones
12. The cannon bone
13. The fetlock, consisting of:
14. The pastern and
15. The coronal bone
16. The coffin bone
17. The sternum
18. The pelvis
19. The femur
20. The patella
21. The lower leg
22. The hock
23. The radial bone or the rear cannon bone
    A. The hip joint   ) The joints of the haunches
    B. The stifle joint)
    C. The poll or the occipital crest
    D. The point of the shoulder
        EF. The center of gravity of horses that are in balance.
        GH. The center of gravity with greater flexion in the haunches.

IK. The line of the haunches.

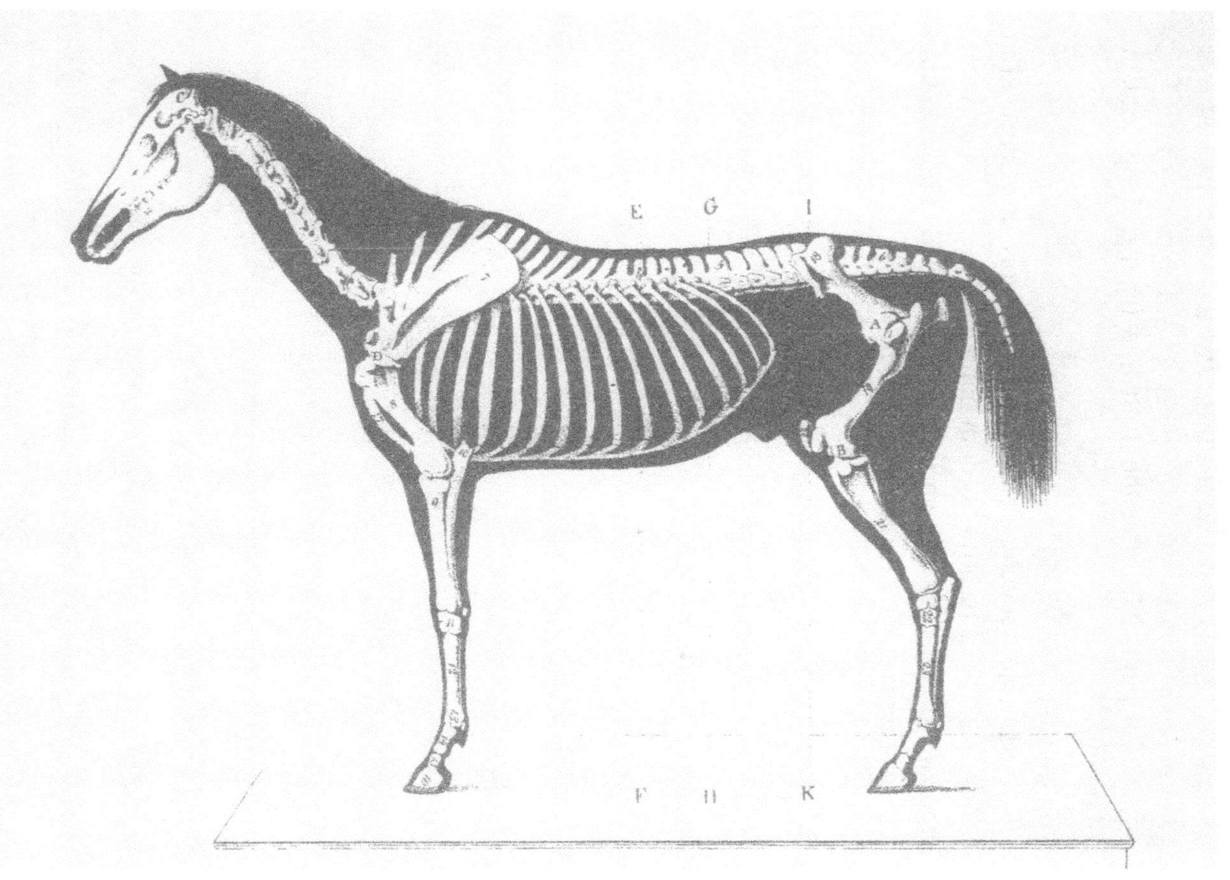

E G I
F H K

<u>Complement</u>

On page 258 after the 10th line from the top, add the following:

If these collecting aids work even more strongly and in a more sustained fashion on both haunches, then the courbette, croupade, balotade, and capriole are developed. These School jumps comprise the "Airs Above the Ground."[7]

---

[7] Translator's Note: This will be on page 185 of this translation.

About the Translator

Cynthia F. Hodges has a Doctor of Jurisprudence from South Texas College of Law in Houston, Texas and an LL.M. in Environmental/Animal Law from Lewis & Clark Law School in Portland, Oregon. She also has a Master's of Arts in Germanic Studies from the University of Texas at Austin. Hodges has a Certificate of Proof of German Language Ability (required to study at a German university), the International Business German Certificate (German American Chamber of Commerce), and passed the U.S. Department of Defense's written German test. She also taught high school German and worked as a professional translator.

Hodges has approximately 20 years experience riding, training and showing dressage. She is a United States Dressage Federation (USDF) Qualified Rider, has shown successfully through Third Level, and has schooled to FEI. She has trained with Karl Mikolka, Rachel Saavedra, Gerhard Politz, Gunnar Østergaard, Franz Rockowansky, Hans Biss, and other prominent riders. Hodges has participated in USDF Instructor Certification workshops and also trained in Germany.

Hodges has written a number of articles on dressage, many of which have appeared in *Topline Ink Equestrian Journal*, local newsletters, and national magazines such as *Dressage Today* and *Dressage & CT*. Hodges has also published law review articles on animal and equine law, which are available on the Michigan State University Animal Legal & Historical Center website. Hodges also translated *Monsieur Baucher and His Arts: A Serious Word with Germany's Riders* by Louis Seeger (1852) and *Anatomy of Dressage* by Heinrich Schusdziarra.

Hodges maintains a website dedicated to classical dressage at cynthiahodges.com/dressage.

About the Artist

Bonnie M. Hodges is a fine artist located in Edmonds, Washington (near Seattle). Hodges has a B.A. in Studio Arts from the University of Maryland and worked as an illustrator for the U.S. State Department in Washington, D.C. Hodges also taught oil painting at a community college.

Hodges works with a variety of media, but prefers oil, pastel, and digital media. Hodges paints lovely landscapes, portraits (animals and people), still lifes and also does photo restoration and graphic design. Hodges' beautiful and life-like paintings have been featured in galleries, national and international art shows, and are on display in collections in the USA and Europe.

Hodges' portfolio can be viewed online at bonniehodges.com.